'Timely and engaging . . . the unlikely and remarkable story of how an English doctor, Thomas Dimsdale, and Catherine the Great, the Empress of Russia, showed great personal courage and took serious personal risks to promote inoculation against smallpox using a method that had originated in Asia. The success of these early efforts led directly to the first vaccine by Jenner, and over the next two centuries saved millions of lives that would have been lost to many different diseases, culminating in the recent vaccines against Covid-19. A truly fascinating book that reads like a thriller.'

Venki Ramakrishnan, Nobel laureate and
former President of the Royal Society

'A rich and wonderfully urgent work of history which engagingly recounts one of the greatest moments in modern science and public health: a story of Enlightenment conviction, court intrigue, Anglo-Russian relations, and timeless, personal bravery. An expertly recounted eighteenth-century tale of political leadership and medical progress with obvious insights for today.'

Tristram Hunt, director of the Victoria and Albert Museum

'*The Empress and the English Doctor* honours Catherine the Great's pioneering scientific journey, demonstrating her personal bravery, her exacting insight and her resolve to protect others against smallpox.'

Teresa Lambe, professor of vaccinology and immunology, University of
Oxford, and co-designer of the Oxford AstraZeneca vaccine

'Packed with political intrigue and scientific insight, this is a fascinating narrative revealing how early inoculation pioneers overcame superstition, prejudice and misinformation. Move forward more than two centuries and the parallels with the current Covid-19 pandemic are incredible!'

Jonathan Ball, professor of virology, University of Nottingham

'This is a wonderful book. It tells the story of the greatest medical discovery before Pasteur, inoculation against smallpox, through the life of a Quaker doctor, Thomas Dimsdale, and his journey to Russia to treat Catherine the Great . . . It's a long time since I've read a history book as beautifully constructed as this – it's a remarkable achievement.'

David Wootton, anniversary professor of history,
University of York, and author of *The Invention of Science*

'This is a remarkable and fascinating story of scientific discovery, break-through medicine and inspirational female leadership by Catherine the Great. The revelations in this book resonate with today's battle against Covid-19. Lucy Ward has undertaken brilliant detective work . . . This is a must-read book.'

Sir Norman Lamb, former UK Health Minister

'Timely . . . The author demonstrates beautifully how London has histori-cally led on the science with first "inoculation" and then "vaccination" – indeed, longer than most people realise.'

Professor Dame Sally Davies,
former Chief Medical Officer for England

'A tale of multiple and intertwining themes – private and public health, public administration, and the politics of Empires . . . Although the book is about things that happened over 250 years ago, the hopes and fears of the people facing those difficult choices resonate with our own times.'

Laurie Bristow, former UK ambassador to the Russian Federation

'A fascinating deep dive into a neglected topic in the history of vaccines, with many lessons for the prevention of viruses today. Lucy Ward blends history and personality to shed light on a story that has been overlooked in favour of Jenner and his milkmaid.'

Dr John Tregoning, Reader in Respiratory Infections,
Imperial College London

'This is a fascinating and meticulously researched book . . . a remarkable story of female leadership and personal courage. Lucy Ward uses her brilliance as a narrator combined with her insight as a former Lobby journalist to bring to life one of history's most powerful women who really did "follow the science".'

Harriet Harman MP

The
Empress
and the
English
Doctor

How
Catherine
the Great
defied a
deadly
virus

LUCY WARD

ONEWORLD

A Oneworld Book

First published by Oneworld Publications in 2022

This paperback edition published 2023

Copyright © Lucy Ward 2022

The moral right of Lucy Ward to be identified as the Author of this work has been
asserted by her in accordance with the Copyright, Designs, and Patents Act 1988

ISBN 978-0-86154-518-6
eISBN 978-0-86154-246-8

Map © Erica Milwain
Typeset by Hewer Text UK Ltd, Edinburgh
Printed and bound in Great Britain by Clays Ltd, Elcograf S.p.A.

Oneworld Publications
10 Bloomsbury Street
London WC1B 3SR
England

For Liam

Note on names, places and dates

As Thomas Dimsdale discovered, Russian names, with their patronymics and multiple affectionate diminutives, can be something of an obstacle course for non-Russian readers and speakers. I have chosen not to keep rigidly to any rule on transliteration or anglicisation: I've tried instead to aim for clarity and ease of reading. Where there is a familiar version, I have used it – hence Catherine and not Ekaterina/Yekaterina; I have omitted patronymics. Occasionally spellings in direct quotations differ from my chosen form.

Many place names mentioned in the book have changed over the last 250 years, as European borders have shifted with the tides of history. The names Thomas encountered on his journeys are used here; their modern equivalents can be found in the footnotes. Both are included on the map.

Alongside names and places, time can also cause confusion, as two separate calendars were in use in Europe in the eighteenth century. Russia used the Julian calendar, which at the time of the inoculations ran eleven days behind the newer Gregorian calendar, introduced in Britain and across the continent to address a growing divergence between dates and the astronomical year. Writers used the notation OS (Old Style) or NS (New Style) to differentiate between the two. Most sources for the events of Thomas's long first visit to Russia use Old Style dates, and I have done the same. The account of the second trip is drawn largely from Elizabeth Dimsdale's journal, and I have followed her lead and stuck with New Style dating.

Contents

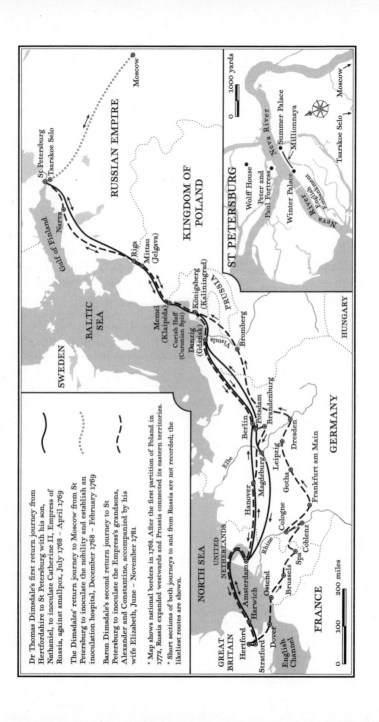

Dr Thomas Dimsdale's first return journey from Hertfordshire to St Petersburg with his son, Nathaniel, to inoculate Catherine II, Empress of Russia, against smallpox, July 1768 – April 1769

The Dimsdales' return journey to Moscow from St Petersburg to inoculate the nobility and establish an inoculation hospital, December 1768 – February 1769

Baron Dimsdale's second return journey to St Petersburg to inoculate the Empress's grandsons, Alexander and Constantine, accompanied by his wife Elizabeth, June – November 1781

* Map shows national borders in 1768. After the first partition of Poland in 1772, Russia expanded westwards and Prussia connected its eastern territories.
* Short sections of both journeys to and from Russia are not recorded; the likeliest routes are shown.

GREAT BRITAIN

Hertford
Stratford
Dover
English Channel

NORTH SEA

UNITED NETHERLANDS

Harwich
Ostend
Amsterdam
Brussels
Spa
Cologne
Coblenz

Rhine

FRANCE

GERMANY

Hanover
Magdeburg
Leipzig
Gotha
Frankfurt am Main
Dresden

Elbe

Berlin
Potsdam
Brandenburg
Bromberg

Danzig (Gdańsk)
Vistula
Königsberg (Kaliningrad)
PRUSSIA

Memel (Klaipėda)
Curish Haff (Curonian Spit)

BALTIC SEA

SWEDEN

Riga
Mittau (Jelgava)

KINGDOM OF POLAND

HUNGARY

Gulf of Finland

Narva
St Petersburg
Tsarskoe Selo

RUSSIAN EMPIRE

Moscow

0   100   200 miles

ST PETERSBURG

Wolff House
Peter and Paul Fortress
Winter Palace
Summer Palace
Millionnaya
Neva River

River Fontanka

English Embankment

Tsarskoe Selo
Moscow

0   1000 yards

Preface

The Silver Lancet

'You are now called, Sir, to the most important employment that perhaps any gentleman was ever entrusted with. To your skill and integrity will probably be submitted, no less than the precious lives of two of the greatest personages in the world, with whose safety the tranquillity and happiness of this great empire are so intimately connected.'

> *Count Panin, chief advisor to Catherine II*
> *of Russia and tutor to her son the Grand Duke*
> *Paul, to Dr Thomas Dimsdale, August 1768*

'Собою подала примѣръ' (She herself set an example)

> *Commemorative medal marking the inoculation of*
> *Catherine II of Russia against smallpox, struck 1772*

At nine o'clock on a chill evening in October 1768, a carriage arrived at the gates of Wolff House, on the outskirts of St Petersburg, with an urgent summons. After weeks of secret preparations, the call had come at last from the Winter Palace, where the Empress Catherine II waited impatiently for her English doctor, Thomas Dimsdale.

Prepared but uneasy at the task ahead, Thomas climbed quickly into the coach with his son Nathaniel, a medical student. Nathaniel carried a sleeping child, a six-year-old boy named Alexander, small for his age and swaddled in a fur against the autumn cold and the beginnings of a fever.

Leaving the guarded gates of Wolff House, a merchant's summer residence requisitioned as an isolation hospital, the trio sped through lanes lit by an almost full moon towards the river a short distance to the south. The wide, grey waters of the Neva were not yet frozen, and the coach crossed over a pontoon bridge, then made its way to the rear of the Winter Palace, away from the bustle of the embankment. Drawing up as agreed at a gate close to the grand facades of Millionnaya Street, the two doctors and the boy were ushered quickly up a back staircase. At the top waited Baron Alexander Cherkasov, the Cambridge-educated President of the St Petersburg Medical College, who would act as interpreter.

As they hurried through richly decorated passages to the appointed room, Thomas had reason for trepidation. Over decades of experience, the 56-year-old physician had refined the practice of smallpox inoculation: deliberately infecting patients with a small, controlled dose of the deadly virus itself to give them future immunity against the brutal disease. His landmark treatise explaining his methods, published just a year previously in 1767, was already in its fourth edition, its influence stretching across Europe and confirming England's place as the global centre of expertise for the preventative treatment.

Yet, despite his flawless record of thousands of successful inoculations, from wealthy aristocrats paying handsome sums to the poorest foundlings he immunised for free, Thomas knew the stakes were now at their highest. Not only did his own reputation hang in the balance, so too did that of the medical procedure he firmly believed could counter one of the greatest threats to human health ever known. If disaster struck – and his Russian test cases at Wolff House had produced disturbingly erratic results – the name of science itself would be tainted, to the benefit of prejudice and superstition.

And if the fear for his profession was not enough, there was his safety and the impact on his country to consider. Back in Britain, King George III himself was following his progress, while diplomats in London and St Petersburg exchanged anxious updates and wished the whole politically hazardous affair swiftly over. In the English market town of Hertford, the family he had reluctantly left almost three months before prayed for his safe return. For Thomas, the danger was only underlined by the Empress's promise – should things go wrong – of a carriage waiting to spirit him to the safety of a yacht anchored in the Gulf of Finland ready to sail for England. Her death at the hands of a foreigner would spark immediate vengeance: he had witnessed the sparkle of the Russian Court but also the dark brutality of life outside it. If he failed to escape immediately, he expected to pay with his life.

All this preoccupied the mind of the Quaker doctor as he entered the small chamber where Her Imperial Majesty, the Empress Catherine II, waited alone, her mind settled and her countenance perfectly composed. Marvelling at her resolution, Thomas took out a mother-of-pearl and silver case no bigger than his palm and opened the hinged lid to reveal three pearl-handled blades slotted inside. Extracting one, he knelt beside the half-awake Alexander, exposing the boy's arm to find the place he had inoculated him a few days previously. With the lancet, he pierced the blister, transferring a drop of the infected matter within on to the blade. The Empress pushed back her brocaded sleeves, and the Doctor made the smallest of punctures in her pale skin, one in each upper arm, guiding a drop of the fluid into each incision.

In barely the time needed to throw a set of dice, the procedure was over. The Empress of Russia had been deliberately, and willingly, inoculated with smallpox: the ancient and terrible disease that had killed an estimated sixty million over centuries and disfigured and blinded countless more. Thomas's record was impeccable, but every jab of the blade carried risk. Now, as Catherine retired to bed and the doctors and the boy stepped back into the cold St Petersburg night, there was nothing to do but wait.

Early in the morning after the secret appointment at the Winter Palace, Catherine travelled by carriage to Tsarskoe Selo, an elegant royal estate some twenty miles south of St Petersburg. There, wrapped up against the cold, she walked in landscaped parkland that stands barely changed today, pacing the tree-lined paths as late leaves scattered and were swept away. She dined simply that day on weak soup, boiled chicken and vegetables, sleeping for almost an hour afterwards and waking refreshed.

The Empress's mood, her doctor noted, was 'easy and cheerful', but during the night pain would build around the two incisions on her arms, her joints would begin to ache, and giddiness and fever would strike the following evening. The smallpox virus, one of the most virulent ever known, had entered her bloodstream and, as her body prepared to resist, there was no turning back.

Doctor's lancet, eighteenth century.

Introduction

The Speckled Monster

'The most terrible of all the ministers of death'
Thomas Babington Macaulay

This is the story of an encounter of a most intimate kind. But it is not a love story; at least, not in the conventional sense. The connection between the English physician Thomas Dimsdale and Catherine the Great of Russia was not a romantic one, but it was in its own way more deeply physical – and more dangerous – than the sexual liaisons that have too often overshadowed her legacy. Her relationship with the doctor, which lasted until her death aged sixty-seven, was more significant than the fleeting dalliances with some of her lovers. It protected her own life, that of her son and heir, and, later, two of her grandsons, and launched a programme of inoculation across her vast empire.

Together, both the Empress and her doctor also risked their lives: she through the operation itself, though she had carefully weighed the odds, and he through the likely dire consequences if the worst happened. The pair had discussed their secret plan in detail beforehand, sometimes with the physician sitting on his patient's ornate bed with her lover, Count Grigory Orlov, beside them. As summer ended and the colder days of autumn drew in, a bond of respect had developed that would last a lifetime. The doctor was anxious and the Empress determined, but the two were of one mind.

The inoculation of the Empress of Russia, once it was made known, became famous throughout the world: reported in newspapers in America, remarked on in London coffee houses, celebrated in French and German poetry. While other European royal houses, led by

Britain's Georgian kings, had inoculated their children, Catherine II was the only reigning monarch to undergo the procedure – an act of courage that has since been all but forgotten. She did her best to publicise her action for many reasons, but her goal was to demonstrate, using her own body, the most powerful means then available to fight the greatest scourge of the eighteenth century: smallpox. Her aim was to challenge prejudice and to promote science.

The Empress and her doctor shared a common purpose, but their connection was in many ways a meeting of opposites. Catherine, ruler of Russia for six years by 1768, had not only seized the crown by force from her unstable husband Peter III but had retained it after his assassination by her allies a few days later. Bold, charismatic and politically highly astute, the 39-year-old Empress presided over a glittering, pleasure-loving St Petersburg court. Her style was informal, playful even, but her intellect was quick and curious. 'I am one of those people who love the why of things,' she would write to the journalist Baron Friedrich Grimm, one of her many correspondents among Europe's intellectual elite.

Born a minor German princess and locked early into a strategic marriage to the heir to the Russian throne, Catherine had swiftly understood the diplomatic value of display. She had used her baptism into the Orthodox faith and her theatrical coronation as tools to promote her love for her adoptive country, and harnessed the iconography of state portraits to present her unique version of female power. By the time of Thomas's arrival, even Russia's magisterial geography could not contain the Empress's ambitions. She prepared for a territory-grabbing war with Turkey to the south while turning west to the grand powers of Enlightenment Europe in search of artistic and cultural inspiration and the latest in philosophical and scientific thought.

While Catherine was every inch the public woman, Thomas Dimsdale, a Quaker-born physician living in a substantial farmhouse just outside the English market town of Hertford, was fundamentally a private man. Plainly dressed in a dark suit and tightly curled doctor's wig, the father of seven came from a medical family. He had worked as a surgeon and army doctor before turning his mind to the emerging technology of smallpox inoculation.

Alongside his lucrative medical practice in Hertfordshire, London and beyond, Thomas had developed the latest and most effective techniques for the preventative procedure, publishing them in a treatise that had propelled him to international prominence. Despite his success, personal fame was not his ambition. He meticulously experimented, recorded and analysed his findings, careful not to take any risks that might harm his many patients, or jeopardise the precious reputation of inoculation.

Both Empress and doctor wrote about their encounter: putting the inoculation on the record, in all its stark physicality, was critical to their shared mission of promoting the procedure. It was forgotten partly because others took control of Catherine's history, choosing after her death to depict her body as a weapon of lascivious desire rather than a symbol of pioneering medical practice.

But the event has also vanished because inoculation – a term drawn from the Latin *inoculare*, meaning to engraft a new bud or 'eye' from one plant to another – is itself almost forgotten. New discoveries have obscured a 'missing century' in the history of immunisation, whose remarkable advances paved the way for perhaps the most important medical technique known to humanity: vaccination.

Inoculation worked on the principle of fighting fire with fire. To protect them from smallpox, patients were deliberately given a minute dose of the virus itself by inserting a drop of pus from someone with the natural or inoculated disease into pierced skin, conveying a mild case of the illness and the same lifetime immunity as the natural infection. The procedure, known for centuries in many parts of the world as a folk practice, made its way at the start of the eighteenth century to Europe from Turkey. There, elderly women stored inoculum (infected matter for inoculation) in a walnut shell and delivered the jab to children with nothing more sophisticated than a blunt needle. Pioneers of the practice in Britain gave it a Western medical makeover – introducing dangerous changes they would eventually strip away again – but met instant anti-inoculation opposition anyway from sceptics and religious opponents convinced that God alone should control the spread of disease. The inoculators persisted and, through an unprecedented globalised effort, a safe and reliable method emerged that carried minimal risk. It was so successful in Britain that far-sighted doctors, including Thomas Dimsdale, envisaged the extraordinary prospect that smallpox, a scourge for centuries, could be eradicated completely.

Nevertheless, inoculation had important drawbacks. Live variola virus, the agent causing smallpox, would always be a dangerous medical weapon requiring careful handing. Most importantly, patients inoculated with smallpox were infectious for a short period, running the risk that they could pass the lethal disease on to others while protecting themselves.

It was these concerns that prompted the Gloucestershire doctor Edward Jenner, himself a smallpox inoculator who had suffered a badly botched inoculation as a boy, to investigate rumours that milder pox viruses affecting farm animals might also create immunity to smallpox in humans, without the risk of introducing the disease itself. The technology of inoculation was already available and proven: Jenner only had to modify it to test his theory. When in 1796 he took pus from the cowpox blisters on the hand of a dairymaid infected while milking and transferred it via a lancet into the arm of his gardener's son, he called it 'inoculation with cowpox'. By the time he had trialled, proven and publicised the adapted procedure, it was known by a new name based on the Latin word for cow, *vacca*.

Vaccination, a revolutionary development that deployed the body's immune response to a mild disease to protect against a deadly one, took off around the world within a decade, quickly supplanting inoculation. Its mechanism remained a mystery until much later in the century, when the French microbiologist Louis Pasteur and the German physician Robert Koch proved the germ theory of disease. At Pasteur's suggestion, the word *vaccine* became a generic term for treatments containing bacteria or viruses used to produce immunity against an infectious disease.[*]

---

[*] The terminology of inoculation is complex and often causes confusion, contributing to widespread misunderstanding of the procedure's history pre-Jenner. *Vaccination* is now used generically, but throughout most of the nineteenth century it referred purely to the use of cowpox to prevent smallpox. After Jenner's discovery, old-style inoculation – using smallpox to fight smallpox – was generally termed *variolation* (from the smallpox *variola* virus) to distinguish it from vaccination. The term variolation is not used in this book because it was not introduced until the nineteenth century.

Vaccination was world-changing, but it would not have happened without inoculation. The century of immunological progress into which Jenner was born paved the way for one of the most important medical advances in history, which would save untold millions of lives. Decades before his landmark publication, doctors were trialling and refining the method he later adapted, exchanging knowledge and hammering out an understanding of the principles that would make his crucial next step possible. In a frenzy of international collaboration, medical tracts and treatises flew across borders in Europe and the colonies of America, gradually building a body of knowledge and expertise. Inoculation featured in newspapers, periodicals, sermons, advertisements, letters, cartoons and poetry. Amateur inoculators, aristocratic mothers, enslaved men and women, philosophers, orphans, prisoners and princesses all had their part to play. Edward Jenner is often called the father of vaccination, but it had many grandfathers and grandmothers who also deserve their place in history.

Smallpox, that fearsome 'speckled monster' as eighteenth-century England knew it for its distinctive dense raised rash, was a disease unparalleled in its horror and lethal power. There was no cure, and none would ever be found. Today, as the world faces new health crises, we have lost the inherited memory of the monster's terrible impact, though its dark shadow lives on deep in our imaginations. Bringing down empires and devastating populations, smallpox rampaged around the globe for millennia, changing the course of history as it killed and maimed millions of all strata of society.

At its height, the disease was 'the most terrible of all ministers of death', the historian Thomas Babington Macaulay wrote in 1848. 'The smallpox was always present, filling the churchyards with corpses, tormenting with constant fear all whom it had not yet stricken, leaving on those whose lives it spared the hideous traces of its power.'[1] Skin gouged with pockmarks, burn-like scarring, damaged limbs and blindness provided constant, highly visible reminders of the devastating virulence of the virus. Among those survivors left brutally disfigured was Catherine's husband, Peter, whose scarred and swollen face his young fiancée now found 'hideous'.[2] The virus was deemed virtually unavoidable: as a proverb of the day had it, 'Few escape love or smallpox.'

We know precisely when smallpox ended: it was declared eradicated by the World Health Organization in 1980, and remains the only disease wiped from the face of the earth by human intervention.[3] Over the first eight decades of the twentieth century alone, it had killed an estimated 300 million people.[4] Tracing its ancient beginnings is harder. No one knows where or when smallpox first began to affect humans, though it probably adapted gradually, perhaps originating as one of the relatively harmless pox viruses of domesticated animals as humans first began living in agricultural settlements, or from contact with wild animals. Archaeological finds reveal the virus was well established in the Eastern Mediterranean and Indus Valley three thousand years ago, and smallpox-like lesions scarred the faces of Egyptian mummies from the second millennium BC. In the fourth century AD, texts graphically describing recognisable smallpox symptoms were written in China and India.

Roll on another three hundred years and the disease had gained a foothold in Europe, gradually spreading with the movement of traders, crusaders and invading armies until, in the sixteenth century, it was entrenched across most of the continent. With the conquistadors and the slave trade, the deadly virus travelled to the Americas. Encountering no immunity, its poison helped bring down the Aztec and Inca empires and scythed its way through Native American populations.

In England, Queen Elizabeth I was wrapped in scarlet cloth as she fought the illness in 1562; her physicians subscribed to the ancient but baseless belief that the colour red repelled the virus. She fell into a coma but survived, forever scarred with pock marks she covered with white lead.

A century later, and smallpox had become Europe's biggest killer, overtaking bubonic plague in virulence and claiming hundreds of thousands of lives every year across the continent. Of those who caught the disease, around one in five died, with children by far the likeliest victims.

Even those avoiding the virus in infancy could rarely escape it forever. In March 1685, the writer John Evelyn recorded in his diary the death by smallpox of his daughter Mary, aged nineteen, 'to our unspeakable sorrow and Affliction . . . O deare, sweete and desireable Child, how shall I part with all this goodness, all this Vertue, without the bitterness of sorrow, and reluctancy of a tender parent?' Within six months, his other daughter Elizabeth had also fallen victim to the disease, and followed her sister to the grave.

Monarchs were no safer from a scourge that took no account of rank or station. In Britain, Queen Mary II succumbed to an especially virulent form of the virus in 1694, to the devastation of her husband, William of Orange. William, Duke of Gloucester, the only surviving son of the couple's successor Queen Anne, died of the disease aged just eleven not long afterwards. The boy had been the last heir to the Stuart royal line, and on Anne's death the British throne passed to the House of Hanover. Once more, smallpox had diverted the path of history.

But for all these waves of death, and their political consequences, worse was to come. In the eighteenth century, smallpox unleashed its full destructive power in Europe. There was nowhere to hide. Devastating epidemics swept the continent, ebbing and flowing in repeated cycles to carry off infants and those who had previously evaded the virus. In London and other large cities, the disease was now endemic. An estimated 400,000 people died each year in Europe alone in what became known as the age of smallpox.[5]

Over these decades, the virus infected not only individual bodies but every aspect of society. Its cultural presence in England was inescapable: family letters resonate with fears of contagion and sorrows at the loss of loved ones; diaries record private grief; poetry and novels harness the dramatic power of death and disfigurement to turn plots and heighten emotion. Even the sober burial tallies of parish records offer an occasional glimpse of the true human cost behind the figures.

In Little Berkhamsted, close to Thomas Dimsdale's home in Hertford, the parish register records the burial in January 1768 of George Hodges, a poor village boy of 'about ten years'. After the child had been ill for some days, a note added by the rector states, his desperate parents had sought advice from Thomas, who battled that evening through snow 'a foot deep' to the family's meagre home. Finding George covered in dirt and sores, 'the Doctor with a humanity peculiar to himself washed him, removed all nasty obstructions and by his care preserved his life some days. Upon our return to the Parsonage, he told me it was smallpox of the worst sort.'[6] While Thomas's care may have eased his suffering, George's life could not be saved.

As the children of the poor died in uncounted numbers, the palaces of Europe remained as vulnerable as ever to the scourge. Five reigning monarchs were dethroned by smallpox in the eighteenth century, including in 1730 the Emperor Peter II of Russia, the fourteen-year-old grandson of Czar Peter the Great, in the early hours of his wedding day. In Vienna, the Habsburg Empress Maria Theresa recovered from the disease, but it ripped through her court, killing her son, two daughters and two daughters-in-law by 1767.

It was no wonder that a year later, in Russia, the Empress Catherine II was gripped by fear at the threat of smallpox to herself and her sickly thirteen-year-old son, the Grand Duke Paul. The disease had broken out once more in St Petersburg, and in the spring Catherine moved out of the capital, shuttling between her palaces scattered along the breezy shore of the Gulf of Finland or sheltered in the countryside. 'I fled from house to house, and I banished myself from the city for five whole months, not wanting to put myself or my son at risk,' she wrote later to Frederick the Great, King of Prussia.[7]

But the virus could not be avoided forever. To protect herself, her heir and her throne, the Empress needed a more permanent solution. As summer came, she made the momentous decision that she and her son should undergo inoculation, and set in motion the plan that would bring Thomas Dimsdale from a small English market town on a 1,700-mile overland journey to the capital of Russia.

As this book is written, during the Covid-19 pandemic, vaccination is once more at the centre of global attention. The techniques used to protect us against the latest disease to sweep the planet employ the most cutting-edge technologies, from using protein fragments to mimic the virus to genetically engineering DNA to produce proteins and prompt an immune response.

The sophisticated laboratory-based methods of modern science seem a world away from the 'fighting fire with fire' approach of the eighteenth-century smallpox inoculators, with their needles, lancets and drops of infected pus taken directly from a feverish human body. But the line between them is direct and the principle behind both is exactly the same: to artificially stimulate the immune system in order to marshal the body's defences and protect us from disease.

It is not only the science of Covid-19 vaccination that echoes the experiences of our forebears as they battled to beat back smallpox. Like us, they used isolation and quarantine to try to slow the spread of the virus; they too suffered economic hardships, closed shops and schools, and endured pressures on healthcare as epidemics hit. Wealthy households used smallpox scars as a form of immunity passport when employing servants. Almost 250 years ago, a doctor in Chester came up with a detailed plan for isolation and contact tracing, backed up with furlough-style payments to ensure anyone potentially affected could afford to stay at home and fines for those who did not.

At a time when there was no nationally organised public health provision in Britain, Thomas Dimsdale and others were pressing for nationwide programmes of general smallpox inoculation with the aim of protecting the poor and, ultimately, eradicating the disease from the country altogether. The idea of compulsory inoculation, especially for the children of the poor, was floated by some but never adopted in the eighteenth century outside institutions such as London's Foundling Hospital. Smallpox vaccination became mandatory only halfway through the nineteenth century, when it prompted riots.

From its very first introduction in Europe, inoculation had met opposition and scepticism as well as support. To try to persuade doubters, proponents turned to data, exactly as today's governments have done with their graphs and slides, to show the effectiveness of inoculation compared with natural smallpox. Like their modern-day counterparts promoting the Covid jab, eighteenth-century inoculation supporters quickly discovered that the psychology of risk is complex, and cold statistics and promises of long-term protection generally have less weight in the human mind than an imminent threat, no matter how small.

Where numbers fail, the power of example can succeed. Catherine the Great, even as an absolute ruler who could have forced inoculation on her people, chose instead to become a role model, using her own safe recovery to persuade her subjects to follow. Church services, fireworks and specially minted medals publicised her recovery, while today celebrities, influencers and politicians post Covid vaccine selfies on social media and Buckingham Palace breaks with its usual refusal to comment on royal health matters to announce that the Queen has received her jab.

Vaccination has stood the test of time as one of the most powerful public health interventions on the planet. Smallpox was eradicated over forty years ago thanks to a concerted campaign by the World Health Organization. In 2017, the number of children vaccinated worldwide against a range of diseases was the highest ever reported at over 116 million. The Global Polio Eradication Initiative, the largest internationally coordinated public health effort in history, has seen polio case numbers drop by over 99% since its launch in 1988 and elimination is within sight.[8] As this book is written, Covid vaccination has proved a mighty weapon in the fight against the coronavirus, though its deeply uneven distribution has laid bare the extent of global inequality.

Despite these milestones, vaccination has never succeeded in fully shaking off the scepticism encountered by the first medical inoculators, and vaccine hesitancy – the term for delaying or refusing vaccines despite their availability – and full-blown anti-vaccination sentiment are on the rise again, powered by a complex mix of populist politics, a backlash against experts, and social media platforms that send misinformation round the world in less time than it takes to inoculate one child. Public mistrust of vaccines and the healthcare services that administer them is growing fastest not in poorer countries but in affluent Western nations: a 2016 global study on vaccine confidence found scepticism was higher in Europe than any other region.[9] 'Vaccine anxieties are not new, but the viral spread of concerns, reinforced by a quagmire of online misinformation, is increasingly connected and global,' the report's author wrote in the health journal *The Lancet*.[10] During the Covid-19 pandemic, Western governments intervened to shore up public confidence in new vaccines, demanding social media giants remove misleading posts and promote scientifically accurate messages.

Expert advisors to the WHO warned in 2018, eight years into the organisation's 'Decade of Vaccines', that hard-won immunisation gains can be easily lost. In 2019, the WHO declared an emergency response in Europe after a surge in cases of measles, and stripped four countries, including the United Kingdom, of their measles-free status as immunisation rates fell below the threshold needed for population-wide protection or 'herd immunity'. In the same year, the organisation ranked vaccine hesitancy as one of the top ten health threats in the world.

Like the debates of the eighteenth century, today's vaccine scepticism highlights how closely inoculation holds up a mirror to the times. Enlightenment thought, with its rational weighing of greater and lesser harms, clashed with public reluctance to take an upfront risk or to challenge whatever providence had in store. Harsh economics played a role too: Thomas Dimsdale wryly noted that parsimonious English parishes could sometimes be persuaded to fund inoculations for the poor because burying those dead from smallpox was a more expensive option.[11] Today, governments see Covid vaccination as a public health good, but also a means to help kickstart economies faltering after months of lockdown.

In the age of the internet, mass tools of instant, unfiltered communication combined with a growing suspicion of experts, traditional authorities and even science itself have hurled vaccination into the midst of contemporary culture wars. The concept of herd immunity, by which a large majority must be vaccinated to keep a disease at bay, has introduced new tensions between the freedom of the individual and the interests of the state in promoting collective benefit. Statistics-packed public health messages on the mass safety of vaccines can be drowned out by emotion-tugging shareable claims of alleged individual harm. A procedure with its origins in folk medicine, carried out by elderly women storing live viral matter in walnut shells, finds itself framed as a tool of establishment oppression.

But if inoculation exposes each era's particular preoccupations, its mirror also reflects back at us a constant: the heights and depths of human nature. As the WHO and other public health bodies search for new ways to address vaccine scepticism, they are treading ground crossed repeatedly in past centuries. Inoculation, especially of a child, touches on our deepest and most enduring emotions – love, fear of death – and our darkest vulnerabilities: prejudice, selfishness, irrationality.

Thomas Dimsdale and his royal patient were brought together by inoculation 250 years ago, but their hopes, fears and complex motivations are profoundly recognisable. Catherine II choked down her childhood terror of smallpox to undergo the procedure for the sake of a son she was never close to and a population she half despised but wanted to protect. Her doctor overcame his own anxiety and staked his life on the success of the medical breakthrough he passionately believed in. Courtiers who would no more have undergone the alien new treatment than jump in the icy Neva judged the practice the height of fashion overnight.

Amid all the swirling emotions of Catherine's inoculation, it rested on facts. Whatever fears and ambitions motivated them, physician and patient believed unequivocally in the science of inoculation and its power to defeat one of the greatest scourges of humanity. Both were careful to document the event and publicise it accurately to champion the practice as widely as possible. In their quest to challenge prejudice and promote trust in evidence, both the Empress and her English doctor wanted their story told.

Baron Thomas Dimsdale, Portrait by Carl-Ludwig Christine, 1769.

The Doctor

'A gentleman of great skill in his profession, and of the most extensive humanity and benevolence.'

Little Berkhamsted Parish Register, 1768

The birth of Thomas Dimsdale was recorded in the form of a neat, handwritten certificate. The new baby came into the world on 29 May 1712, the sixth child and fourth son of John and Susannah Dimsdale of the parish of Theydon Garnon in the county of Essex, England. The document was signed by seven witnesses.

A second scrap of paper also listed on one side the birth dates of Thomas and some of his siblings. On the other was something unexpected: a medical recipe. To cure kidney stones, it instructed, mix saffron, turmeric, pepper and elder bark into three pints of white wine, and take the mixture first thing in the morning and last thing at night. 'It is proper', the note concluded, 'to take a vomit first.'[1]

The scribbled remedy was one of many in the Dimsdale household. Thomas's father, John, was a doctor, as his own father, Robert, had been before him. A generation further back, at the time of the English Civil War, Thomas's great-grandfather – an active supporter of the Parliamentarian cause – had combined running an inn in the Hertfordshire village of Hoddesdon with a trade as a barber-surgeon.[2] John Dimsdale had established himself in practice at Epping, a small market town lying among pastures and scattered hamlets in the countryside some seventeen miles north-east of London, just at the tip of the long strip of ancient forest that still bears its name. There, as well as treating those who could afford to pay for his services, he worked on behalf of the Overseers for the Poor of Theydon Garnon, providing basic healthcare for the many impoverished households whose only safety net was parish welfare.

The home-made birth certificate offered another clue to the Dimsdales' heritage. The family were Quakers: members of the dissenting Puritan sect that had emerged from the Civil War the century before. Refusing to recognise the authority of the Church of England and its 'hireling priesthood', members of the Religious Society of Friends, as the Quakers were formally known, rejected parish registers and kept their own independent records of births, marriages and deaths. God was within every individual, the sect believed, and its worshippers trembled at his word.

By the time of Thomas's birth, Quakerism was officially tolerated in England, but the experience of persecution was fresh in the family's memory. Grandfather Robert Dimsdale, born across the county border in Hertfordshire, had been a convert in the revolutionary early years of the movement when, following the restoration of the monarchy in England, Quakers faced violent protests, confiscation of property and prosecution for their refusal to swear an oath of allegiance to the Crown or to pay tithes. For all their philosophy of peace, the Friends were judged a threat to the social order. Robert was thrown briefly into Hertford gaol in 1661 for failing to attend church, only to be imprisoned again almost immediately for nine more years for 'practising physic without a licence'. His work as a doctor, albeit unqualified, had apparently been successful enough to have threatened his conformist rivals.

Enough was enough. Weary of oppression at home, Robert joined thousands of fellow dissenters in search of true religious freedom and 'a peaceable life' in the New World, where the Irish Quaker William Penn and fellow Friends had acquired no fewer than three American colonies. Pausing only to snap up five thousand Pennsylvania acres as a 'first purchaser' in 1682, the year Penn's fleet made its stormy crossing to the new colony, the doctor emigrated with his wife Mary and young family to settle on another parcel of land he had bought earlier in Burlington County, West Jersey.

Lying on the opposite bank of the Delaware river from Pennsylvania, West Jersey was already an established colony flourishing under Quaker principles of tolerance, simplicity and religious and political freedom combined with industriousness, honesty and enterprise. The European settlers found a sparsely populated land rich with plant and animal life and agricultural promise. While they did not doubt their right to colonise, they signed treaties with the Lenni-Lenape Indians of the area, developing peaceful relationships that contrasted starkly with conflicts in other settlements.

Though Robert, perhaps missing the familiar meadows and woodlands of south-east England, would return there with his family in 1689, his temporary emigration and investments brought him increased wealth, public status as a member of both the legislature and county court of Burlington, West Jersey, and the experience of living in a community founded on the tenets of his faith. Described by Penn himself as 'a solid and good man, ingenous [sic] & sufficient', he would hand on those principles to his sons and, in turn, their children, as well as the family profession: medicine.

Thomas, the baby whose birth date was jotted on the back of a medical recipe, was the child of John Dimsdale, Robert's eldest son. The family lived on the edge of Epping in a substantial Tudor house called Kendalls, one of the properties bought by Robert on his return from the colonies and handed on to John, who also inherited his father's medical practice. A cluster of smaller dwellings and outbuildings belonging to the house were occupied by tradesmen, while a meadow attached to the property provided a haven from its noise and bustle and a place for children to play.[3]

Just a stone's throw from Kendalls to the north lay the town's newly built Quaker Meeting House, a thatched, red-brick building attended by the Dimsdales for the modest and mainly silent worship distinctive of their faith. John Dimsdale, in keeping with the tradition of the Friends, had married a fellow Quaker, Susannah Bowyer, who added family money and connections to her husband's profitable profession. 'Marrying out' – choosing a spouse of another faith – was strongly discouraged by the sect, and considerable efforts were made to bring those who strayed back into the fold, as the young Thomas Dimsdale would later discover.

For now, though, Thomas and his seven siblings were brought up in a comfortable household imbued with Quaker values. Principles of truth, equality, non-violence and justice were not simply abstract goals but a code to live by, both individually and in the world. Later in the eighteenth century, Quakers would become leading voices in the movement for the abolition of the British slave trade, social reform, pacifism and public health – all causes Thomas Dimsdale would personally espouse. Susannah Dimsdale, writing in 1751 in her will to Thomas and his only surviving sibling Joseph, was still urging her adult sons to enact their faith, and to educate their own children within it. 'I desire you both to live in true love and affection one towards another, and to live in the practice of what you know to be right in your own hearts and to shun all manner of evil, so that you may be good examples to your children.' The imprint of Quaker family life shaped Thomas Dimsdale, and his loyalty and affection for the faith never left him, despite differences to come. Likewise, his network of Quaker friends and acquaintances would play crucial roles in his career, including in the invitation to Russia that would change his life forever.

Thomas's upbringing gave him a second defining force in his life, besides his faith: the practice of medicine. 'I lived with my father and attended his practice in physick, which was very great and extensive,' he wrote later.[4] John Dimsdale was a surgeon, barred as a Quaker from attending the medical schools at the two English universities of Oxford and Cambridge, who had honed his skills at his own father's side in West Jersey and Essex. He was paid by the parish to treat its residents under the Elizabethan Poor Law, the English system of locally organised poor relief based around the church and funded by local property taxes and tithes. By law, all parishes had to support 'the lame, the impotent, the old, the blind' and others unable to work, supplying those in need with basic necessities such as food, clothing and fuel and providing medical care. There was no centralised national healthcare or welfare system. In Epping, some individual villagers – among them 'Old Queen' and 'Beggar Betty' – received repeated cash payments, while other inhabitants were given provision in kind: waistcoats, stockings, faggots and re-soled shoes.[5]

The resources and generosity of parishes in distributing poor relief varied widely around the country, but records of payments to John Dimsdale (and later to Robert, Thomas's older brother) by the Overseers of Theydon Garnon show substantial contributions for medical assistance. Regular sums were paid, often for unspecified services, ranging from £5 to over £18 right up to John's death in 1730, when a special catch-up payment for any outstanding debts for care of the poor was authorised by the parish. In all, the doctor received over five percent of the Overseers' total annual expenditure – a proportion that prompted occasional grumbling from wealthy ratepayers and disapproving calls for pre-treatment authorisation.

Of all the demands on English parish coffers, one in particular stands out. An entry in the Theydon Garnon record for 1724 reads: 'From April 3rd paid for Mary Godfrey when she had the Smallpox £3/3/0. Paid Mr Dimsdale for Mary Godfrey £1/7/-.'[6] The brief lines shine a light not only on Mary's case, but on a disease so prevalent and severe it absorbed between one fifth and one tenth of all parish poor relief funds.[7] Smallpox patients were particularly expensive to treat, requiring attentive care for several weeks and potentially subsequent treatment for long-lasting disabilities. The poor, unable to work when sick or caring for family members, were left facing severe financial hardship, and the cost of burials placed an even greater strain on parish coffers.

The unrecorded voices of the poor themselves are gone, but glimpses of their suffering remain. In the Essex village of Little Horkesley, a letter records the experience of the family of George Patterson, whose wife and five children contracted the disease.

> The son about 13 years of age who fell down on Thursday is full of purple spots, so that He is not likely to live many days at all appearance . . . The wife is now likely to fall down, having the usual symptoms . . . they begin to be craving for victuals . . . there must be provision made of that kind, they have no firing nor any thing necessary but what is bought by the penny from hand to mouth . . . If the son dye there will be charges to bury him.[8]

Thomas Dimsdale, accompanying his father on his rounds, could not have avoided witnessing the brutal impact of smallpox, both on individual victims and on his community as a whole. A carriage ride away in London, where he would shortly move to train as a surgeon at St Thomas's Hospital, the disease was endemic, accounting in 1725 for one in every eight deaths.[9] In rural areas like his own home county, its presence ebbed and flowed, but the threat of devastating epidemics was always present. And for now, there appeared to be no way to fight back.

The variola virus, the brick-shaped microscopic agent that caused smallpox, was still unknown to the Dimsdales and their medical world, but the symptoms of the disease were all too familiar. After infecting the body through the mouth or nose, the virus would incubate silently for around twelve days, gradually spreading into the patient's bloodstream. Only then, as sufferers became highly infectious, did the first outward signs of illness appear: a fever, headache and sickness were followed by the emergence of a rash on the face and then body. This developed into hundreds of pustules which oozed, giving off a stomach-turning smell, sticking agonisingly to bedclothes and preventing eating or drinking if they blocked the throat. In the worst cases, known as 'confluent' smallpox, thousands of spots merged together in a purple mass, usually proving fatal.

Around a week after the onset of fever, if patients avoided blood poisoning and organ collapse, the pocks dried and scabbed over. Finally, after a month-long ordeal, most survivors were left with pronounced, pitted scars, often accompanied by blindness or irreversible joint damage. Josiah Wedgwood, of the renowned English pottery family, survived smallpox aged eleven in 1742 but suffered an infected and weakened right knee joint that prevented him operating the traditional potter's wheel and ultimately led to amputation.[10]

To try to understand smallpox, early eighteenth-century doctors relied on a medical doctrine based on the classical concept of humours. Defined by Galen, the most influential physician of the Roman Empire who had drawn in turn on Ancient Greek

Hippocratic tradition, the theory identified four vital humours: blood, phlegm, black bile and yellow bile, which had to be kept in balance to maintain health. An imbalance in these swirling bodily fluids caused disease, with symptoms such as diarrhoea, sweating and bleeding interpreted as the body's efforts to restore equilibrium by expelling excess matter through orifices and pores. In the ninth century, Rhazes, a Persian scholar, had built on the idea to identify smallpox as a distinct disease, which he explained as the result of an inherent tendency of the blood to ferment and expel the waste it produced though the skin.[11] According to this influential theory, everyone was born with smallpox latent within the body and expulsion was a natural process.

Drawing directly on these ancient ideas, most doctors in Europe were still treating smallpox by attempting to support and accelerate the body's 'natural' attempt to remove the 'poison' from the blood, pushing it to the surface and away from the organs at the core. Patients were kept as warm as possible, wrapped tightly in blankets in heated, airless rooms, to boost the fermentation process and force both sweat and contagion out through the pores. The colour red, symbolic of heat, was also thought to assist healing, and the Habsburg Emperor Joseph I of Austria was cocooned in '20 yards of English scarlet broadcloth' when he died from smallpox in 1711.[12]

A rival approach, developed by the brilliant English physician Thomas Sydenham fifty years before, held that, rather than seeking to assist sufferers' fever, the key was to suppress it by keeping them cool. The so-called 'cold method' permitted patients to get out of bed, open the windows and even walk outside. The idea, with its direct challenge to humoral theory, was controversial, but was to become critically important in the development of inoculation.

As well as hot or cold treatments, doctors could choose from an array of other methods to adjust a disordered balance of humours by purging the body of morbid matter. Bloodletting, using either the sharp blade of a lancet or live leeches, was widely used to lower fever; dating back to classical times, it was a go-to therapy for an array of ailments until the nineteenth century, when experiments showed it didn't work. Purgatives were prescribed to induce diarrhoea and emetics for vomiting. Diet also played a role in smallpox treatment, not least because luxurious living and over-indulgence in rich foods were blamed for triggering the dangerous 'innate fermentation'. Meat, spices and alcohol were forbidden, replaced by vegetables, broth and other plain fare, and herbal and chemical remedies of dubious value might also be added to the mix.

Uncertainty over the effectiveness of the many bewilderingly contradictory smallpox therapies did not prevent a lively debate among doctors. Pamphlets flew to and fro, each presenting new combinations of established and largely ineffective techniques, based on personal experience. Tempers sometimes flared. In 1719, the distinguished physicians John Woodward and Richard Mead engaged in an undignified impromptu duel over whether smallpox patients were best treated with emetics or purgatives. 'Take your life!' exclaimed Mead (the vomit enthusiast), as his opponent slipped and fell. 'Anything but your physic,' Woodward replied.[13]

For all their passion, doctors of the time could not 'cure' small-pox and could do little even to ease patients' suffering. According to their understanding of the disease, their therapies had a rational basis, but in practice the standard methods – bleeding or sweating patients and sometimes puncturing pustules and administering astringent eye drops – were generally ineffective and often actively harmful. Wealth or fame could not buy successful treatment. Wolfgang Amadeus Mozart, whose father Leopold had chosen to rely on 'God's grace' rather than have his son inoculated, was given 'black powder' from the family medicine chest after being infected with smallpox in Vienna during the epidemic of 1767. The substance, a brutal purgative concoction containing croton seeds and scammony, did nothing to repel the disease.[14] The eleven-year-old prodigy became violently ill, and his eyelids were so badly swollen there were fears his sight would never recover. When he finally returned to health, his father's relief was palpable. In a letter from Moravia on 10 November, he wrote: 'Te Deum Laudamus! Little Wolfgang has got over the smallpox safely!'[15]

Physicians, holding university degrees and positioned at the top of the medical status ladder above surgeons and apothecaries, diagnosed and treated those who could afford their services at the bedside through observation and discussion. They adapted therapies according to patients' symptoms and lifestyle and considered environmental factors such as the season of the year. Where surgeons dealt with the outside of the body, physicians held a monopoly on internal medicine, and used humoral theory and personal experience to predict disease course and outcome. Physical examinations were rare: doctors in Britain limited themselves to listening to breathing, tasting urine for sweetness, measuring the strength and rate of the pulse, and noting skin colour. Ailments were understood as clusters of changing symptoms, placing the patient and their constitution, rather than a specific disease, firmly at the centre of treatment. The most skilled doctors were regarded as those who could best tailor their therapies to the personal needs and habits of individual patients, despite the fact that the interventions of many did more harm than good.

Just as disease was poorly understood, so too was its spread. The sheer universality of smallpox, and the rapid progress of outbreaks, suggested the disorder was innate: existing as 'seeds' within the body that could be activated by certain external conditions. Could it be, doctors wondered, that miasmas – foul, stench-ridden air found in dirty and crowded environments – were triggering the disease, or alternatively somehow conveying it to the patient? Or was infection a matter of contagion, in which some specific and invisible agent was passed between individuals? Might fear itself be enough to activate the dormant seeds?

There was no way to be certain. The only effective strategy available to contain smallpox was isolation: patients were treated remotely as much as possible, increasingly in purpose-built 'pest houses' at some distance from inhabited areas, where basic nursing care could be provided. Fear of contagion from corpses meant burials were conducted swiftly, often under cover of night and in locations out of town rather than the churchyard. 'Due care is taken to bury the dead privately, and to give such as recover proper airings until they may be in a state to return home without danger of infecting others,' Thomas Dimsdale would note in one of his treatises. 'This method, when duly complied with, has prevented the disease from spreading, and preserved the neighbourhood from being generally infected.'[16]

The numbers who died of smallpox could never be counted precisely. Most data in seventeenth- and eighteenth-century Britain are drawn from the London Bills of Mortality, the system introduced in 1603 to record weekly in each parish in the capital the number of baptisms and burials and, from 1629, causes of death recognised at the time. Smallpox was initially bundled in with measles but gained its own separate category in 1652, after which the Bills chart a steady increase in deaths from the disease in London. The recording system was far from perfect, relying on 'searchers', typically elderly women employed to view corpses and identify causes of death. While many had experience of domestic or nursing care, they had no access, as women, to professional medical training and were sometimes open to bribery from those reluctant to have a business premises associated with a fatal and infectious illness. Young children, meanwhile, might die before the identifiable smallpox rash emerged and their deaths would be attributed to 'fevers', again skewing the numbers. Even assuming under-reporting, the Bills showed clearly that by the start of the eighteenth century the disease was becoming more virulent and the epidemic cycle was accelerating. The virus then stepped up another gear. On average, smallpox was responsible for around one in every twenty recorded deaths in the capital early in the century and one in ten by the 1750s. In epidemic years, such as 1752 when the disease claimed over 3,500 victims, the proportion rocketed to over one in every seven deaths.[17]

For the nine-tenths of the English population living outside London, smallpox mortality rates varied dramatically according to the ebb and flow of epidemics. A long gap between attacks meant less immunity within the local community, and the speckled monster could sweep in with irresistible force, leaving many victims in its wake. Fear of the disease was correspondingly strong in rural areas, and some country-dwellers took elaborate steps to isolate themselves from potential contact. The parents of the Quaker poet John Scott moved their family from London to the village of Amwell, Hertfordshire to escape the disease, shielding the talented child by keeping him away from school and cutting off connections in the literary world. Only in 1766, when he was successfully inoculated by Thomas Dimsdale aged thirty-five, did he finally free himself from 'fear of that distemper' and was again able to visit the capital, where he had been just once in twenty years.[18]

For most people, especially the poor, such draconian avoidance measures were impossible. As the French mathematician Charles-Marie de La Condamine would later declare in a landmark address making the case for inoculation, smallpox resembled a deep, fast-flowing river that almost everyone must cross, while those who had not yet done so lived in fear of being forced to plunge in at any moment.[19] There was little alternative to a level of fatalistic acceptance, and even a preference for children to suffer smallpox early when the economic loss to the family was less significant. Nevertheless, children made up the vast majority of smallpox deaths – ninety percent of those killed by the disease in British towns were under five, while a seventh of all Russian infants and a tenth of those born in Sweden died of the disease each year.[20] Parents were advised not to count their offspring until they had survived its clutches. A memorial in St Michael's Church in Bishop's Stortford, the Hertfordshire town where Thomas Dimsdale's sister lived, is inscribed with the names of seven children of the Maplesden family. Six of the children, aged five to twenty, died within five weeks in the autumn of 1684, and the seventh followed them the following June.

The economic effects on communities of the ravages of smallpox were as stark as the impact on individual families. The crippling expense of caring for the sick poor and supporting households when breadwinners died had a direct impact on the ability of parishes to fulfil their obligations to maintain infrastructure such as roads and bridges. In 1712, three parishes responsible for a wooden bridge on the busy Chelmsford to Braintree road in Essex explained in a petition to the local quarter sessions court that, 'in this very sickly season by reason of the smallpox', funds were too short to pay for repairs.[21]

An outbreak of smallpox in a town disrupted everyday life, damaging trade as fairs and markets closed and buyers and sellers stayed away. Schools were often shut for weeks to prevent the spread of the disease, interrupting learning and plunging their proprietors into debt, and church services and rites such as baptisms and marriages were also affected. The machines of law and government juddered to a halt as outbreaks interrupted their routines, causing assizes or quarter sessions to be suspended or moved away from areas of infection. Joseph King wrote to the Clerk of the Chelmsford Sessions to excuse himself for missing jury service:

> I should have readily attended but am informed that the Small Pox is very much about Chelmsford and its neighbourhood and neither my Self Wife nor any of my Children have had it, it strikes such a Dread and Horror upon me that I dare not venture to attend so I humbly beg of your Worship for this time to excuse me.[22]

Even once an epidemic subsided, the crowds stayed away, prompting town authorities to publish public notices declaring the community free of smallpox and open for business.

The sheer visibility of the disease, not only during an attack but in the physical scars it left behind, haunted daily transactions. Wealthy families wary of contagion advertised in local newspapers for servants who had already had smallpox, as their skin would testify. Conversely, those seeking employment made clear they had passed safely through the disease and, being immune, would pose no risk to those who hired them. A young woman looking for a post as a dairymaid or housemaid described herself as 'A sober girl, who has had the smallpox, and who can be well recommended for her honesty.'

Indentured apprentices who ran away from their masters found their complexions mentioned in notices offering rewards for their return. The *Ipswich Journal* gave a description of a trainee blacksmith, Robert Ellis, aged 'about twenty', who had run away in Lowestoft: 'Has red Hair, is pitted with the Small-pox, has a face a good deal freckled, and crooked legs.'[23] An advertisement for the capture of the highwayman Dick Turpin in 1735 described the outlaw as 'a tall, fresh-coloured man, very much mark'd with the Small Pox . . . wears a Blew Grey Coat and a light natural Wig'.[24]

Readers of the many newspapers that sprang up during the

eighteenth century found numerous advertisements for ointments and salves to soothe smallpox scars, posted by the enterprising but unqualified 'quack' doctors who occupied the lowest level on the ladder of medical prestige. 'Dr Daffy's Famous Cordial Elixir', offered at the never-to-be repeated price of two shillings per half pint, purportedly cured everything from scurvy and gout to hangovers and piles, as well as being 'a certain Remedy in the Small-Pox and Meazles'.[25] Family recipe books, commonly containing medicinal remedies as well as recipes for food, also featured directions for home-made herbal treatments for smallpox symptoms and scarring.

For women, especially those of higher social rank, disfigurement caused by the disease brought especially damaging consequences. The loss of unblemished beauty was not simply a matter for personal sorrow: a ravaged face equalled reduced marriage prospects. Scarred survivors paid a significant economic price as their market value, measured by attractiveness as well as rank, diminished overnight. To spare wealthy victims the horror of their own changed reflections, mirrors were removed from their walls, while masks and veils ensured their altered looks did not in turn terrify strangers. But the gestures only underlined the loss not only of a woman's social position but of her very identity: if to be female was to be beautiful, could a scarred individual be fully a woman at all?

Even amid such existential questions, ways were found to ensure the marriage market continued to function. A genre of gallant smallpox poetry emerged, in which ready-made verses with titles such as 'To a Lady, on her recovery from the smallpox' set out to provide templates for suitors eager to declare their love was more than skin deep. Clunking metaphors were pressed into service in an effort to acknowledge the unignorable yet reclaim the idea of beauty: 'Say, does the sun less bright appear tho' spots o'er-spread his face?'[26]

Faced with the scourge that was smallpox, however, poetry, together with salves, elixirs, leeches and the rest, would never be enough. Only a radical new approach would challenge the increasingly virulent disease as it claimed ever more victims. As the young Thomas Dimsdale began to study the art of medicine at his father's knee, news of the medical innovation that would finally change the odds in the battle with smallpox was arriving just a few miles away in London. It would first be championed in Britain not by a doctor but by a woman who bore the emotional and physical scars of the disease.

Lady Mary Wortley Montagu was an aristocrat, a mother and a woman of penetrating intelligence, determination and courage. She was also rebellious, fashionable, exquisitely well connected, and fully understood the power of influence. It was an unstoppable combination: she recognised the medical significance of inoculation and knew she could promote it by example.

The daughter of the Whig Member of Parliament Evelyn Pierrepont, Earl of Kingston, Lady Mary grew up exposed to political and court networks, gaining an early sense of the public world and her place within it. She read voraciously, wrote poetry and taught herself Latin. 'I am going to write a history so uncommon, that in how plain a manner so ever I relate it, IT will have the Air of Romance, tho there shall be not a sillable feign'd in it,' she declared in her teenage autobiography.[27]

In 1712, the year Thomas Dimsdale was born, Mary defied her father's wishes over her arranged marriage to the Anglo-Irish politician Clotworthy Skeffington and eloped with the aristocrat and politician Edward Wortley Montagu. Famed for her beauty, wit and intellect alike, she swiftly gained prominence at Court and among London's aristocratic and literary elite.

Social status was no protection against smallpox, however: the disease attacked 'the quality' just as readily as the poor. In 1713, Mary's beloved younger brother William died of the disease, and two years later, aged twenty-six, she too fell victim. She recovered, but suffered a scarred face and lost her eyelashes, leaving her with a distinctive piercing gaze and a lifelong sense of beauty lost.

Fresh from these traumatic experiences, the Montagus travelled in 1717 to Turkey, where Edward had been appointed ambassador to the Ottoman court at Constantinople. Soon after arriving, Mary encountered the traditional medical practice that, to her amazement, defied the brutal virus: inoculation. Families, she observed, would hold smallpox parties every September at which as many as sixteen children might be treated. Under the Turkish method, she wrote excitedly to her childhood friend Lady Sarah Chiswell, old women used a needle to deliver a drop of pus from the pustules of a smallpox patient into a child's veins in several places, then covered the wound with pieces of walnut shell. A mild dose of the disease

LADY MARY WORTLEY MONTAGUE.

Lady Mary Wortley Montagu.

followed, then lifelong immunity. 'The smallpox, so fatal, and so general among us, is here entirely harmless, by the invention of *ingrafting*, which is the term they give it,' she reported. 'Every year thousands undergo this operation . . . there is no example of anyone that has died in it . . . I am patriot enough to take pains to bring this useful invention into fashion in England.'[28]

Mary was as good as her word. She had her five-year-old son Edward painfully but successfully inoculated by 'an old Greek woman' using a blunt and rusty needle, with the Embassy surgeon, Charles Maitland, in attendance, and then returned to London eager to promote the practice.[29] Her timing, for her purpose, was perfect. In April 1721, after a winter so warm that roses bloomed in January, smallpox rampaged 'like a destroying angel' in the capital. As growing numbers of her own acquaintances succumbed to the disease, Mary called on Maitland to inoculate her three-year-old daughter, also Mary.[30] Reluctantly, the surgeon agreed, but insisted two physicians should be present during the operation, 'not only to consult the health and safety of the child, but likewise to be eyewitness of the Practice, and contribute to the credit and reputation of it'. The little girl was inoculated in both arms with no preparatory bleeding or purging, and experienced a 'fair and favourable' case of smallpox with just a few distinct spots.[31] When three eminent members of the Royal College of Physicians, probably including its President Sir Hans Sloane, arrived to view the young patient, they found her 'playing about the room, cheerful and well, with the Small Pox raised upon her'.[32] It was the first official inoculation performed in Britain.

The event was a milestone, but, as with many scientific waymarks, the same point might have been reached by another route. Reports of inoculation in China and the Ottoman Empire had begun to arrive in England from the very start of the century, most influentially from the Greek-born physician Emanuele Timoni, whose brief written account of the method used in Constantinople was presented in 1714 to the Royal Society.[33] Inoculation had reached the city in around 1672, Timoni reported, introduced by Circassians and Georgians from the Caucasus region across the Black Sea to the east. After overcoming 'suspicion and doubt', it was now widely accepted and triumphantly successful: 'since the operation, having been performed on persons of all ages, sexes, and different temperaments . . . none have been found to die of the smallpox'.

Members of the Society, the eminent national scientific academy founded fifty years earlier and boasting Sir Isaac Newton as its president, asked for more information. A second doctor, Giacomo Pylarini – a Venetian born in Greece who had practised in Moscow, Smyrna and many cities in between – confirmed the technique and reported in 1716 that inoculation had been successfully used in the Balkans and Caucasus for many years before spreading to Christian communities in Turkey.[34] In both cases, the papers were published in the Society's journal, the *Philosophical Transactions*, and members of the august body discussed the ideas. There was no attempt to go further: entrenched medical conservatism ensured that, for twenty-one years, not a single clinical experiment was conducted to test the strange procedure conducted by old women in foreign lands.

Equally, England's medical establishment did not deign to notice the folk practices employed on its own doorstep to tackle smallpox. In parts of Scotland and Wales, it had long been a custom for villagers to 'buy the smallpox': paying a few pence for scabs to be held in the hands or rubbed on children's skin, perhaps with the idea of transferring the disease from one person to another as a cure for the afflicted.

In the end, neither scientific reports nor existing practice launched inoculation in Britain. Instead, the catalyst was the example set by a determined and informed woman, passionately convinced of the value of her cause and willing to stake her children's lives on it. The inoculation of little Mary Montagu was not reported in the newspapers, but her mother's connections and profile ensured word quickly spread within London's influential social networks. One of the physicians who observed the child's recovery, Dr James Keith, immediately ordered the procedure for his own six-year-old son, Peter, having lost his two older boys to smallpox in the 1717 epidemic. By having her daughter inoculated in England, in the presence of powerful medical witnesses, Lady Mary had given credence to 'exotic' oriental customs previously considered little more than a scientific curiosity. Her private act as a mother took on public significance.

For the elites of the capital, inoculation became the new fashion, exactly as Mary had hoped. Taking her daughter with her as evidence of a healthy recovery and confidence in immunity, she toured the drawing rooms of London promoting her cause. The continuing smallpox epidemic gave added edge to her one-woman campaign, and she was in exhaustingly high demand. Horace Walpole (youngest son of the Prime Minister Robert Walpole), was among the first aristocratic infants to undergo the operation, along with the children of the Austrian ambassador and the future novelist Henry Fielding and his siblings.[35] By 1723, Mary was reporting to her sister that, 'Lady Bing has inoculated both her children . . . I believe they will do very well . . . The whole town are doing the same thing and I am so much pull'd about and solicited to visit people, that I am forc'd to run into the Country to hide my selfe.'

Of the prominent households who swiftly followed her example, one held more influence than all the others together: the royal family. With her lineage, charm and wit, Mary was already well connected at Court, often visiting St James's Palace. There, she played cards with King George I, the Hanoverian prince who had succeeded to the British throne in 1714 on the death of Queen Anne, and joined the circle of his intelligent and scientifically minded daughter-in-law Caroline of Ansbach, the Princess of Wales.

When Caroline's eldest daughter, Anne, narrowly escaped death by smallpox at the same time as little Mary Montagu's inoculation, it was no wonder her mother, anxious to protect her two younger daughters from the disease, sought more information about the new procedure. Encouraged by the Princess, a group of physicians including Sir Hans Sloane successfully petitioned the King for permission to conduct an inoculation trial on condemned prisoners at Newgate gaol, offering a pardon to the chosen volunteers.

With Caroline and her husband, the future George II, as official sponsors, the so-called Royal Experiment went ahead in August 1721 in a blaze of publicity. There was no concern with ethics. Three men and two women, all thieves convicted of stealing goods including wigs, cash and Persian silk and all swearing they had never had smallpox, were each inoculated in both arms and right leg by Maitland under the watchful eye of Sloane and the King's personal

Anuconi Pinx.   A.Van hecchen Fecit: 1736.

Serenissima Carolina D.G. Mag: Brit: Fran: et Hib: REGINA,

Caroline of Ansbach, Princess of Wales.

physician. A third woman had ground smallpox scabs put up her nose, in an effort to mimic an alternative inoculation technique used in China. Some twenty-five physicians, surgeons and apothecaries witnessed the trial.

Five of the prisoners developed the expected few dozen spots and light fever and quickly recovered (though the nasal approach proved deeply uncomfortable), while one man had no symptoms and turned out to have lied in a bid for freedom: he had had the disease before. The experiment convinced Sloane that inoculation produced mild smallpox, and that it had no effect on those who had already had the disease naturally.

There was one key fact left to check: would the mild illness conveyed artificially through inoculation really confer full immunity to the natural disease? The only way to be sure was to expose one of the inoculated prisoners to smallpox, and Elizabeth Harrison, nineteen, was sent to nurse a series of patients including a schoolboy whose bed she was instructed to share during his illness. Elizabeth stayed well and Sloane and his fellow doctors had their proof.

Princess Caroline, debating having her two younger daughters inoculated, was not yet convinced. To test the procedure on children, she paid for a further clinical trial on another group whose bodies were effectively seen as the property of the state: six young orphans drawn from the parish of St James at Westminster. The youngsters also recovered well and an advertisement in *The London Gazette* announced they would be on display to 'satisfy the curious' at a house in Soho each morning and afternoon.[36]

With the blessing of their grandfather George I, and the permission of Parliament, Princesses Amelia, eleven, and nine-year-old Caroline were finally inoculated by the King's surgeon, Claude Amyand, assisted by Maitland and overseen by Sloane, in April 1722.[37] The girls, like the prisoners and orphans, were soon well again, and the Prince and Princess of Wales showcased them prominently at court occasions, where they performed specially choreographed dances to demonstrate their blooming health.[38] Like Mary Wortley Montagu, and Catherine II of Russia in decades to come, Caroline of Ansbach recognised that scientific facts alone were often not enough to allay doubts over inoculation: human connection and the power of example were essential too.

The Hanoverian royal family were now firm advocates of smallpox inoculation and would remain so throughout the eighteenth century. George I sent Maitland to Hanover to inoculate his grandson Frederick, and wrote recommending the procedure to his daughter Sophia Dorothea, Queen of Prussia.[39] Princess Caroline and the future George II continued to treat their growing family. Later, George III and Queen Charlotte would inoculate all of their fifteen children and, despite losing two sons to the practice, supported it unwaveringly, endorsing its dissemination abroad by English doctors such as Thomas Dimsdale.

But as the Prince and Princess of Wales promoted the ground-breaking medical advance, an anti-inoculation backlash was already beginning. In the rush to meet elite families' demand for the operation, two widely reported tragedies occurred: the four-year-old son of an Earl inoculated by Maitland died following the procedure, while a footman in Hertford succumbed after catching smallpox from an inoculated child in the household. The first case showed that the procedure itself carried risk, while the second revealed a difficult truth: inoculated patients could still, while recovering, infect others with natural smallpox.

William Wagstaffe, a physician at St Bartholomew's Hospital and Fellow of the Royal Society, highlighted the danger of accidental infection in a lengthy public letter, published just weeks after the Royal Experiment.[40] Inoculating a patient, Wagstaffe argued, was like deliberately setting one house on fire and reducing a neighbourhood to ashes even if the first house survived. 'When not only those who are inoculated, but those infected from them, shall die of the distemper, 'tis time for every parent to examine what he is doing, and for the inoculator to consider that he is answerable for all the consequences,' he thundered.

Attempting, like all his medical contemporaries, to understand the new technology in terms of classical humoral theory, he warned that pustule matter added to patients' blood could not be properly discharged from the skin, and argued that the appropriate dosage for an individual patient was not understood. There was 'all manner of uncertainty in this experiment', with no guarantee that the immunity apparently conferred would be permanent.

Physicians should not be overhasty in encouraging a practice not yet sufficiently supported by reason or fact, wrote Wagstaffe, acidly noting with a sideswipe at the trendsetting royal parents that 'the fashion of inoculating the small pox has so far prevailed, as to be admitted into the greatest families'. Where Mary Wortley Montagu had had the insight to seize on and disseminate the wisdom of elderly Turkish women, the prejudiced doctor dismissed inoculation precisely because of its Eastern, female-centred origin. 'Posterity perhaps will scarcely be brought to believe, that an Experiment practiced only by a few Ignorant Women, amongst an illiterate and unthinking People, should on a sudden, and upon a slender Experience, so far obtain in one of the Politest Nations in the World, as to be receiv'd into the Royal Palace.'

Another critic, the surgeon Legard Sparham, branded inoculation 'one of the scandals of the age', comparable with the recent South Sea Bubble, the infamous financial collapse caused by greed and stock market manipulation.[41] Sparham, who believed the process injected 'poison' into the bloodstream and produced dangerously severe smallpox, was early in voicing the fundamental objection that would always be raised against inoculation and its successor, vaccination: why should individuals be deliberately exposed to an immediate health risk in order to counter a future one they might yet avoid?

The practice was the equivalent of a man with toothache advising his friend to pull his own tooth out just in case he too suffered in future, Sparham argued, or of a soldier asking his comrade to shoot at him to ready him for possible death in battle. 'In a sound and healthy state, by the mercenary and cunning artifice of some, Wretches are persuaded to change their sound condition for a diseas'd; the expectation of one day falling ill, for a certain sickness now, under pretence of future security.'

Sparham, never a man to use a plain phrase where a flowery one would do, was also one of the first critics to refer to inoculation in terms of chance – a concept that, in a more rigorous form, would later become central to promotion of the new technology. 'That the inclinations of Mankind should prompt them to throw a Dye for their Lives, when no Necessity obliges, because there is a Possibility of surviving the Chance, is Matter of the greatest Admiration,' the surgeon wrote with heavy irony. He concluded with one of the earliest swipes at the pioneering doctors responsible: 'Our condition is desperate and these Gentlemen, these new Operators, are kindly furnishing us with materials for our Dispatch.'

Sceptical medical practitioners with their tracts and pamphlets were not the only group opposed to the newfangled procedure: some churchmen too objected, warning that it defied the will of God. From the pulpit of St Andrew's Church in Holborn, London, the Reverend Edmund Massey denounced inoculation as a sinful, diabolical practice, claiming that the Devil himself had been the first inoculator when, as recounted in the Bible, he tortured Job with a plague of boils.[42] God sent disease 'either for the trial of our faith, or for the punishment of our sins', he argued, therefore preventing it interfered with the divine plan. With no fear of retribution, what sins might man indulge in?

By seeking to control disease, the cleric raged, doctors were, effectively, playing God. 'I shall not scruple to call that a Diabolical Operation which usurps an authority founded neither in the laws of nature or religion, which tends in this case to banish Providence out of the world, and promotes the increase of Vice and Immorality.'

The assaults on the effectiveness and morality of inoculation prompted an immediate counterblast from its supporters. John Arbuthnot, a Scottish physician, mathematician and satirist, leapt to the defence of the practice, rushing out a withering point-by-point rebuttal to Woodward and Massey to be chewed over in the coffee shops and public houses of London and beyond.[43] His pamphlet, published anonymously in September 1722, pulled no punches, accusing both men of prejudice and accusing the 'Anti-inoculators' (possibly the first written use of the term for the forerunners of today's anti-vaxxers) of holding 'inconsistent and changeable' opinions in their headlong rush to discredit the new technology.

Arbuthnot countered with numbers, using the London Bills of Mortality to calculate deaths from natural smallpox at one in ten cases while estimating those from inoculation at only one in a hundred. The argument laid down the important principle of comparison, but the mathematician did not provide data supporting his estimate.

Inoculation gave patients a much better chance of surviving smallpox than if they caught the disease naturally, Arbuthnot reasoned, since it allowed them to choose advantageous circumstances: a favourable season of year; a time when the body's humours were balanced and in a 'temperate and cool state'; the chance to prepare with a modest diet and not a 'drunken bout'. The procedure was not seen as a means of avoiding or fending off small-pox: rather it was a way for individuals to pass through a mild version of the disease as safely as possible with the maximum amount of preparation and control.

To Woodward's complaints that it was wrong to artificially produce a disease, Arbuthnot noted that in many standard medical practices – purging, bleeding, amputations – doctors themselves instigated a natural process as a means of prevention as well as cure. Indeed, without experiments, how would any medical discovery ever be made? 'In all these matters, Mankind generally govern themselves by common Sense and strong Probabilities; there being no absolute certainty in any human Affairs.'

The sharp-tongued physician had even less time for Reverend Massey, who seemed to have 'cast aside the divine' and was playing doctor. The cleric had not shown any evidence that inflicting disease for good purposes was unlawful in the eyes of God, and – given that anyone who had not yet had smallpox had the 'seeds' of the poten-tially fatal disease within him – a doctor had a duty to do whatever was most likely to save him from danger. Likewise, opting for inoc-ulation was not a sign of a lack of faith in God on the part of the patient. If a man leapt out of a window for fear of fire, wrote Arbuthnot, 'surely that can never be reckoned a mistrust of Providence, even if he did it before he was much in danger'; after all, God might through Providence save him from a fire in future anyway.

Within a few short months of the royal inoculation, battle lines had been drawn in Britain. In a passionate pamphlet war, propo-nents and critics of the new technology were establishing, and loudly voicing, arguments that would echo down the century and beyond. The introduction of smallpox inoculation, the world's first preventative medical procedure, had already shaken established beliefs and dramatically divided opinion. And as controversy raged, the disease continued on its savage path, claiming more victims than ever before.

*   *   *

News of the dramatic medical breakthrough filtered out of the capital in pamphlets and newspapers, but there is no evidence it changed the practice of the Quaker doctor John Dimsdale on his rounds in Essex, his young son Thomas learning at his side. The surgeon continued to treat smallpox victims, as he did other patients, with the techniques of traditional humoral medicine, relying on bleeding and purging to rebalance the body and drive out disease.

In 1730, aged just fifty-five, John Dimsdale died. His eldest surviving son, Robert, took over his practice, and Thomas, by now eighteen, was sent to complete his medical studies in London. Unlike his grandfather, imprisoned decades previously for practising physic without a licence, and his father, Thomas was able to train as a surgeon at a hospital, St Thomas's in Southwark. At the start of the century, alongside an extensive building programme, medical education at the hospital had been formalised: a haphazard process by which students were apprenticed to surgeons on an ad hoc basis was replaced with basic regulations to control entry and restrict the numbers attached to each practitioner. There was also the opportunity to attend lectures and dissection classes provided by eminent experts at the hospital.

Thomas was apprenticed, he wrote later, to 'that able anatomist Mr Joshua Symonds, who was then one of the surgeons of St Thomas's, and gave lectures of anatomy in the theatre there, and soon after my coming to him was elected Demonstrator of Anatomy at Surgeons Hall'.[44] The study of anatomy was the most prestigious course offered at the hospital, providing top quality practical instruction. Students crammed the hall as cadavers were expertly dissected by the cream of the medical profession. When Symonds died, the young Quaker doctor signed up for further training with his successor and three physicians 'of distinguished character, whose practice I had daily advantage of attending'. It was a far cry from home visits in Theydon Garnon. Thomas was learning in the country's most cutting-edge hands-on medical environment, and from the best of the best.

In the middle of his apprenticeship, an all too familiar tragedy struck the Dimsdale family. Thomas's older sister Susannah, married and living in Hertfordshire, died aged twenty-four of smallpox and premature childbirth. 'My dear child ... departed this life 20 February 1732 of the smallpox and lying in coming before her expected time and her son died in a few days after her and was buried in her grave at Bishop's Stortford,' wrote her mother Susannah Dimsdale in her diary.[45] Like Mary Wortley Montagu, Thomas had lost a beloved sibling to the speckled monster. Beating back the fatal disease would always have personal resonance.

His training completed two years later, Thomas set up as a surgeon aged just twenty-two: a handsome young man with an open face, dimpled chin and serious expression. He began his career not in Essex but in Hertford, where he had inherited property and a medical practice from his father's childless cousin, Sir John Dimsdale. In keeping with Quaker tradition, the Friends at the new arrival's previous place of worship, Enfield, provided a handwritten certificate of recommendation to the Hertford Meeting of the Society, signed by six witnesses. On 29 May 1734, they reported that:

> his conversation has been orderly during his residence amongst us and was also free and clear from all persons in relation to marriage so far as appeared to them. We therefore recommend him to your tender care and oversight as he has descended from valuable parents; we hope and desire he may be preserved in a humble state walking in the Truth.[46]

For five years, the young surgeon developed his new practice and fulfilled the weighty expectations of the faith he had been immersed in from birth. But in 1739, he did something entirely unexpected, that would, at least for a while, drive him away from the puritanical Friends. He married out.

Dr James Jurin, Secretary of the Royal Society.

2

The Deadly Lottery

'Everyone has his ticket, and many every year must draw the
blank of Death'

Charles-Marie de La Condamine[1]

Light flooded down through the high arched windows of the
Church of St Benet Paul's Wharf in the City of London as Thomas
Dimsdale married Mary Brassey, only daughter of the MP for
Hertford, on 13 July 1739. The church, designed by Christopher
Wren in ox-blood-hued brick and Portland stone, lay squarely
between the River Thames and Wren's masterpiece, St Paul's
Cathedral, in the very heart of the capital. Inside, the couple made
their vows in front of a priest of the Church of England, in direct
defiance of the Quaker rejection of the priesthood in favour of each
individual's 'light within'. The marriage was entered in the parish
record, while the Friends' own assiduous record-keeping documented their consternation that Thomas had chosen a wife from
outside the sect – and their efforts to persuade him to repent.

Socially, the match was suitable, even advantageous, for the
ambitious young surgeon. Mary's father, Nathaniel Brassey, was a
banker and politician, the son of a wealthy Quaker banker though
not a Friend himself. Her mother Bithia was the daughter of Sir
John Fryer, a baronet, merchant and prominent Presbyterian
layman. For the Quakers of Hertford, however, marrying out of the
sect was 'a disorderly practice' that challenged the purity of their
community and could not be ignored. Two local members of the
sect, John Pryor and Thomas Grubb, were appointed to visit Thomas

at home and 'endeavour to make him sensible' of his offence.[2] They duly paid their call, but the records of the Hertford Meeting show that, while he was prepared to listen politely, the men's efforts proved fruitless. 'He did not seem at present disposed to hear the Truth,' noted the record, pledging a further visit. This too failed, but the persistent Friends decided, 'in tenderness . . . towards him', to offer a further chance to acknowledge his offence.

At this third visit, in 1741, Thomas informed Pryor and Grubb that he had nothing further to offer the Meeting, and the members finally gave up hope 'of his being brought to a due sense and acknowledgement of his said offence'. A Testimony against the doctor was drawn up, noting that he had married a person 'not of our religious Society, and in such a way as is contrary to the Good Order and discipline established amongst Friends', and had failed to respond adequately to repeated entreaties to apologise. The meeting found his actions 'inconsistent with the Truth he made profession of with Us as a people' and declared that 'we cannot have unity with him as a member of our Religious Society, until he comes to a sincere Sorrow for his said offence'. The testimony was read out and, in 1742, delivered to Thomas. The young man brought up as a devout Quaker, whose heritage stretched back to the beginnings of the sect, had been – in its distinctive terminology – 'disowned'.

To defy the strictures of his faith community in a small market town, and the likely disapproval of his family, took courage on the part of Thomas Dimsdale, and a measure of stubbornness. Having come carefully to a conclusion, he was not a man to change his mind. He loved Mary Brassey, and if marrying her meant standing before a priest, he was willing to take the consequences, and perhaps even welcome them. Disownment offered escape from the claustrophobic discipline of the Friends, freeing him to pursue his medical ambitions and build the wealth he valued more than he allowed himself to admit.

The newlyweds could not foresee that Thomas's sacrifice would buy them just a few short years of happiness. In February 1744, after less than five years of marriage that had produced no children, Mary died. Thomas was heartbroken. Widowed at thirty-two and lost without the woman for whom he had left his faith, he turned for advice to his friend and fellow Quaker Dr John Fothergill, a talented Yorkshire-born physician who had begun his training at St Thomas's Hospital just as Thomas was completing his own studies.

Fothergill, already an influential figure in London's medical and Quaker circles and a man whose patronage would later prove life-changing for Thomas, offered a practical diversion. He encouraged the inconsolable young widower to join his campaign to raise funds for the English army fighting the Jacobites, the Scottish rebels seeking to overthrow the Hanoverian King George II and regain the British throne for the Catholic Stuarts.[3] With most British troops tied up on the continent by ongoing war in mainland Europe, the Scots, led by the 'Young Pretender' Prince Charles Edward Stuart, were able in late 1745 to push south into England, reaching Derby on their march towards the capital. English volunteer regiments massed to defend the royal cause, but with few supplies and thin clothing they were ill-equipped for the cold of an especially severe winter. The Quakers, forbidden by their pacifist principles from fighting for their country or funding arms, opted instead to raise money to provide every soldier – some ten thousand men – with a double-breasted woollen waistcoat and breeches.[4] It was a practical cause to which Thomas could donate in good conscience.

Inadequate clothing was not the only problem besetting English troops as they sought to halt the advance of Bonnie Prince Charlie and his Jacobite rebels: there was widespread concern at a lack of physicians and surgeons to help the sick and wounded. Here, at last, was a chance for Thomas to provide not only charitable donations but specialist help. Still grieving, with no responsibilities to keep him in Hertford and 'totally disengaged with business', he again sought the advice of Fothergill and volunteered his services for free as a military doctor.[5] He travelled north to join the royal army under Prince William Augustus, Duke of Cumberland, at Preston, Lancashire, and continued on with the troops to Carlisle, where the garrison surrendered as the Scots retreated over the border.

Relieved to have been at least 'usefully employed', Thomas returned home to Hertford, where, unexpectedly, new happiness awaited him. In June 1746, just two months after the Jacobite army was brutally and finally crushed by British forces at the Battle of

Culloden, he married for a second time, once again choosing a wife from outside his own sect. He exchanged vows with Ann Iles, a cousin of his first wife, in the chapel of Aske's Hospital in Hoxton, London, a handsome colonnaded building belonging to the Worshipful Company of Haberdashers, one of the ancient merchant guilds of the capital. Thomas Dimsdale the Quaker outsider was now an accepted establishment man. Ann, from the village of Roxford, near Hertford, brought a dowry of £9,000, a sum so substantial that her family drew up a prenuptial agreement setting out what should happen to the funds should the marriage not go to plan.

After a period of mourning, endured in self-imposed exile from his local Quaker community, Thomas was no longer alone. Despite his in-laws' caution, his second marriage would last for over thirty-two years, produce seven surviving children and, on Ann's death, he would write that 'we both considered our union as the most happy that could possibly be'. This he would attribute to his wife's 'engaging and compliant temper and her tender regard for me', confessing, 'I am sensible for my own heart that I had faults tho my love was very great.'[6] He was also financially secure, easing the concern that always nagged at him even as his career blossomed. Just three generations from poverty and the gaol house, and born a dissenter, he knew money secured his place in the world. Ann's fortune added to his own substantial inheritance from his father's cousin John Dimsdale, recently further enhanced following the death in 1745 of Dame Susannah Dimsdale, John's widow. Susannah's will, with its references to 'all my carriages, chariots, chaises, horses, stock in husbandry, cattle', reflected not only the travelling arrangements but the comfortable wealth of a successful English doctor.[7]

In a few short years Thomas had known love and loss, and twice shown his readiness to follow his own heart and mind in defiance of his virtuous but prescriptive religious community. He had established his medical practice and been willing to give up his comfortable life in a market town to treat the sick and wounded in a testing winter conflict. Maintaining his Quaker pacifism, he had nevertheless seen first-hand something of the reality of war, and the politics that drove it. At about this time, too, he had begun to introduce a new procedure into his practice, a breakthrough so important he immediately hoped it would be used universally. The technique was smallpox inoculation.

By the time Thomas Dimsdale began inoculating patients in Hertford and beyond, the debate over the technology had moved in Britain from furious pamphlet war to broad positive consensus, at least among the medical community. The publicity surrounding the campaign of Mary Wortley Montagu and the subsequent Royal Experiment had generated intense interest and controversy over the preventative treatment, but the high-profile examples themselves had not settled the matter. Stories of princesses, thieves and orphans gave way to a new development that would prove crucial to the acceptance of inoculation. It was all about statistics.

Soon after the inoculation of the Newgate prisoners in August 1721, newspaper reports of the trial reached Thomas Nettleton, a physician educated at the progressive Dutch university of Utrecht and working in Halifax in his native West Riding of Yorkshire. The smallpox epidemic sweeping England was raging in the woollen-cloth-making town and its surrounding hillside hamlets, carrying off children and adults alike. Nettleton's experience of visiting desperately ill patients, 'whose cases were so deplorable, as to admit of no relief', prompted him to take a radical decision: he would personally test out the new technique, 'which promised to carry many persons thro' that cruel Distemper, with so much ease and safety'.[8] Using as a manual the accounts of inoculations in Turkey published in the journal of the Royal Society a few years before, he made a cut on the arm and opposite leg of his first patient and inserted two or three drops of pus from a smallpox sufferer. To his delight, the procedure worked 'beyond my expectation'. The trial patient recovered, and Nettleton inoculated over forty local people using his own improvised technique with no resulting deaths and few serious side effects. The brutality of the natural disease was clear at every turn: he recorded he had inoculated a girl 'in a family where they had formerly Bury'd three Children successively of the small pox'.

There was only one downside: to his distress, his efforts had met with 'vigorous opposition' from many 'honest, well-meaning' critics who believed the practice to be unlawful, including some who spread 'false and groundless reports, whereby this matter has been very much misrepresented'. The rumours had put off some parents from inoculating themselves or their children, who had since died of smallpox. No sooner was inoculation under way than anti-inoculation fake news was out and spreading.

Nettleton, experimenting alone far from London and looking for support there that might convince his local opponents, shared his findings with William Whitaker, a friend and fellow doctor in the capital. Whitaker passed the letter to James Jurin, Secretary of the illustrious Royal Society, and himself a prominent physician and skilled mathematician. The connection was to prove invaluable. The sensational report from Halifax was read to the Society in May 1722, shortly after the inoculation of the two Princesses, and Jurin immediately requested more information. Nettleton replied with accounts of his own research, in which he had decided to gauge the safety of the new procedure by 'making a comparison so far as our experience will extend' of the relative dangers of natural and inoculated smallpox.[9]

Gathering data on smallpox mortality rates in Halifax and other towns in Yorkshire and nearby Lancashire and Cheshire, Nettleton found that of 3,405 people who had caught the disease naturally during the epidemic, 636 had died – almost one in five – while all sixty-one people he had by now inoculated had survived. He placed the figures in a simple table listing smallpox cases and deaths for each location, and recommended the comparative approach to Jurin, adding: 'I am very sensible You will require a great Number of Observations before you can draw any certain Conclusions'. Even if there were deaths from inoculation, Nettleton pointed out, it would at least be possible to weigh up the numbers using what he called 'the Merchant's Logick'. 'State the Accounts of Profit and Loss to find on which side the Balance Lyes . . . and form a Judgement accordingly.'

Nettleton's direct comparison of death rates seems unremarkable today, yet it represented a landmark in the history of medicine. His 1722 analysis of the safety of smallpox inoculation is arguably the first known example of the use of numerical quantification to evaluate a medical practice.[10] Instead of the subjective opinion of an individual physician based on a clutch of cases, or a tradition relying on established authorities stretching back to classical times, the Yorkshire doctor was using directly acquired data to assess the new technology, and letting the numbers do the talking.

As the anti-inoculation backlash began in London in the wake of the Newgate prisoner experiment, Jurin seized on Nettleton's approach to help get to the truth about the risks of the new procedure. He too had begun to explore numerical analysis, but, like Arbuthnot, had based his attempts to work out the fatality rate of natural smallpox on historic data in the London Bills of Mortality, the notoriously unreliable cause-of-death statistics collected by each parish in the capital. Using the Bills, which he adjusted to allow for the fact that many infants died of other diseases before encountering smallpox, he produced tables suggesting that, on average, a person who survived infancy had a one in seven or eight chance of dying of natural smallpox.

Nettleton's example showed that it was possible to go further and quantify not only mortality rates from a particular disease but the risk of death from the intervention used to tackle it. Comparing the two figures – using the 'Merchant's Logick' – would help answer at least the first of the two key questions raised by inoculation: was the procedure significantly less risky than natural smallpox, and did it provide permanent immunity? Jurin, like Nettleton, now sought out live data on the new practice. Where the Yorkshire doctor had gathered information through his own house-to-house enquiries and personal contacts in northern towns, the Secretary of the Royal Society was able to crowdsource information from across England and beyond. His first sweep identified fifteen pioneer inoculators, mainly medical professionals including Nettleton and the royal surgeons Charles Maitland and Claude Amyand, but also 'a woman at Leicester' who had successfully treated eight patients. Between them, the group had inoculated 182 individuals, of whom just two had died.[11]

In a remarkable coincidence of timing, experiments were also under way across the Atlantic in colonial Boston, New England. There, a prominent Puritan minister, Cotton Mather, had first heard an account of inoculation from his enslaved servant, Onesimus, who explained the practice – which he had undergone himself – was a routine part of traditional medicine in his homeland in North Africa.[12] Like Nettleton, Mather had read reports of inoculation in the Ottoman Empire in the *Philosophical Transactions*, and, recognising the technique described by Onesimus, had written incredulously to the Royal Society: 'How does it come to pass that no more is done to bring this operation into experiment and fashion in England?' When a visiting ship brought smallpox to Boston in 1721, he persuaded a local physician, Zabdiel Boylston, to trial the procedure. The initiative sparked vicious controversy – a lighted hand grenade was even thrown into a room where a group of patients were sleeping, though its fuse fortunately fell out. An attached note read: 'Cotton Mather, You Dog, Dam You; I'll inoculate you with this; with a Pox to you'. The results of the experiment proved more robust than the grenade: only five of almost three hundred people inoculated died following the procedure, compared with nearly nine hundred deaths out of over five thousand Bostonians who caught the natural disease during the epidemic.[13]

At the Royal Society's London headquarters in Crane Court, off Fleet Street, Jurin, heavy-jowled under his shoulder-length wig, bent over his desk, methodically crunching the real-time numbers from both continents. Finally, he blew the ink dry on a set of new tables. The latest figures, based on direct observation from sources he stressed were authoritative, indicated that almost one in five, or nearly nineteen percent, of people of all ages who had contracted smallpox naturally in the recent epidemics had died of it. Of those inoculated, meanwhile, the mortality rate in Britain was just one in ninety-one, or just over one percent. In Boston, where the inoculators had treated a wider range of patients including pregnant women and those in labour, the rate was one in sixty.[14]

The case for the relative safety of smallpox inoculation already looked clear, but far from halting his data collection project, Jurin ratcheted it up a gear. He decided to draw up annual reports, 'till the Practice of inoculation shall either be establish'd on a firm and lasting Foot, or shall be justly exploded'. Only 'fact and experience' would determine the answer. Each year, he published advertisements in the *Philosophical Transactions* calling on small-pox inoculators to send him complete and accurate case histories of all their patients' outcomes, prompting a flood of responses from physicians, surgeons, apothecaries and a handful of lay operators in Britain and abroad. Boylston crossed the Atlantic to present to the Society in person a book detailing each inoculation he had conducted in New England, including enslaved people as well as white Bostonians, and speculating on why the procedure seemed to work.

Painstakingly checking each case, chasing up missing details and extracting key numbers, Jurin and his successor as Royal Society Secretary Dr Johann Gaspar Scheuchzer published annual data tables showing mortality rates from natural and inoculated small-pox, broken down by age. Their reports also included clinical details of inoculation deaths in a bid to demonstrate transparency and allow readers to make their own assessments. 'I shall make it to my constant endeavour, free from any private views, to act the part of an historian and with all possible faithfulness and impartiality to represent facts, as upon enquiry I shall find they are,' pledged Scheuchzer, fending off brickbats from both sides as the inocula-tion debate raged. By the time the project ended in 1729, reports had been produced on 897 individuals inoculated in Britain and 329 in Boston and other countries.[15] The overall mortality rate was just below one in fifty – far lower than from natural smallpox at over one in six.

Jurin's mathematical approach would prove game-changing, not only for the weight of evidence it produced in favour of inoculation but because the method itself represented fact-based impartiality in the face of a heated and often emotional debate. Anecdotal experi-ences, by definition subjective and expressed through language, could be distorted or interpreted to confirm existing opinions; anonymised numbers, with all data equally weighted, allowed cooler analysis. Thomas Dixon, an Aberdeen-trained physician from Bolton, Lancashire, was one of many correspondents to congratulate the Royal Society Secretary, writing in 1726: 'I think the method you pursue of convincing the world by matter of Fact is fair & Just, & prejudices in reference to Inoculation can, I think, be removed by no other means.'[16] Dr John Woodhouse of Nottingham sent his 'hearty thanks', predicting that Jurin's annual accounts would 'convince all Enemys to this practice and establish it for the great benefit of mankind'.

For all the enthusiasm of Dr Dixon and his fellow medics, the task of 'convincing the world' would prove far more challenging than anyone could envisage. No sooner had numerical arguments been introduced in medicine than they met the objections familiar to any modern statistician: were the right facts being counted, and were comparisons fair? Critics pointed out that because in England those inoculated were mainly affluent people in good health, their outcomes could not reasonably be set against those of the poor and often unhealthy who so often died of natural smallpox.

A 1724 article praising Jurin's efforts to use 'clear matter of fact to establish or explode this Practice' noted wryly that his numbers had by no means tamed opposition to inoculation:

> With what Violence, and Malice, has it not been rail'd at, and oppos'd? – How many False Affirmations have we seen, with unblushing Boldness, insulting Truth, in our Publick News-Papers! – Nay, the Pulpits, too, have trembled, under the Zeal of Reverend Railers ... It has been represented, as a Wilful Murder! A new, and wicked, Presumption! An Assault on the Prerogative of Heaven! And a taking God's own Work out of his Hands, to be mended by Man's Arrogance![17]

Even as accusations flew, the ground on which knowledge was built was changing irreversibly. The shift towards measurement reflected a growing focus in Britain on the value of experience and directly acquired evidence rather than inherited theory. Medicine came somewhat belatedly to the empirical approach, whose principles had been laid down during the Scientific Revolution of the seventeenth century. The English philosopher Francis Bacon had set the scene for the reform of 'natural philosophy', as the new science was known, one hundred years before, urging the rejection of the dogmas of traditional authorities in favour of scientific enquiry grounded in first-hand, methodical observation of nature and inductive reasoning. The process of counting as a basis for analysis was critical: in his *New Atlantis*, a utopian account of an ideal scientific society, Bacon depicted a research institute in which 'compilers' organised experimental findings into tables, 'to give the better light for the drawing of observations and axioms out of them'.

The immense influence of the 'father of empiricism' shaped the founding in 1660 of the Royal Society, with its focus on the acquisition of knowledge through first-hand experimental investigation. Members' determination to verify all statements by an appeal to facts was encapsulated in the Society's crisp motto, *Nullius in verba*: take nobody's word for it.

One of the Society's earliest Fellows, and later President, was Sir Isaac Newton, another giant of the Scientific Revolution whose 1687 masterpiece, *Philosophiæ Naturalis Principia Mathematica* (Mathematical Principles of Natural Philosophy), revealed nothing less than the physical laws governing the universe. Newton's explanations of the laws of motion and universal gravitation provided a revolutionary new model of Nature in which quantifiable forces operated according to general rules which were capable of mathematical expression. Natural philosophy consisted in 'establishing these rules by observations and experiments, and thence deducing the causes and effects of things', Newton wrote in the programme he proposed to the Royal Society on beginning his twenty-four-year presidency in 1703.

Medicine, embedded so firmly in classical humoral tradition and the theory-driven authority of individual physicians, had resisted empirical thinking, though surgery, more open to direct observation, had long been readier to evaluate treatments. Now, medicine too began to absorb the new evidence-based approach and become more scientific or, in contemporary terminology, 'philosophical'. If the motions of the planets and tides could be measured and mastered, why not the internal organisation and mechanisms of the body? In place of divine will, chance or superstition, could sickness instead be understood by reason and Nature's laws?

Smallpox inoculation, that new and counter-intuitive practice whose effectiveness was proven by experience rather than ancient theory, perfectly fitted the emerging scientific spirit. Systematically evaluated by Jurin, a follower of Newton trained at the University of Cambridge in both mathematics and medicine, its comparative risk could be quantitatively measured, and the results subjected to rational enquiry. The very nature of the intervention spoke of mastery: rather than struggle, often fruitlessly, to treat a frequently fatal disease, physicians could now control its onset, manage its severity and reduce, almost to nothing, its power to kill and maim.

Emblematic of the scientific method and promising the possibility of improving the health and happiness of mankind, inoculation would come to exemplify the defining tenets of the eighteenth-century European Enlightenment, with its optimistic drive for intellectual and cultural progress achieved through reason, in pursuit of greater freedom and a better world. The French 'philosophe' Voltaire, one of the disparate movement's pre-eminent thinkers and an outspoken proponent of inoculation, included an entire letter extolling the procedure in his *Lettres sur les Anglais*, a series of commentaries on English government, politics, religion, literature and science based on his experiences living in London from 1726 to 1728. Applauding the pioneering inoculation advocates Lady Mary Wortley Montagu ('A woman of as fine a genius and endowed with as great an intellect as any of her sex in the British kingdoms') and Princess Caroline ('an amiable Philosopher on the Throne') for their insight and leadership, he positioned inoculation firmly as an enlightened subject, rubbing shoulders in his book with analyses of the ideas of Bacon and Newton.[18] Voltaire praised the increasingly influential quantifying efforts of James Jurin as he contrasted the acceptance of inoculation by the pragmatic English with resistance in his home country and elsewhere. Some forty years later, the philosophe's continuing passionate support for inoculation as both a medical intervention and a symbol of enlightened thinking would help persuade Catherine II, Empress of Russia, to undergo the procedure and introduce it in the Russian empire.

By the time Voltaire returned to France, inoculation was sufficiently recognised in England to feature in one of the first general encyclopaedias to be published in English, Ephraim Chambers' *Cyclopedia*. The 1728 publication, subtitled *An Universal Dictionary of Arts and Sciences*, defined the procedure as 'used for

Voltaire (François-Marie Arouet).

the Transplantation of Distempers from one Subject to another, particularly for the ingraftment of the Small-Pox, which is a new practice among us, but of ancient Original in the Eastern countries'. The advantages were clearly spelt out: inoculation offered the chance to choose a favourable time of year and optimal age and health of the patient, providing the same immunity as natural smallpox with 'the danger next to none'.

The *Cyclopedia*'s account of the 'best method' reflected the fact that, for all the simplicity of the folk practice witnessed by Lady Mary Wortley Montagu in Turkey, physicians in England had from the outset modified the procedure to fit their own established thinking. In place of the uncomplicated pricking of the skin with a blunt needle practised by the women of Constantinople, doctors used a lancet to make deep incisions in the patient's arm and opposite leg and embedded small wads of lint impregnated with smallpox pus inside, bandaging them in place for several days before removal. In accordance with the tenets of classical medicine, inoculees underwent three weeks or more of preparation to balance the humours and ensure the body was in the best state to receive the transferred poison. Diets were kept plain and largely vegetarian, alcohol was banned, and patients were bled and purged to achieve an equilibrium of bodily fluids and help prevent fever. The regimen continued after the inoculation, with physicians tailoring therapies and medication to suit the age, constitution and lifestyle of individual patients. Including convalescence, the whole process could take two months, even without complications such as infections in the large incision wounds.

Some critics, including Lady Mary herself, accused doctors of deliberately complicating an inherently simple procedure in an attempt to reinforce their professional authority and rake in higher fees from their gullible aristocratic clients. But, while inoculation would certainly eventually prove a money-spinner for some, the costly preparations and treatments were less about greed than an attempt by practitioners – and their clients – to integrate the new scientific discovery into existing long-held paradigms. Enlightened thinking and quantitative analysis had opened the way for the radical innovation, but it was shaped at first by centuries-old humoral theory and established medical practice.

The complexity, length and resulting high cost of inoculation ensured that for some twenty years after its introduction in Britain the procedure was limited mainly to upper-class families, who had their children protected and often, to prevent household infection, their servants. Reports of some deaths and fears that inoculated patients could infect others with the natural disease raised public concern, but it was primarily a fall in smallpox incidence that saw enthusiasm for the procedure wane. Even the royal family, staunch advocates of inoculation, took their eye off the ball. In November 1743, five-year-old Prince George, eldest son of the Prince and Princess of Wales and the future King George III, caught smallpox, but was reported to be, 'it's hop'd, out of Danger, having a favourable sort'.[19]

The pause was brief. A resurgence of smallpox in Britain in the 1740s, rising to a new nationwide epidemic at the start of the following decade, produced a renewed sense of threat. Public fear had always been the most powerful promoter of inoculation, and revival of the practice was swift. While the few deaths that occurred could alarm potential patients, with the poor still far less convinced than the wealthier classes, lingering reservations among medical practitioners over the safety and efficacy of the technology had vanished. Thomas Frewen, a doctor in Rye, Sussex, noted in his 1749 essay on inoculation that, 'the Success, with which it has been attended for some Years past, seems, at this Time, to have established it on so firm a Basis, as to stop the Mouths of its Antagonists, and to let it make its own way'.[20] Opponents of the practice had been many, he acknowledged, but 'for the most Part, Men of little Note; who endeavoured to vilify the Art, more, by promulgating false Reports and trumped-up Stories, than by having Recourse to either Argument or Experience'. He urged a return to the clarity of big picture data: instead of making what he termed 'an ill-natured Bounce' at inoculation's few failed cases, Man should 'but weigh the Advantages accruing to numbers by this practice'.

Prince George's younger siblings Prince Edward and Lady Augusta were inoculated as soon as his illness emerged, using infected matter from their brother's pustules. The Georgian Royals' active support for inoculation within their own family gave the procedure endorsement at the highest level in Britain, although the absence of any nationally organised public healthcare meant there was no corresponding top-down government promotion of the practice during the eighteenth century. Instead, the ineffectively regulated medical profession, with its weakening hierarchies and lack of any uniform system of education and qualifications, simply got on with inoculating according to the demands of the marketplace.

For those who could not pay, the gap again left by government began to be filled by private charitable initiatives. While organised campaigns to provide general inoculation for the poor would emerge only later in the century, the London Foundling Hospital, founded in 1739 by the philanthropist and sea captain Thomas Coram, introduced routine inoculation of the 'exposed and deserted young children' – usually those born to unmarried mothers – entering its care from 1744. There was strong support for the policy among the hospital's eminent governors, including its medical consultant Dr Richard Mead, the renowned physician and larger-than-life polymath, collector and poisons expert who had once fought a duel over smallpox treatment. As the foundlings were in the hospital's care, and inoculation was a proven procedure that saved lives, compulsion was deemed entirely acceptable. By the end of April 1756, 247 children had been inoculated and only one had died: a fact the governing committee proudly publicised in the newspapers.

The same philanthropic spirit directed at the practical alleviation of suffering saw the foundation in 1746 of another groundbreaking charitable institution: the Middlesex County Hospital for Smallpox and Inoculation, later known as the London Smallpox Hospital. As well as treating sufferers of natural smallpox, who were banned from admission to other hospitals in the capital to avoid infection, it pioneered institutional inoculation. Smallpox prevention was beginning its shift from expensive personalised treatment in aristocratic homes to a wider approach targeting all classes. After all, the governors' report observed, 'the inferior sort of people are at least equally liable [to smallpox] with those in a higher sphere of life, though utterly unable to support themselves under so dreadful a Malady'.[21]

The new institution, the first of its type in Europe, started life in canvas tents before moving to permanent buildings in which patients underwent four weeks of preparation and quarantine. Once it was clear they did not already have natural smallpox, they were inoculated and spent three weeks recovering in a separate house. The lengthy process severely limited the number of potential patients, and, though it gradually expanded to inoculate around one thousand people annually and boasted just one death in almost six hundred cases, the hospital was criticised for serving mainly the servants of its wealthy patrons. Local neighbours, fearing the spread of disease, unsuccessfully petitioned for its closure, and abused departing patients so fiercely they had to be discharged under cover of darkness.

Despite its shortcomings, the Smallpox Hospital's unique specialism and successful method swiftly attracted foreign physicians anxious to learn from England's progress in the new technology. Eminent doctors from Geneva, Sweden, Holland and France took their new expertise back to their home countries and beyond as the hospital's influence spread through Europe. There was even a visitor from Russia: Baron Alexander Cherkasov, who had studied at Cambridge University and spoke perfect English, came to observe institutional inoculation in action. A few years later, the Baron – now President of the new Medical College in St Petersburg – would act as interpreter for Thomas Dimsdale, greeting him on his secret visit to the Winter Palace to inoculate the Empress of Russia.

Outside institutions, the increasing demand for inoculation in Britain saw the blurring of the old divisions within the medical profession. Surgeons, traditionally in charge only of the manual incision element of the procedure, and apothecaries, the prescribers and dispensers of medicines, muscled into the more lucrative aspects of preparation and aftercare typically overseen by physicians, specialists in the body's internal workings and, in theory at least, highly trained. The latter in turn complained bitterly at the incursion and opted to wield the lancet themselves, offering a competing 'full service' inoculation for patients with at least ten guineas (almost a hundred days' wages for a skilled tradesman) to spend. Amateur operators – some effective, some no more than quacks – began to emerge to fill gaps in the market, opening the procedure to those unable to afford physicians' weighty fees. High charges for inoculation 'must necessarily exclude a great part, nay I may say the greatest part of mankind, from the benefit of it', warned a contributor to the monthly *Gentleman's Magazine* in 1752, in one of the earliest calls for universal access to the procedure. 'The poor in general are absolutely cut off from all share in it.'[22] Even farmers and tradesmen, living well above the poverty line, could not afford to protect their whole family, yet the operation was simple and could be safely performed by non-specialists, right down to house-wives with no fear of needles, the writer observed. He offered a bold solution. A kingdom-wide network of charities along the lines of the Smallpox Hospital was needed to extend the procedure to 'all ranks of people', individuals should choose whoever they felt competent to perform the operation, and physicians should lower their rates and inoculate the poor for free.

In his 1754 *Analysis of Inoculation*, one of numerous treatises on the subject now flying off the presses and circulating in Britain and beyond, the Irish-born doctor James Kirkpatrick also floated the idea of a nationwide system of isolation hospitals, lower fees and even universal inoculation of children from age five.[23] But he attacked the sidelining of physicians, arguing their professional expertise was essential to adapt each operation to suit individual patients' health and humoral state. Nevertheless, his own lengthy publication, swiftly regarded as the go-to authority in the field, set out in precise detail preparatory regimens to suit specific ages and constitutions, recommending a few grains of rhubarb as a laxative to remove worms in children and, for adults, bleeding, vomiting and purging with the poisonous metal antimony and calomel, a compound of mercury widely used as a cure-all. Dietary guidelines were exhaustive: the doctor favoured 'good mellow turnips and succulent spinach' when in season and acknowledged he had over-come his initial caution over the benefits of asparagus. For all his focus on the physician's judgement, Kirkpatrick's prescriptive approach based primarily on patients' age signalled a growing shift towards standardisation of inoculation that would, ultimately, open the way for its wider use.

The *Analysis*, translated and read across Europe, was more than a medical manual. It opened with a furious counter-assault against continuing religious objections to inoculation. Far from challeng-ing the will of God, Kirkpatrick argued, the procedure was 'a method discovered by Providence', and man's God-given Reason should actively direct him to pursue 'a practice so incontestably favourable to life'. Inoculation aligned precisely with enlightened values: it was situated squarely in the 'serene expanse of Reason and sunshine', while its prejudiced critics were lost in darkness. And after Providence and Reason, royal example was almost as valuable an endorsement – another British lesson that would make its way to Russia. The treatise was dedicated to King George II, whose 'sagacity and resolution' in having his daughters inoculated twenty-five years before had 'eventually preserved so many thousands of his subjects, His political children'.

If some clerics remained unconvinced, there were no such doubts in the British medical establishment. In 1755, the Royal College of Physicians gave smallpox inoculation its official stamp of approval. Noting that the success of the practice in England had been 'misrepresented by foreigners', the College announced its view that early objections had been 'refuted by experience, and that it is at present more generally esteemed and Practised in England than ever, and that they Judge it to be a Practice of the utmost benefit to Mankind'.[24]

While support for inoculation had surged ahead in England, neighbouring states on the European Continent were still sceptical or fiercely opposed. Smallpox was no less devastating across the Channel, but despite an initial flurry of experiments with the new technology at the time of the highly publicised royal inoculations in Britain, the practice did not take hold in Germany or Italy. In France it became the subject of a culture war in which leading intellectuals locked horns with a conservative medical establishment and fiercely resistant Catholic Church, prompting profound debates on the nature of decision-making and risk.

In his polemical letter on inoculation, published in 1733 and promptly banned in France, Voltaire observed that 'it is whispered in Christian Europe that the English are fools and madmen: fools because they give their children smallpox to prevent their catching it, and madmen because they wantonly communicate a certain and dreadful illness to their children, merely to prevent an uncertain evil'. The English, meanwhile, 'call other Europeans cowardly and unnatural: cowardly in that they are afraid of giving a little pain to their children, and unnatural because they expose them to death from smallpox sometime in the future'.[25]

Even allowing for Voltaire's taste for satirical provocation and frustration with the rigid institutions of his native country (and his memories of his own brutal experience of smallpox in the Paris epidemic of 1723), it was a broadly accurate summary of mutual perceptions. In France, despite the death of his grandfather the Grand Dauphin from smallpox in 1711, King Louis XV rejected the pioneering example of his royal counterparts in London and never risked inoculating his children, three of whom died of smallpox. Where in Britain Church and state were separated and neither the government nor the Royal College of Physicians held responsibility for public health, in France medical regulation was tightly controlled by faculties of the main universities. Limited numbers of doctors were permitted to train in each faculty and were licensed to practise only locally, keeping the medical profession locked into a top-down, corporate system that resisted new, especially foreign, ideas. The Paris Faculté de Médecine at the Sorbonne held complete autonomy over medical affairs in the capital, leading to a permanent power struggle with the King's royal physicians and further strangling innovation. Entrepreneurial English practitioners could treat anyone who would trust them to handle a lancet; their French counterparts would have to break the law to do so.

Backing for inoculation in France came not from the country's physicians and scientists, as it had in Britain, but from the philosophes: the prominent public intellectuals of the Enlightenment whose self-declared mission was not only to understand and critique the world but to live within it and change it for the better. The *Encyclopédie*, the monumental general encyclopaedia of new thinking edited by Denis Diderot and Jean d'Alembert and published from 1751, defined the philosophe as 'a civilised man who acts in all things according to reason, and who combines a spirit of reflection and precision with morals and sociable qualities'. Such a man actively strove to be guided by reason but was no 'insensitive sage' remote from society who wished to deny human emotions. The true *philosophe* gloried in humanity, working at not being dominated by the passions but 'at benefitting from them, and at making reasonable use of them . . . because reason directs him to do so'.[26]

Smallpox inoculation, bringing together empirically driven science and the deepest fears of parents seeking to protect their children from harm, epitomised the combination of reason and sensibility that underpinned enlightened thinking. French intellectuals weighed into the debate not only to fight for medical progress over dogma and superstition but to encourage individuals to direct their emotions in a reasonable way. Theirs was not so much a scientific debate as a cultural campaign, and, through articles, pamphlets and even poetry, they pitched their arguments not at a resistant medical profession but at enlightened public opinion. To the men of letters, inoculation was not simply a medical matter: it concerned the welfare of wider society.

In 1754, two years after a smallpox epidemic in Paris that had almost killed the King's eldest son, the mathematician and scientist Charles-Marie de La Condamine delivered a landmark address in support of inoculation to a public session of the Académie Royale des Sciences in Paris.[27] Smallpox, which he believed was caused by 'seeds' carried within the blood, was practically universal, he argued: the disease was 'a deep and rapid river' that almost everyone must cross, and one in seven lost their lives as they tried to swim to shore. Inoculation, which he had witnessed himself on expeditions to Peru and Constantinople, offered a God-given boat across the raging torrent and saved ninety-nine lives out of every hundred, according to Jurin's statistics. The process contained some risk, the academician acknowledged, but it was both legally justifiable and rational for a loving father voluntarily to expose his son to a limited danger to protect him from one far greater. There was no middle option.

'If prejudice does not totally extinguish the light of reason in the father, if he loves his son with an enlightened love, he cannot hesitate one moment,' La Condamine told his enthralled audience. 'This is not a question in morality, it is a matter of calculation. Why should we make a case of conscience of a problem with arithmetic?' In the lecture theatre, the rhetoric sounded persuasive, though in practice parenting by numbers was – and still is – impossible. The cool truths of anonymised statistics were a world away from the emotional reality of parenthood, where protecting an infant meant exposing it to a lancet full of live virus.

Charles-Marie de La Condamine.

La Condamine had no such qualms. Parental love, reasonably expressed, was all about balancing risk, just as individuals daily weighed up lesser hazards such as long voyages, hunting or cricket. Inoculation, he argued, dramatically changed the odds in the 'enforced lottery' of smallpox: a fateful tombola in which all took part and many every year drew out 'the blank of death'. Now at last the number of blanks could diminish, soon shrinking to just one in one thousand.

Having sought to harness private sentiment to his cause, La Condamine turned to a motivation still barely raised in Britain in connection with inoculation: national interest. The English, 'a wise and learned nation, our neighbours and our rivals', had tamed the smallpox 'Minotaur', while the French remained idle spectators. By failing to follow the English example in adopting smallpox inoculation in 1723, he thundered, France had lost almost a million lives, 'by our ignorance, our prejudices, our indifference to the good of mankind. Surely we must confess we are neither philosophers nor patriots.' The case for inoculation not only rested on saving individual beloved children: the practice would also preserve the population for the benefit of the state. Since the labour force was critical to increasing a nation's wealth and trade – the mercantilist goal of France and its European neighbours – it was in the economic interests of a country to increase the health and number of its citizens, and governments should officially sanction inoculation. He stopped short of calling for compulsion but concluded: 'In an affair that relates to the public welfare, it is incumbent on a thinking nation, to enlighten those who are capable of receiving light, and lead that crowd by authority, who are not to be wrought upon by evidence.'

The colourful address, cheered in the Académie and widely disseminated in print, spread new interest in inoculation among elite families in France and across Europe. In 1756, the Bourbon Prince the Duc d'Orléans set a new fashion in Parisian aristocratic circles when he invited from Geneva the celebrity physician Théodore Tronchin, six feet tall and 'as handsome as Apollo' according to his patient Voltaire, to inoculate his two children. Tronchin, who would pen a lengthy essay promoting inoculation for the *Encyclopédie*, was soon the talk of Paris, reported the writer and fellow Encyclopédiste

Friedrich Melchior Grimm. 'All of our women are going to consult him; his door is besieged, and the street where he lives is full of coaches and cars, like the entertainment districts.'[28] Voltaire wrote the first of several poetic tributes to doctor and patient, likening the medical breakthrough to Newton's articulation of the laws of the universe (and reminding readers he had been an early exponent). Designers created '*bonnets à l'inoculation*', smallpox-themed head-wear featuring red-spotted ribbons, and '*tronchines*', loose-fitting morning gowns the physician recommended to encourage sedentary aristocratic women to take more exercise. Among the titled families of continental Europe, the power of French royal example and of fashion began to triumph where argument had failed. The Duchess of Saxe-Gotha, reporting the inoculation of her children to Voltaire in 1759, wrote: 'You see we are very much à la mode and free from prejudice.'[29] 'You are wise in all things,' he replied.

But for most, including the medical establishment, distrust of the new technology remained. As fierce debates continued in France over the relative risks of natural and inoculated smallpox, a new means emerged to demonstrate the advantages of inoculation: the calculus of probabilities. Encouraged by La Condamine, the Swiss mathematician and physician Daniel Bernoulli employed sophisti-cated mathematical modelling to answer one question: should a rational government promote universal inoculation for its popula-tion at birth, even though the operation was sometimes fatal? In 1760, breaking new ground as Nettleton and Jurin had done before him, he presented the Académie with what is regarded as the world's first epidemiological model for an infectious disease. His complex algebraic formula calculated life expectancy at different ages, then factored in the impact of inoculation and smallpox mortality, concluding that inoculating all infants, even allowing for some risk from the procedure, would increase a citizen's life, on average, by up to three years.[30] On that basis, Bernoulli concluded, it would always be in the interest of the state to 'favour and protect inoculation by all possible means; likewise the father of a family with regard to his children'.

No sooner had probability – still a relatively new branch of math-ematical theory – been applied to inoculation, than it too was challenged. Later the same year, the French mathematician Jean d'Alembert responded with a warning against reducing the matter 'to equations and formulae'.[31] Bernoulli's calculation, he argued, had provided a rational case for the state to support inoculation, but the state's interest was not necessarily the same as that of individuals, and the two should be treated separately. A government might rationally sacrifice some lives to save others, as it did in war; a parent would always prioritise protecting the life of their child. Not only that, probability did not accurately reflect the psychology of risk, d'Alembert pointed out. Most people, particularly mothers thinking of their children, would weigh the immediate danger of inoculation, however small, more highly than the benefit of a few more years of life sometime in the future.

Angelo Gatti, a prominent Italian physician inoculating in France using his own pioneering simplified method, also rejected the philosophes' contention that sentiment could be governed by reason and mathematics.[32] The only way to make inoculation universal was to make it safe, he countered, recommending abandoning complicated medical and dietary preparations that he rightly believed did more harm than good. 'Till it is quite safe, it can never become general; and all computations to show that a lesser risk ought to be incurred rather than a greater, will be found of little weight with the multitude.'[33] Gatti perfectly summed up the perennial shortcomings of statistics as a tool of individual persuasion. 'Mankind will always be more affected by a present danger, though exceedingly small, than by a much greater one, if remote, and in some degree uncertain.'[34]

The French debates over inoculation generated new and resonant ideas, innumerable pamphlets, books, poems and letters and even breakthroughs in epidemiological modelling, but beyond aristocratic circles there were more disputes than actual experiments. Where mathematical arguments had proved decisive for doctors in England, the French medical establishment was not persuaded by them, not least as France had little quantitative information about its own population. In 1763, following yet another smallpox epidemic and claims that infections from inoculations were responsible, the Paris Parlement, France's leading court, took action. It banned inoculation within its jurisdiction – to the fury of the philosophes – and asked the Faculties of Medicine and Theology at the Sorbonne to come to a view on the safety of the practice. The medical faculty went first, inviting submissions from physicians across Europe, and still ended up split down the middle, producing two conflicting reports and ultimately recommending 'toleration'. Inoculation continued without official endorsement, but it was the death of Louis XV in 1774 from smallpox that finally changed attitudes in France. The new king Louis XVI and his two brothers were quickly inoculated, as the French royal family became the last reigning monarchs in Europe to accept the procedure. The delay did not lessen the opportunity for display: Louis XVI's queen, Marie Antoinette, sported a towering, powdered hairstyle, dubbed '*pouf à l'inoculation*', featuring a serpent decoration to represent the power of medicine. The Italian economist Ferdinando Galiani wrote in 1777: 'One death caused by smallpox is worth more than the dissertations of La Condamine.'[35]

While the French were probing inoculation's philosophical implications, in England the practice surged forward. With medical opinion firmly on board by the mid-eighteenth century, and backing from senior churchmen, the only limitations were public trust and affordable access to the operation. Benjamin Pugh, a surgeon and inoculator in Chelmsford, Essex, wrote in 1753 to *The Gentleman's Magazine*: 'This universal good is inoculation, and notwithstanding envy has laid such batteries upon it, yet happy for this kingdom it gains ground daily; the lower class of people coming into it very fast in these parts.'[36] The erosion of rigid boundaries within the medical profession saw physicians, surgeons and apothecaries alike offer inoculations at a greater range of prices, gradually bringing the practice within reach of more of the population.

Among those surgeons was Thomas Dimsdale, who later recorded that inoculation had formed 'a considerable share' of his employment since his return from the army and second marriage in 1746. Although his inherited fortune and his new wife's wealth had allowed him to step back from his medical practice for some years, the couple soon had a substantial family to care for. Of ten children born, seven survived, and Thomas's mother Susannah had left clear instructions that they should be brought up according to the family's Quaker faith. In her will she wrote:

> And I can't be easy without reminding you to take a very particular care that [your children] are religiously educated, which most certainly is your duty to do, and to take care that you don't let a coldness and indifferency take any place in you in respect of keeping to meetings of the profession you have been educated in I hope you will take the same care of your offspring.[37]

Despite his clash with his local Hertford Monthly Meeting over his 'disorderly practice' and unapologetic decision to marry outside the sect, Thomas was still considered by his family as an observant Quaker, who would continue to live according to the faith himself and pass it down to the next generation. His first wife, Mary, had been buried in the Friends' Burial Ground in nearby Bishop's Stortford, suggesting a reconciliation had been made after the disownment. Thomas's flourishing professional career also centred on Quaker connections: he had maintained his friendship with the high-profile physician and prominent Friend Dr John Fothergill, now living in Bloomsbury with a second house in Upton, Essex, that boasted a garden said by the naturalist Joseph Banks to be second only to Kew in all of Europe. By 1768, the pair would both be governors of St Thomas's Hospital, where they had trained almost forty years before.

In 1761, Thomas obtained an MD degree from King's College, Aberdeen – a qualification that could then be bought from the university without even a visit, though he was vouched for by two London doctors. Now a physician, his professional ranking matched his enhanced social status, and he could charge his wealthy patients fees to match. Although he was barred from full membership of the Royal College of Physicians, which – to growing opposition – required a degree from Oxford or Cambridge and therefore excluded non-members of the Church of England, he was admitted to the elite body as an Extra-Licentiate, officially permitting him to practise medicine outside London. Two years later, a small isolation hospital known as the Pest House and funded by charitable subscription was built on land adjoining the substantial garden of Port Hill House, the family's new home in the village of Bengeo, just outside Hertford. Here, Thomas could now safely treat smallpox patients from the local parishes, together with wealthier individuals recovering after inoculation at his home surgery.

Over more than twenty years practising inoculation, Thomas had lost only one patient, a child who had died of a fever he believed had no connection to smallpox, though he admitted that in other cases the symptoms had caused him 'not a little anxiety'. He was a skilled doctor, but his technique was still broadly the conventional one developed in England when the practice first arrived in the country: preparation of the patient with diet, medicines and purging; the insertion of pus-infused threads into an inch-long incision; a managed recovery in a hot environment. But at around the time the Pest House opened, he began to hear rumours of a new, far simpler inoculation method that upended all established theory, devised by an operator with no formal medical qualifications. The practitioner, Daniel Sutton, was based in Essex, not far from Thomas's own birthplace at Theydon Garnon. He was treating thousands of patients, apparently with great success, and earning more than the Prime Minister.

The 'Suttonian Method' was nothing short of a revolution: it would transform the safety and availability of inoculation. After decades in which individual doctors had practised variations of a costly and imperfect technique, Sutton found the key that would unlock the practice for the masses. Combining his new method with buccaneering business instincts, he set about making his fortune.

Sutton's secret would provoke and intrigue his rivals, who used every means – honourable and otherwise – to glean the details, only to be shocked by its simplicity. Among the most curious was Thomas, who, assiduous as always, subjected the new technique to his own 'repeated trials' in order to 'bring the practice still one step nearer to perfection'. Then, in 1767, he took a step his entrepreneurial counterpart had avoided: he published his findings. Even if the method could not 'exterminate' smallpox entirely, he wrote, at least it would lessen its deadly power.

His treatise, *The Present Method of Inoculating for the Small-Pox*, was an instant hit, running to seven editions and positioning Thomas as the leading global expert in inoculation. It would also bring him to the attention of the eighteenth-century world's most powerful woman: the Empress of Russia.

Catherine II astride Brillante, Vigilius Eriksen, 1762.

3

The Empress

'She is of all that ever I saw of her sex the most engaging'
Thomas Dimsdale[1]

Less than two weeks after arriving at the royal court in Moscow aged fourteen, the German Princess Sophie Friederike Auguste of Anhalt-Zerbst – the future Catherine II of Russia – fell gravely ill. As she dressed for dinner with her mother Johanna and the Grand Duke Peter, heir to the Russian throne and her husband-to-be, she collapsed with a high fever and excruciating pain in her side. Johanna, desperate to save not only Sophie's life but her uniquely advantageous marriage, urged doctors to treat her daughter for smallpox. But when they suggested the teenager should be bled – believing that syphoning away a quantity of her blood would bring down the heat of her fever – her mother refused outright. She had her own reasons for distrusting Russian medical expertise: her older brother, Sophie's uncle, had died of smallpox in St Petersburg as he prepared for betrothal to the reigning empress, Elizabeth.

Sophie suffered for five more days before Elizabeth stepped in, barring the demanding and unsympathetic Johanna from the sickroom, sitting at Sophie's bedside herself and freeing doctors to bleed her. 'I hung between life and death for twenty-seven days, during which I was bled sixteen times and sometimes four times a day,' Catherine later recalled.[2] The illness turned out to be pleurisy, brought on, it was said, by pacing her cold bedroom barefoot at night as she drove herself to master the challenging Russian language. As she drifted in and out of consciousness, she refused a visit from a Protestant pastor of her family's Lutheran tradition. Instead, to the Empress's delight, she asked for Father Semyon Theodorsky, her instructor in the Orthodox Christian faith to which she would convert ahead of her marriage, changing her name in the process. As she began to recover at last, still weak through illness and loss of blood, the young princess lay in her chamber feigning sleep. Her eyes were tightly closed, but she listened intently to the gossip of her ladies-in-waiting. As her fever eased, she learned that her conniving mother was much out of favour, but her own star was already rising.

Catherine described the episode in the detailed memoirs she wrote secretly in three bursts from her mid-twenties almost up to her death aged sixty-seven. The memoirs – frank, vibrant and repeatedly revised and reshaped – were a key platform she could use to control her image and frame her legacy as the longest-serving, and most startlingly successful, female ruler in Russian history.

On her sickbed in Moscow, just days after arriving as an outsider, she was able to demonstrate her devotion to her adoptive country through two defining aspects of its identity: language and faith. She had sacrificed her health to master her Russian vocabulary (never mind that she had had similar illnesses before), and then sought comfort during her illness from whispered Orthodox prayers. Her eavesdropping was revealing too. It showed she had guile – essential in any leader – but also innate political instincts, with a remarkable ability to judge character and motive. She knew where power lay, and how, through strategically publicised actions, she could win hearts and minds. Her experience also gave her an early insight into the public nature of her body and its workings in the Russian Court, and of the brutality of medical treatment even by skilled physicians. In future years, her doctors would pull out a section of her lower jaw as they extracted a tooth, and almost kill her with the botched handling of a miscarriage.

On 21 April 1744, her fifteenth birthday, Sophie was well enough to appear in public again for the first time since her illness, though she was still 'thin as a skeleton', with her dark hair falling out and her face deathly pale. The Empress Elizabeth sent her a jar of rouge and ordered her to wear it, creating a lifelong habit, with its hint of a theatrical mask.

The young princess was brought up far from the decadence and intrigues of the court of Elizabeth, daughter of Czar Peter the Great. Sophie was born in 1729 in the grey garrison town of Stettin on the windswept Baltic coast of Prussian Pomerania, where her father, the minor German prince Christian Augustus of Anhalt-Zerbst, commanded an infantry regiment. Her mother was Princess Johanna Elisabeth of Holstein-Gottorp, another of the multitude of toy-sized sovereign states that covered the expanse of present-day Germany in an intricate jigsaw. Johanna came from a higher-ranked family whose diminishing wealth saw her married off at fifteen to a husband twenty-two years her senior. When Sophie was born the following year, her mother – weakened by an agonising birth that almost proved fatal – handed the baby straight to a wet nurse. Johanna passed on to Sophie her heart-shaped face, neat mouth and slight double chin, but not the love and warmth she would search for in her adult relationships. Neither her birth nor baptism were officially registered. 'My father thought I was an angel; my mother did not pay much attention to me,' Catherine wrote in her memoirs. She noted that Johanna adored her sickly younger brother, born eighteen months later. 'I was merely tolerated and often I was scolded with a violence and anger I did not deserve.'

The adult Catherine recognised her ill-treatment, but little Sophie was a survivor. Known by the boyish family nickname Fike, she had an appealing rebellious quality and a lively, independent mind. In place of her mother, she turned to her French Huguenot governess, Babet Cardel, who provided the encouragement, patience and affection she needed to flourish. Babet taught the German-speaking princess fluent French but also passed on another precious gift: a lifelong passion for the pleasures and possibilities of language.

Sophie loved Babet but granted no such respect to Pastor Wagner, the humourless army chaplain charged with tutoring her in religion. Forced to rote-learn long passages of scripture – a discipline she was skilled at but hated – the young pupil retaliated by subjecting articles of faith to rational questioning. Her mischievous humour was irresistible: she embarrassed her tutor during Bible study by asking the meaning of 'circumcision'. 'I bear no grudge against Monsieur Wagner,' she later wrote with characteristic directness, 'but I am intimately persuaded that he was a blockhead.' Only Babet's kind approach convinced her to learn. 'All my life, indeed, I have preserved this inclination to yield only to reason and gentleness: I have always resisted pressure of any kind.'

Outside the classroom, Sophie's lively mind was matched by a boisterous physical energy. Sedate walks in the park were not enough to tire her: she played outside with the local children. In her memoirs, she portrayed her childhood self as a budding leader, directing her playmates in imaginative games. 'I never liked dolls, but quite liked any kind of exercise, there was no boy more daring than I, I was proud to be that and often I hid my fear . . . I was quite secretive,' she recalled. Her love of physical movement would later see her develop as a bold and exceptionally skilled horsewoman, while her ability to master her fears and conceal her emotions prepared her for the power games of court life to come. Here too, perhaps, came the first stirrings of her sexual appetite: Catherine's memoirs depict her at around thirteen placing a hard pillow between her legs at night as an imaginary horse 'on which I galloped until I was quite worn out'. When the servants came in to check on the noise, she pretended to be fast asleep.

The freedom the young princess found in exercise came to an abrupt temporary halt when, aged seven, she was confined to bed with a cough and chest pain, a forerunner of the pleurisy she would suffer in Moscow. After three weeks enduring a range of medications, doctors found she had developed a curvature of the spine: a deformity that risked damaging her marriage prospects. Her horrified parents turned in desperation to the town's hangman, reputedly skilled in resolving back problems. He recommended not only that Sophie wear a specially designed corrective corset and a black ribbon tied across her body to wrench it into shape but that her 'zigzag' spine and shoulder should be rubbed at six o'clock every morning with the saliva of a local servant girl. By the age of eleven, her back was straighter, but the experience added to the sense of ugliness already embedded by her mother, pushing her to work still harder to acquire 'inward accomplishments'. The bizarre and humiliating folk treatment can only have reinforced her impatience with superstition and preference for the rationality of proven science when it came to tackling the far more dangerous threat of smallpox.

As Sophie's teenage years approached, the ambitious Johanna finally paid her attention. The time had come to arrange a suitable marriage. Her daughter had already begun to accompany her on trips to stay with relatives in grander north German courts than austere Stettin, and the girl's intelligence and wit had been noted. On a visit to Johanna's elder brother, Adolf Frederick, the pair met Sophie's second cousin, Karl Peter Ulrich, the eleven-year-old Duke of Holstein-Gottorp and only surviving grandson of Peter the Great of Russia. The boy's mother, Peter's daughter Anna, had died shortly after his birth, and he had just lost his father, a nephew of Charles XII of Sweden. Now he was in the care of Sophie's uncle, a cousin of his father. The bereaved only child was pale, sickly and undeveloped, isolated from other children and ruthlessly tutored and drilled by military instructors in the north German duchy. Already, Sophie observed, he was drowning his misery with drink.

In 1741, the powerful chess game of European royal politics unexpectedly placed Karl Peter in a prominent new position. His unmarried aunt Elizabeth, the only living daughter of Peter the Great, seized the throne of Russia in a bloodless coup. Thanks to a law passed by her father, the empress was free to choose her own successor, and settled on her nephew. The boy converted to the Orthodox faith and, aged thirteen, became His Imperial Highness the Grand Duke Peter Fyodorovich. As heir to the Russian throne, he had to renounce his claim to the throne of Sweden, which passed instead to Sophie's uncle, Adolf Frederick.

For the scheming Johanna, the double move was a perfectly timed gift. She was already connected to the new Empress through her late brother, who had died of smallpox as he was about to marry Elizabeth. Now her family was elevated through its connection to the future Emperor of Russia. Wasting no time, Johanna sent

Elizabeth effusive good wishes for a long reign, followed by a portrait of Sophie. To her delight, a letter arrived in return on New Year's Day 1744 inviting both mother and daughter to Russia.

Johanna and Sophie arrived by sleigh in St Petersburg after a freezing and uncomfortable journey along the Baltic shore. The Empress and Grand Duke were in Moscow, but the weary visitors were met by theatrical celebrations featuring fireworks, mountainous ice slides and a troupe of elephants performing circus tricks in the courtyard of the Winter Palace. The superficial grandeur of the city, built at the start of the century by Peter the Great as part of his great mission to turn Russia's face west to Europe, belied a behind-the-scenes reality of an unfinished marshland construction site dominated by mud, puddles and rickety wooden buildings. Even in 1774, the visiting philosophe Denis Diderot would observe 'a confused mass of palaces and hovels, of *grands seigneurs* surrounded by peasants and purveyors'.[3] Catherine would later highlight the difference her own improvement programme had made: 'I shall say that I found Petersburg almost made of wood and that I will leave buildings adorned with marble.'[4]

After just two days in the capital, the two German princesses set off for Moscow in a caravan of over twenty sleighs, all racing against time to reach the city by the Grand Duke's birthday.[5] Thanks to a final breakneck dash, they met the deadline, and were greeted by Peter before being formally presented to the Empress in her apartments. Elizabeth, a sturdy woman of thirty-four whose beauty and majestic bearing impressed Sophie, kissed and hugged the visitors, while Johanna delivered an effusive speech of thanks.

The meeting had gone well, but the royal betrothal was not yet a done deal. The match was supported by one court faction seeking closer links with Prussia, but opposed by another favouring a marital alliance with Austria or England. Alongside her lessons in Russian, the Orthodox faith and dancing, Sophie needed to learn the survival skills required to negotiate the complex politics and relationships of the Russian Court. She recovered from her illness, but found herself caught between her unpopular, plotting mother and her unpredictable putative fiancé. 'My situation grew thornier each day ... I strove to obey the one and to please the other,' she recalled in her memoirs.[6]

Sophie swiftly got the measure of Peter, playing games and sharing practical jokes with him: 'neither of us lacked childish vivacity.' Wisely, she refused his tutor's request for help in correcting the immature, increasingly wayward boy on the grounds that, 'I would become as odious to him as his entourage already was.' More complicated still was the task of pleasing the capricious, spendthrift Elizabeth, who would shower her with expensive gifts, then abruptly withdraw affection. Sophie, eternally fearful of being disliked, did all she could to win over the woman on whose patronage her fate depended. 'My respect for the Empress and my gratitude to her were extreme,' she wrote.

Her efforts worked. Despite her frustrations with the meddling Johanna, Elizabeth settled on Sophie as her nephew's bride, and the young princess wrote to her father in Stettin for permission to convert to Orthodoxy.

On 28 June 1744, dressed in scarlet and silver, anointed with oil and reciting a Slavonic text she had learned 'like a parrot', Sophie was received into the Orthodox Church in an elaborate ceremony in Moscow. She had never been personally devout, but she instinctively understood the central importance of the rituals and extravagant performance of faith in Russia. As Empress, that insight would be invaluable. With her baptism came a new name, Ekaterina Alekseyevna; in English, Catherine. The following day she and Peter were formally betrothed, bringing her a new title: Grand Duchess.

The autumn passed in a whirl of theatrical court amusements: parties, masquerades and 'metamorphoses', the cross-dressing balls demanded by Elizabeth as an opportunity to dress as a man and show off her elegant legs. The diversion was short-lived. In December, on the journey by sleigh from Moscow back to St Petersburg, the Grand Duke fell into a high fever, and, as red sores appeared on his body, doctors delivered their chilling diagnosis: smallpox. Peter was immediately quarantined, and Catherine and her mother continued on to the capital, while the Empress, remembering her own lost fiancé, rushed to her nephew's side. For several weeks, she nursed him through the illness, updating Catherine on his progress by letter.

When the engaged couple were finally reunited in late January, the meeting was held in a darkened room, but Catherine was still shaken by the traumatic experience. 'I was almost frightened to see the Grand Duke, who had grown a great deal but whose physiognomy was almost unrecognisable. All of his features were enlarged, his face was still completely swollen, and one saw that he would doubtless be quite scarred.' Peter's hair had been cut and he wore an immense wig that only increased the disfiguring impact of the disease. 'He approached me and asked if I found it hard to recognise him. I stammered my congratulations on his recovery, but in truth he had become hideous.'

Peter, weakened and pock-marked, did not appear in public for a long time afterwards. 'There was no hurry to exhibit him in the state in which smallpox had left him,' Catherine wrote pitilessly in her memoirs. As she awaited her future husband's reappearance, she practised her Russian and read incessantly, while maintaining her carefully controlled court persona. 'I treated everyone as best I could . . . I showed no preference for any side, did not meddle in anything, always had a serene air, much kindness, attentiveness and politeness for everyone, and because I was naturally quite cheerful, I saw with pleasure that from day to day I gained the affections of the public.' It was a powerful lesson: the teenage princess now knew she could please the people, and she had learned that she enjoyed their adoration. She had internalised, too, a deepened dread of smallpox.

While Catherine studied public opinion, the future emperor played games. Resentful at trading his familiar Holstein parade grounds for the spectacle-obsessed Russian Court, he marshalled elaborately modelled toy soldiers dressed in Prussian uniforms, compelling his valets to wear the same costumes and accompany him as he changed the guard. His unhappiness turned into sadistic violence: when not scraping a tune from his violin he would whip his pack of hunting dogs from one side of his room to another, punishing those who did not obey. Once, when he held up a little King Charles spaniel by the collar and beat it, Catherine interceded, only for the blows to rain faster. She retreated to her room, noting:

'In general, tears and cries, instead of arousing the Grand Duke's pity, made him angry; pity was a painful, even unbearable, sentiment for his soul.'

As the couple's wedding date approached in August 1745, Catherine felt no excitement but a deep sense of melancholy. 'My heart did not foresee great happiness,' she recorded in her memoirs. 'Ambition alone sustained me. At the bottom of my soul I had something, I know not what, that never for a single moment let me doubt that sooner or later I would succeed in becoming the Sovereign Empress of Russia in my own right.' She could never have risked publicly articulating her vision of her future power, even if she genuinely felt it clearly. In her later writing, she could impose on her rule a retrospective sense of destiny.

Ten days of extravagant marriage festivities did not bring the royal couple closer. Peter joined his sixteen-year-old bride late on their wedding night and promptly fell asleep. Despite the increasingly urgent encouragement of the Empress and her ladies-in-waiting, the couple did not consummate their marriage for some nine years, by which time both had taken other lovers. Catherine, seduced by the philandering chamberlain Sergei Saltykov, became pregnant and miscarried twice, the first time haemorrhaging violently and the second confined to bed for six weeks after a remnant of placenta remained stuck within her body. Finally, on 20 September 1754, she gave birth to a son, Paul Petrovich. Her memoirs hinted that her lover was the father, though the boy would grow up to resemble her husband. The new prince was immediately taken away to be brought up by Elizabeth; Catherine barely saw her baby and did not take part in the mass public celebrations marking his birth.

As the mother of the future heir to the throne, and not merely the wife of the heir apparent, Catherine's position was now more secure, but her patience with court life under Elizabeth was fraying. Always keen to contrast the period with more civilised life under her own regime, she wrote later:

High stakes card games ... were necessary in a court where there was no conversation, where people cordially hated one another, where slander passed for wit . . . One carefully avoided speaking of art or science because everyone was ignorant; one could wager that half the group could barely read, and I am not quite sure that a third knew how to write.

Catherine increasingly pursued her own interests. Royal life meant constant shuttling with her husband and retinue between the Winter Palace in St Petersburg and the outlying royal estates at Peterhof, Oranienbaum and Tsarskoe Selo. While Peter hunted, drank to excess and recruited the servants for giant games of soldiers, she found an outlet for her restless physical – and perhaps sexual – energy on horseback. 'I cared not at all for hunting but I passionately loved riding,' she wrote. 'The more violent this exercise, the better I liked it, so that if the horse broke loose, I chased after it and brought it back.' The English side saddle preferred by Elizabeth was too sedate to permit her wild galloping, so she adapted it to allow her to ride astride when not in view of the Empress, dressed in a man's riding attire and letting her pale face tan in the summer sun. In winter, she loved to toboggan down the perilously steep ice slides that delighted Russian crowds on snowy holidays. Elizabeth commissioned a wooden version for summer use and Catherine flew up and down its undulating slopes in a wheeled cart at terrifying speed.

When not riding, she loved to dance. Her looks were now at their finest, and she was pleased to find that, despite her mother's early criticism, her expressive blue eyes, pale skin and thick dark hair, worn curled, attracted admiring comments. After she dressed simply in white for one ball, she recalled, onlookers praised her as 'very beautiful and particularly radiant. To tell the truth, I have never believed myself to be extremely beautiful, but I knew how to please and I think that this was my forte.'

Alongside physical exercise, Catherine began reading in earnest. Her memoirs portray her spending the winter after Paul's birth voraciously consuming Voltaire's *Histoire Universelle* and works on the history of Germany and of the Church, before discovering Montesquieu's *The Spirit of Laws*, the seminal text of eighteenth-century political philosophy. The treatise, with its exploration of political systems from republicanism to despotism, transformed her understanding of the machinations she saw around her at Court and among the competing powers of Europe, jostling for supremacy across the globe during the Seven Years' War. The landmark work would provide the inspiration once in power for her own *Nakaz*, or *Great Instruction*, intended to guide reform of the Russian legal system. 'I began to see more things with a black outlook and to seek the causes that really underlay and truly shaped the different interests in the affairs that I observed,' she wrote. The Grand Duke's lack of interest in fulfilling his own responsibilities gave her scope to cut her political teeth advising on the management of his home duchy of Holstein.

The Grand Duchess's political awakening coincided with the declining health of the Empress and accompanying fevered speculation on the succession. As the volatile Grand Duke's unsuitability for leadership became ever more apparent, some at Court suggested installing Catherine as co-ruler alongside her husband. She began to acquire allies, demonstrating an ability to judge character and to trust accordingly that would prove indispensable in power. After a relationship with the adoring Polish aristocrat Count Stanislaw Poniatowski, and the birth and brief fifteen-month life of their daughter, Anna, Catherine embarked on an affair with her third lover, the dashing young Russian war hero Grigory Orlov. One of five brothers, all officers in the Imperial Guard, Orlov brought physical passion and cheerful companionship – both still absent in her marriage. Catherine was quickly pregnant with his child, her third, but by now had learned to keep the relationship, and the pregnancy, secret amid the factions and jealousies at Court. Orlov was more than a lover: he and his soldier brothers provided a connection with St Petersburg's four elite Guards regiments, crucial allies in any future struggle for power. Another new ally was a diplomat: Count Nikita Panin, court chamberlain and tutor to her son, Paul. Panin, cosmopolitan and well educated with extensive political experience, provided brains alongside the Orlovs' patriotic brawn. Sharing Catherine's enthusiasm for Enlightenment political theory, he hoped she could replace Peter and rule as regent until Paul could inherit the throne.

Count Grigory Orlov.

The reality was far more dramatic. When Elizabeth died in January 1762, the cannons of the St Peter and Paul Fortress thundered to mark the accession of the Emperor Peter III, but his reign lasted just 186 days. No coronation was ever scheduled. In a few short months, the wildly unpredictable ruler delivered some moderate reforms, but also managed to alienate the Orthodox Church, the army (whose Russian greatcoats he traded for close-fitting Prussian uniforms) and his European allies, having dramatically ended Russia's five-year war with Prussia. When he threatened to imprison Catherine and marry his mistress, his opponents seized their moment. On 28 June, in a dramatic dawn coup supported by Panin, the Orlov brothers and the army, Catherine proclaimed herself Empress from the Winter Palace to the sound of cheering crowds and the ringing of church bells. Then, dressed in the striking bottle-green regimental uniform of the elite Preobrazhensky Guards, riding a white stallion and armed with a sword, she led fourteen thousand marching soldiers from St Petersburg to arrest her husband.

Catherine's victorious ride was a potent visual statement, and her instinct for political image-making immediately kicked in. She commissioned a monumental portrait by the Danish artist Vigilius Eriksen showing her in her soldier's attire with her dark hair flowing behind her, riding astride in full command of her horse, Brillante, and holding an upright sword in her right hand. The depiction radically subverted perceptions of gender roles, borrowing the masculine, military iconography of the traditional equestrian portrait to present a revolutionary image of female power. Here, riding boldly from clouds into sunlight, was a warrior queen who had saved Russia and now led her country forward in triumph.

The new Empress had reason to deploy every available propaganda tool to establish her legitimacy. Six days after the coup, Peter, imprisoned in his country estate at Ropsha, was dead, killed by his officer guards in a drunken act that may have been an accident or murder. Alexei Orlov, older brother of Grigory and a coup protagonist who was present on the fateful night, despatched a frantic note to Catherine, insisting he did not know how Peter had died. Addressing the Empress as Matushka or Little Mother, the traditional term for female rulers of Russia, he scrawled: 'He is no more, but no one intended it so . . . We ourselves know not what we did. But we are all equally guilty and deserve to die.'

There is no evidence Catherine ordered her husband's death, or was complicit in any plan for his murder, but his removal was in her interest as ruler. She was perceived, even by association, to have blood on her hands. Her grip on power was far from stable, and she moved rapidly to change her image from usurper to reformer. She was still justifying her actions in her final memoir many years later: 'Things took such a turn that it was necessary to perish with [Peter], by him, or else try to save oneself from the wreckage and to save my children, and the state.'

Ordering a post-mortem for her husband that conveniently concluded – to widespread ridicule abroad – that he had died naturally of haemorrhoidal colic, the new Empress Catherine II deployed her personality, sense of theatre and a swathe of reformist policies to strengthen her political position. Her coronation in Moscow on 22 September 1762 mobilised the full spectacular force of Russian pageantry: crowds crammed the streets over a three-day holiday, cannons roared, and Catherine wore a gleaming gown of silver silk beneath a golden mantle trimmed with ermine for her anointing as ruler of 'All the Russias' at the Assumption Cathedral. The elaborate Orthodox ceremony saw her lift the specially commissioned imperial crown, encrusted with diamonds and pearls and the largest in Europe at her request, on to her own head. She was depicted in her magnificent regalia, confidently holding the orb and sceptre that symbolised her vast power, in two life-size coronation portraits, one by Eriksen and one by the Italian artist Stefano Torelli. The Torelli image was chosen to hang in the Holy Synod, with a duplicate in the Senate: the churchmen and politicians of Russia were left in no doubt who was in charge. Copies of Eriksen's work were despatched to the courts of Europe as a reminder that the Russian empire was under new leadership.

Barely pausing for breath, the 33-year-old Empress embarked on the double mission she had planned during her long years studying Enlightenment philosophy: to make Russia love the culture and political ideas of Europe, and to make Europe, in turn, respect Russia. As a native German and ardent Russophile, she felt herself uniquely positioned to speed Russia forward politically, economically and culturally into line with European civilisation. At the same time, she would challenge prejudiced Western characterisations of her adoptive country as primitive, barbaric and swimming in vodka.

As Grand Duchess, Catherine had read the works of the philosophes Diderot and Voltaire; as Empress, she wrote to them directly. Within weeks of taking the throne, she offered to arrange printing of the *Encyclopédie*, the bible of enlightened thinking edited by

Diderot and d'Alembert, amid opposition to the progressive text in France. The proposal was rejected – her credentials were still too uncertain – but the gesture won approval in Europe as a symbol of enlightened sympathies. In 1765, in a masterstroke of cultural propaganda, Catherine bought Diderot's library, put up for sale by the impoverished philosopher, but allowed him to keep it for his lifetime and paid him a salary. 'I prostrate myself at your feet,' he gushed in gratitude. 'Oh Catherine, be sure that you do not reign more powerfully in Petersburg than in Paris.'

The Empress's exchanges with Voltaire, the witty, provocative evangelist-in-chief of enlightened thought, flourished into a mutually flattering lifelong correspondence once the philosopher reassured himself of her commitment – in principle at least – to ideals of justice and tolerance. His outspoken advocacy for smallpox inoculation, symbolising the rational thinking he found so lacking in his native France, would be one of the prime influences persuading Catherine to adopt the procedure in Russia. Books on the practice were among over 6,700 volumes in his personal library, which she would buy up and transport to St Petersburg on his death.

Less than five years after coming to power, Catherine synthesised her ideas on enlightened political philosophy as applied to Russia in a landmark document: the *Nakaz*, or *Great Instruction*. Opening with the declaration 'Russia is a European state', an unequivocal echo of the Westernising vision of Peter the Great, her treatise presented her view of the country and how it should be governed, providing guiding principles by which its laws could be rationalised. Russia was so vast that only the firm hand of an absolute sovereign could control it, she argued, but it was not a despotism: the power of that autocratic leader should be limited by fundamental laws determined by reason. The document, borrowing extensively from Montesquieu and others and rapidly translated for distribution in Europe, was designed not only as a compendium of practical principles but a public statement of values with which Catherine wanted to associate her country and herself. It was also, almost certainly, a unique example of a work of political philosophy written in conjunction with a needlework project: she wrote to a friend that she worked on the Instruction for three hours from six each morning and on her tapestry while being read to in the afternoon.

Putting the *Nakaz* into practice proved more challenging. In 1767, Catherine convened a Legislative Commission comprising delegates of all sections of society bar the enslaved serfs to help guide the creation of a proposed new code of laws. The Commission met in 203 sessions before being prorogued and ultimately abandoned after less than two years as Russia went to war with Turkey. Even so, its chaotic deliberations provided the Empress with a vital insight into the competing interests of her stratified nation's diverse social groups. The experience confirmed her view that maintaining stability in Russia required autocratic leadership.

Though her legal code came to nothing, the self-proclaimed Little Mother of the Russian nation had other enlightened projects to improve the lot of her family of subjects, ninety percent of whom were peasants. With an intense work ethic and ability to manage multiple tasks simultaneously, the Empress launched initiatives in health and in education. Finding that educational reforms begun by Peter the Great had been allowed to disintegrate, she appointed a Commission to explore enlightened ideas for a national school system for children of both sexes. In 1764, it proposed a radical system which would isolate children from age five completely from the harmful influences of their parents and brutal and corrupt society, in order to create a 'new kind of person': good citizens shaped through moral persuasion rather than corporal punishment. In the same year, Catherine set up a foundling hospital in Moscow in which the new theories could be trialled. Operating under the Empress's direct command, the institution protected the anonymity of mothers unable to care for their children by allowing them to ring a bell in the street and place the baby in a basket lowered from an upper floor and then hauled up again. A maternity wing enabled mothers to give birth with some level of care. All abandoned children, legitimate or not, were accepted and cared for, trained in a craft or skill then released for work, further study or marriage.

The hospital, copied in St Petersburg and elsewhere, was a private foundation, not a state body, but its mission to reduce infant mortality reflected Catherine's wider concern to boost the health and size of Russia's population. She drew on the German theory of cameralism, which advocated strong management of a centralised economy for the benefit of the state. To strengthen national wealth, the argument went, rulers must strive to increase their productive populations. Russia had vast tracts of unsettled land, and a high death rate. 'If you go to a village and ask a peasant how many children he has,' Catherine observed, 'he will say ten, twelve and sometimes even twenty. If you ask how many of them are alive, he will say one, two, three, rarely four. One ought to remedy this mortality.'[7] There was a need to consult with doctors, she concluded, but also to establish some rules for estate owners, who carelessly allowed small children to run about, barely dressed, in ice and snow. 'There are those who remain robust, but nine-tenths die, and what a loss for the state!' In addition to child welfare, she determined to tackle the communicable diseases that wiped out millions of her subjects annually: syphilis, bubonic plague and the most dreaded affliction of all – smallpox.

To achieve her goals, she needed reform. Like education, health-care in Russia was woefully inadequate and barely existent in many parts of the empire, with far too few practitioners, especially in the countryside, and too many expensive – often incompetent – foreign doctors. There were just ninety-four physicians practising in the whole of Russia from 1760 to 1770, of whom only twenty-one were Russian and Ukrainian.[8] Again, the Empress established a Commission, read around her subject and took advice. In 1763, she issued a decree to set up Russia's first Medical College, charged with expanding medical care for the population at large and with recruiting more native Russian physicians, surgeons and apothecaries. Professional training was set up on a European model, and a new medical faculty at Moscow University was opened to provide an elite class of doctors. Specialist hospitals were established to treat venereal disease. To fill the post of first President of the College, she appointed Baron Alexander Cherkasov, the English-speaking Russian who had visited the London Smallpox Hospital some twenty years before. Reform was under way: a broader conception of public health was emerging, and it was seen as the business of the state.

By 1768, six years after the coup, Catherine's multiple reform-ing projects and efforts to present herself at home and abroad as an enlightened ruler in a distinctively Russian mould had stabi-lised her grip on power. Her lover Grigory Orlov remained at her side as a favourite but not a threat, and Count Panin had proved an indispensable advisor and a skilled tutor to her son, the Grand Duke Paul. Foreign observers, initially sceptical, expressed admiration at her understanding of the mystery that was Russia. 'The Empress is perhaps the woman in the world the most able to conduct so complicated a machine,' the British ambassador in St Petersburg, Lord Cathcart, wrote home to London. 'She is carrying on great public works, and magnificent institutions; the army of Russia never was on such a footing, her finances are reckoned to be in good order, and the balance of her trade higher than ever.'[9]

The threat to Catherine's plans that spring did not come from an enemy nation or internal plot. Instead, it appeared in the form of a deadly virus: smallpox. Sweeping St Petersburg in a fresh epidemic wave, the disease struck down Countess Anna Sheremeteva, the beautiful and wealthy fiancée of Count Panin. As the young woman fought for her life, the Empress quickly summoned Paul to her side at her estate in Tsarskoe Selo, terrified that her son and heir, who slept in the same room as his tutor, would fall prey to the dreaded virus that had so brutally disfigured his father. She had led thou-sands of soldiers in a coup and survived on the throne as a usurper, using her wits, courage and force of personality to outflank her opponents. In smallpox, she had finally encountered an enemy she feared she had no means to vanquish.

No records exist to date the arrival of smallpox in Russia, but the disease may have entered the country via trade routes as long ago as the fourth century. Accounts of unnamed fatal illnesses charac-terised by spots on the body are found in fifteenth- and sixteenth-century chronicles, but the first specific reference to smallpox appeared in 1610, when the infection was identified among the indigenous peoples of western Siberia.[10] More epidemics followed in Russia's vast Siberian lands and the Kamchatka region of the far east, wiping out communities unprotected by immunity and prompting fears of evil demons seeking dead bodies to feast on. Under the guidance of shamans, terrified inhabitants sacrificed livestock to appease the evil spirits, dressed in borrowed clothes to confuse them, and used burned wood to blacken false 'pocks' on to their bodies to trick the demons into believing they had already had the disease. When the virus struck, the healthy abandoned the sick in their villages, sacrificing homes and employment as they fled to safety.

With few doctors and no reliable means of treating the disease, objects were assigned healing powers. In 1653, in a bizarre collision of medical officialdom and folk belief, records show Russia's central pharmaceutical institution was offered the chance to purchase a slice of unicorn for eight thousand roubles. The item was billed as a radical means of curing plague-like diseases, including smallpox. It came with its own Latin authentication certificate signed by seven Hamburg doctors.[11]

More plausible, if less colourful, methods of stalling the virus were already emerging. In 1640, amid fears infections could be contracted from livestock, the first government decree banned the removal of skins from dead animals, on pain of whipping. More decrees followed, enforced by a new cadre of medical police. In 1680, Czar Feodor III Alexeyevich ordered that all cases of small-pox, fevers and other serious illnesses must be officially reported, and a warning painted in red letters on the house of those afflicted. Householders were ordered to isolate themselves indoors until given permission to leave, and severe punishments were issued for non-compliance, including requisition of property and enforced bankruptcy. The main aim was not to shield the population but to protect the health of the Czar and his entourage.

Subsequent decrees, with the same objective, were stricter still. Czar Peter the Great directed that anyone leaving a quarantined area, no matter what the reason, would be hanged on gallows posi-tioned on main roads as a warning to others. In 1722, a command issued on behalf of Peter's grandson, Emperor Peter II, decreed that the owner of any house where smallpox was present must inform the police or face severe punishment. The chief of police was then obliged to request a doctor to assess the illness and decide on any necessary measures to prevent contagion. To protect the royal household, the young Emperor ordered that no one from a house infected with smallpox could enter Vasilievsky Island, the location of his residence in St Petersburg. The precaution failed: the disease still spread to the court. In 1730 Peter II died of smallpox aged fourteen on the morning of his wedding.

The boy's fate cast the shadow of the disease over the Russian royal family. His successors followed his lead and used police enforcement to try to control the virus and protect the imperial line. The Empress Elizabeth, who had lost her fiancé to smallpox and later saw her nephew disfigured by it, renewed Peter's decree when she took the throne in 1741, and added new restrictions. Individuals with a red rash were banned from court and church. In 1765, after 116,000 citizens had died in a smallpox epidemic the previous year, Catherine II yet again reissued the order to inform the police of all cases.[12]

While the Russian state relied on strictly enforced isolation and quarantine in its efforts to tackle smallpox, news of the pioneering experiments in inoculation made its way to the empire from western Europe. The first public call for inoculation, focusing on children, appeared in a Russian periodical in 1732, some ten years after the practice had been introduced in London.[13] Within two decades, as inoculation took off in earnest in Britain, knowledge of the new technology was common in learned medical circles in Russia. *Monthly Essays*, an influential journal launched in the St Petersburg Academy of Sciences, published an enthusiastic account in 1755.[14] The article explained the 'English method' by which pus-soaked threads were placed in a scalpel cut, opening the way for interested practitioners to try the technique. Word spread to Russia that towering intellectual figures such as Voltaire and the American polymath and politician Benjamin Franklin supported inoculation, and Western developments in the practice were reported in the St Petersburg *Vedemosti* newspaper.

As the latest scientific updates came from the West, inoculation was already happening on Russian soil. Despatches from travellers and scientists exploring the empire revealed a range of folk practices present among peasant populations in some provinces. In Ukraine, mothers took pus from a patient with a mild case of smallpox and applied it to their children's bodies, bandaging it until the fever emerged. Further east in Kazan, on the Volga river, smallpox scabs were collected in a pot and mixed with honey before being rubbed on the skin, while according to another custom in some villages a coin was wetted with pus and then placed in the hand or under the armpit. In Samarkand, a traditional method involved mixing scabs with water in a copper spoon, pouring the concoction on to cotton wool in a wooden container and letting it ferment until it smelt. It was then applied with a multi-pronged needle to a scratch between the thumb and index finger. The peoples of Kamchatka, far from Western influence on Russia's eastern coast, were unique in using fish bones dipped in pus as makeshift inoculation needles.[15]

The traditional practices, scattered and specific to individual territories or communities, never extended outside their regions or reached beyond peasant populations to higher society. It was not until inoculation was introduced from above, via professional medical practitioners, that its use spread in Russia.

The first official attempts at inoculation began in 1756 in the city of Dorpat in Livonia,[16] the westernmost region of the empire, where a German doctor, August Schulenius, trialled the operation on two servants' children. He did not stop to ask the parents' consent; fortunately, both survived. Next, he operated with permission on two of the children of a Lutheran pastor, Johann Eisen, who had lost three other infants to smallpox. Using the proven Western method of scalpel incision, Schulenius went on to inoculate more than a thousand children with just one fatality, developing a reputation that would eventually bring him to the attention of the new Empress.

Pastor Eisen shared Catherine's view that a state's wealth lay in its people. By introducing inoculation to the poorest rural children as well as the rich, he hoped both to reduce suffering and enlarge the population. Eisen quickly recognised there were too few doctors to carry out the plan, and instructed peasant mothers to inoculate their children themselves with two or three light needle pricks to the hand, too shallow to draw blood. The method, he noted to a friend, was the same as Lady Mary Wortley Montagu had learned from the old women of Turkey: after fifty-seven years he had 'given the practice back into their hands'.[17]

Back in St Petersburg, the promotion of inoculation in the *Monthly Essays* encouraged some doctors to experiment with the practice, but medical authorities focused on treating natural smallpox. In 1763, with Catherine now on the throne, a specialist smallpox hospital was opened in Tobolsk, in western Siberia, in response to repeated devastating outbreaks. A treatment handbook published in the Russian capital three years later opened with a description of inoculation, 'this useful invention, so advantageous to the human race', but noted that the method was 'not yet in use among the people here'.[18]

The operation had, however, been secretly considered by the Empress herself. On a visit to Riga as part of a tour of her Baltic provinces in June 1764, she had proposed to her advisors that she inoculate her son, who had accompanied her on the journey despite his precarious health. The practice was established in the region, and she may have heard of it there for the first time, immediately seeing its value in protecting her heir so soon after the coup. Her favourite, Orlov, supported her but, according to Lord Buckinghamshire, the British ambassador to Russia, 'the idea was overruled by M. Panin and by many others'.[19] It was too outlandish, and too risky, to be considered.

For Catherine, sheltering in the countryside at Tsarskoe Selo as smallpox once again ripped through St Petersburg four years later, isolation was still the only way to avoid the terrifying threat to herself and her heir. The disease was no respecter of rank: exactly a year previously in May 1767 the Empress Maria Theresa of Austria and her daughter-in-law, Maria Josepha, the wife of her son and heir Joseph II, had both contracted smallpox. While Maria Theresa was scarred but recovered, Maria Josepha died within a week with no surviving children to inherit the throne. Just a few months later, Maria Theresa's fifteen-year-old daughter Josepha also fell victim to the virus. The devastation to the family and to the Habsburg dynasty had caused shockwaves across Europe.

Catherine and Panin had been exceptionally careful to protect the Grand Duke, now fourteen, from any exposure to smallpox.

Both were conscious that, until he had safely survived the disease, a question mark remained over his succession. Their restrictions had kept him away from crowds and other possible sources of infection, to the boy's understandable frustration. Asked aged twelve if he wished to attend a masquerade, he complained that he was likely to be prevented from going in any case. 'Mr Panin will tell me that there is a great monster called Smallpox, walking up and down the ballroom. This same monster has very good foreknowledge of my movements for he is generally to be found in precisely those places where I have the most inclination to go.'[20]

Horrified that, with the infection of Panin's young fiancée, Paul would now be exposed to the deadly virus, Catherine secretly wrote ordering her son be brought to her from the city. She worried at the distress the move would cause Panin, caught between his duties as tutor and his desperate concern for his beloved Anna Sheremeteva, but there was no choice. Aside from her maternal desire to protect Paul, there were wider implications to consider. She was all too aware that if she allowed her heir to catch the disease, it 'would not be without reproach from the public'. Her personal decisions – as a mother, a lover and every other role – would always be political.

On 15 May 1768, Catherine wrote to Panin passing on her own doctor's assurances that Anna would soon recover, but two days later she received word that the 24-year-old countess had died at five o'clock that morning. Immediately, she penned another message, expressing her 'real sorrow' and adding: 'I am so touched for you by this grievous misfortune that I cannot sufficiently explain it. Please watch your own health.'[21] Henry Shirley, straight-talking secretary to the British ambassador Lord Cathcart, shared her concern. He wrote in a despatch to London: 'By the anxiety [Count Panin] was in during all the time of her illness he must be inconsolable. He loved her so much, that we are not without apprehension for him.'[22]

For seven more weeks, Catherine and Paul sheltered at Tsarskoe Selo, spending the rest of the summer staying at the coastal estates of Peterhof and Oranienbaum to avoid the smallpox outbreak in St Petersburg. The arrangement kept them safe but it was not sustainable: an Empress could not abandon her capital. Searching for a solution, perhaps with encouragement from her correspondent Voltaire or of Baron Cherkasov, President of the Medical College, she revisited the idea she had considered four years earlier. She had been dissuaded then, but now she made a landmark decision. She would have her son inoculated against smallpox and, to avoid any suggestion she had rashly exposed him to harm, she would first undergo the procedure herself.

The proposal was unprecedented. Royal children, including those of the Georgian kings in Britain, had been inoculated before 1768 but no ruling European monarch had ever personally risked the operation.

No European monarch, on the other hand, was quite like Catherine II of Russia. Her reading of Enlightenment texts, and correspondence with their authors, had convinced her of the primacy of reason and of carefully weighed evidence. Just as she had with matters of law, health and education, she researched inoculation and took advice from those she trusted. The accounts she saw of the procedure in its latest, newly simplified manifestation were positive; the statistics showed the operation was far safer than natural smallpox.

Catherine began to recognise new possibilities besides the benefit of protecting herself and her heir from a terrifying disease. Talented politicians capitalise on events, and the Empress was a consummate operator. By her own pioneering example, she could demonstrate the safety of inoculation, and then introduce the practice across her dominions. The move fitted neatly into her planned health reforms. It would save untold numbers of lives, winning her adulation as the caring Little Mother of her adoptive nation and reinforcing her legitimacy on the throne. Abroad, it would help her position Russia as a centre of cutting-edge scientific practice instead of a hotbed of superstition. Once the operation had passed off safely, she would be ready to put her ideas into action.

The only task left was to choose a doctor to perform the operation. There was no physician in Russia with the status and experience to take on the enormous responsibility she had in mind. In France, the philosophes were vocal supporters of the practice, but the Sorbonne was busy banning it. The obvious place to turn was

Britain, the global centre of excellence in inoculation and home of the less invasive 'new method', with its remarkable success rates.

Catherine gave her orders. In June, a messenger was despatched to Russia's ambassador in London, Count Aleksei Semyonovich Musin-Pushkin, charging him with selecting Britain's leading expert on inoculation. The mission, to be cloaked in secrecy until fully complete, was not to be divulged: even the chosen doctor would not learn the full truth until he reached St Petersburg. The Empress of Russia was preparing to risk her life.

THE

PRESENT METHOD

OF

INOCULATING

FOR THE

SMALL-POX.

To which are added,

Some EXPERIMENTS, inſtituted with a
View to diſcover the Effects of a ſimilar
Treatment in the Natural Small-Pox.

By THOMAS DIMSDALE, M. D.

THE SECOND EDITION.

LONDON:

Printed for W. OWEN, in Fleet-Street.
MDCCLXVII.

*The Present Method of Inoculating for the
Small-Pox by Thomas Dimsdale, 1767.*

4

The Invitation

'A letter from His Excellency Mr Pouschin'

Thomas Dimsdale[1]

One summer's evening early in July 1768, a horseman rode up to the gates of Port Hill House, Thomas Dimsdale's home a few miles from Hertford. Dismounting, the visitor announced himself to the physician with a flourish: he came from the Russian embassy in London, and brought a letter from the ambassador, Count Aleksei Semyonovich Musin-Pushkin. Breaking the seal, Thomas found an extraordinary invitation. Catherine II, Empress of Russia, had resolved to introduce the practice of inoculation across her empire, and wanted to engage a skilled physician to oversee the project. Dr Dimsdale, renowned author of *The Present Method of Inoculating for the Small-Pox*, was invited to meet the ambassador to discuss the plan at his earliest possible convenience.

Thomas's first instinct, he recalled in his own account of the events that followed, was to say no. He had not, he wrote, 'the most distant intention of engaging to go abroad', much less travel some 1,700 miles to a country of which he knew almost nothing.[2] His medical education had been excellent, but his language skills were lacking: he spoke only poor French and certainly no Russian. Nevertheless, an instant refusal would be dishonourable: it was his duty to answer the call. He sent the courier back to London agreeing to a meeting.

A few days later, the doctor paid his respects to Count Pushkin, meeting him at the London home of his old Quaker friend Dr John

Fothergill in fashionable Harpur Street, Bloomsbury. The ambassador's approach was flattering: he had consulted eminent physicians who were united in recommending Thomas as the man to lead the Empress's ambitious scheme. He worked hard to persuade his serious, plainly spoken guest, promising that with respect to status, remuneration and 'the most perfect freedom of returning' when he chose, everything should be done according to his wishes. The possibility of any further task was barely mentioned; only the merest hints were dropped that 'some persons of the highest rank' might also be the objects of the proposal.[3]

Thomas resisted. He admitted that a young man starting out in his career would have jumped at the opportunity, but his own situation was different. At fifty-six years old, with a busy and lucrative medical practice built up over more than three decades, he was in no need of challenging foreign adventures. His money worries were behind him; by now he was 'happy in the possession of a fortune equal to my wishes'. His comfortable career and income were not the only reasons to stay safely in the gently rolling countryside of Hertfordshire: the 'still more endearing attachment to a large family' of a wife and seven children tied him even more strongly to the home and work he loved.[4] The prospect of leaving all this behind for months, even years, weighed too heavily for him to take up the royal invitation. The glamour of a foreign court held little attraction to overcome his reservations: he regularly inoculated in the finest homes in England, but his social ambitions came a distant second to his passion for medicine. He declined the offer, but promised to do his best to find an alternative and equally suitable candidate.

To confirm his decision, Thomas met again privately with the affable Fothergill, who counted the Russian ambassador among his array of clients and had heartily recommended his friend as England's leading expert in inoculation. The two Quaker physicians knew each other well: they had been meeting often to discuss the revolutionary developments in inoculation that had led Thomas to write his treatise. They shared a talent for making money through hard work and medical innovation, and for philanthropy, both treating the poor for free.[5] Fothergill, perhaps with inside information or simply a worldlier mind, agreed his fellow doctor was right to turn down the invitation to introduce inoculation in the Russian empire, but stressed that, if any of the Imperial family should turn out to be the real object of the mission, he must accept. Thomas, not a man for the public eye, remained cautious, but his well-connected Quaker friend was insistent. Such a summons would be 'a call of honour which ought to be obeyed'.[6]

Barely had Thomas begun his search for a substitute than a second invitation arrived from the Russian ambassador, even more

Dr John Fothergill.

urgent than the first. Count Pushkin informed him that another courier, a distinguished military officer employed 'only on extraordinary occasions', had made the journey from St Petersburg to London in an astonishing sixteen days – galloping well over a hundred miles a day.[7] This time, the message was unequivocal: the Empress Catherine II and her son, the Grand Duke Paul, wished to be personally inoculated by Dr Thomas Dimsdale. The unprecedented request had enormous implications: for the Empress and her heir, for Russia, for Thomas and his country, and for the reputation – even the future – of inoculation itself. There was no time to delay, and no possibility of consultation. Thomas put doubts aside and accepted the 'call of honour'. He pledged absolute secrecy and assured the ambassador he would prepare for the journey as fast as possible.

There was just one more matter to be settled before departure: payment. Count Pushkin asked the physician to name his own terms, adding that his orders were to provide whatever was asked. The unlimited offer, to the ambassador's surprise, had precisely the opposite effect to the one expected. Thomas refused to stipulate any reward for his services, leaving his remuneration entirely in the hands of the Empress. 'Lucrative motives had little weight with me from the beginning,' he wrote later, though that did not stop him fretting over payment during his trip.[8] He certainly did not need the money, but his decision not to set a fee could not have worked more strongly in his financial favour if he had planned it. Count Pushkin immediately presented him with £1,000 simply for the expenses of his journey to St Petersburg, recommending he travel by land, not the stormy Baltic Sea, for the most reliable arrival time. The ambassador also invited Thomas to bring a relative or friend with him on the visit. Relieved, the physician chose his twenty-year-old son, Nathaniel, a medical student at the University of Edinburgh and well versed in his inoculation methods. It was a wise decision: the young trainee, fresh-faced with large brown eyes softening his father's craggier features, would prove an invaluable assistant.

Just days later, the father and son medical team was ready for departure. Thomas prepared his medical instruments, checking the lancets and securing them in their silver and mother-of-pearl case. Cases were packed; carriages booked. The doctors' lives were about to change for ever.

The treatise that had catapulted Dr Thomas Dimsdale to international prominence was published in April 1767 and announced with little fanfare in the newspapers. In the *London Evening Post*, wedged between an advertisement for women's silk gloves made in Nottinghamshire ('exactly after the manner of the French') and another presenting a scientific essay on the powers of chemistry, was a third notice promoting '*The Present Method of Inoculating for the Small-Pox*, Containing a succinct account of the preparation, both in respect to diet and medicine, the operation, and subsequent management of the distemper; together with some experiments, instituted with a view to discover the effects of a similar treatment in the natural smallpox'. It cost two shillings and sixpence.

The Present Method opened with a remarkably bold statement. From the very start of his medical career, Thomas wrote, the dangers of natural smallpox had firmly convinced him that inoculation should 'become general' among the population. He had begun his training in 1730, less than a decade after Lady Mary Wortley Montagu had brought the practice to Britain, so the claim placed him as one of the world's first ever advocates of universal preventative healthcare.

Despite his enthusiasm for inoculation, Thomas acknowledged that the traditional methods used in Britain had sometimes led to worrying side effects and a small number of deaths. That had damaged confidence in the practice, even though it was far less risky than natural smallpox. The memory stayed with him of the child who had died under his care, and other patients had cost him 'not a little anxiety' during over twenty years as a busy inoculation specialist. But there was good news. A simpler, safer technique was now available that would reduce the risks to almost nothing – and he would explain it. The ambitious aim of his treatise was:

> to bring the practice still one step nearer to perfection, and lessen the ravages of a distemper, which is not a native of Britain,

but, like the plague, has been imported from a foreign country, and demands the exertion of all the powers we are possessed of, either to exterminate it from amongst us, which perhaps is not practicable, or to render it less unsafe, if not wholly without difficulty or danger.[9]

Thomas's vision of wholesale smallpox eradication was two hundred years ahead of its time, but his practical handbook for controlling the invading foreign virus through inoculation came at precisely the right moment. The manual would spread the word of the new and improved method just as resistance to the concept was crumbling, almost entirely in Britain and, more gradually, elsewhere in Europe and in America. Between 1767 and 1793, *The Present Method* would run to eight English language editions, including six in London, one in Dublin and another in Philadelphia. There were three translations each into French, German and Italian, and one apiece into Dutch, Swedish, Russian and Portuguese.

The treatise explained the latest techniques in inoculation with clarity and economy. Thomas referenced his own professional findings at all times and set out the rationale behind his conclusions, based on a set of detailed case histories from his own patients. His directions, he wrote, were 'the result of extensive practice ... founded on repeated trials and impartial observations'. Readers, whether practitioners or the many non-specialists following the debate, were receiving a despatch from the frontline of eighteenth-century science. They would find no inherited dogma: the author was a man of the Enlightenment. He promised simply the reasoned analysis of experience.

There were two key elements of the new practice of inoculation. First, a far smaller, lighter incision was used in place of deep cuts containing threads soaked in viral matter. Second, feverish patients were no longer wrapped up to sweat out the smallpox 'poison' once the pocks emerged. Instead, the aim was to keep them cool by encouraging them to walk outside in all weathers, drink cold water and even return to manual work while recovering. This so-called 'cold regimen', in particular, was 'new and opposite to all established theory'.[10] The idea was so shockingly in conflict with traditional humoral medicine, with its focus on reinforcing the body's natural processes of expulsion, that Thomas felt the need to reassure incredulous readers of its effectiveness.

> When a practice so foreign as this, and almost totally different, is inculcated, it is no wonder if men's minds are alarmed ... Experience, however, and instances of so many thousands succeeding by this method, without any considerable bad effects from it, either immediate or remote, are irresistible arguments for its support and justification, and the best proof of its utility and safety.[11]

In the face of tried and tested inoculation practice, centuries of medical theory were beginning to crumble.

The incision, meanwhile, was to be 'not more than one eighth of an inch' long, made with the tip of a lancet dipped in pus taken directly from a smallpox patient. The tiny wound, just deep enough to pierce the skin's surface, would then be gently stretched open and moistened with the fluid matter, with no bandaging or ointment applied. The steps would be repeated on the opposite arm. Despite the non-invasive nature of the technique, Thomas wrote, 'these methods of producing the disease never once have failed me.'[12]

The Present Method also provided guidance on a greatly shortened preparatory regimen for patients undergoing inoculation. Instead of preparing for some three weeks, they could get ready in just nine days. Thomas recommended the plain vegetarian diet that was standard to ensure the humours were balanced, together with three doses of a purgative powder. He gave the precise recipe: a mix of calomel – the mercury compound widely used to clean out the bowels – powdered crabs' claws, and the antimony compound emetic tartar, commonly used to induce vomiting. This medication could be adapted according to the category of patients: children needed only a mild purge (which had the extra benefit of expelling worms), and a light touch was also recommended for older people, those with delicate constitutions and menstruating or pregnant women.

Silver and mother-of-pearl medical instrument case
owned by Thomas Dimsdale. The lancet is thought
to be the one used to inoculate Catherine II.

Thomas shared his personal inoculation practice and experiments in the treatise, but he also acknowledged an important fact: the radical techniques he described were not his own discoveries. He knew of the benefits of the 'cool treatment' in principle – the famed seventeenth-century physician Thomas Sydenham had controversially prescribed it to cure natural smallpox – but he had not previously dared risk it on his patients. Bold experimentation was not his way: he was naturally cautious and reluctant to damage the reputation of inoculation. He had continued to keep his patients warm, and to cut their skin and insert cotton threads. Then, several years previously, he had begun to hear 'incredible accounts' of a new and more successful inoculation method being practised in some parts of England, made even more marvellous because it seemed the operators 'could lay but little claim to medical erudition'.[13]

The assessment was uncharacteristically patronising, but it reflected the weight he placed on hard work and study. He was proud of his rigorous hospital training and his years of experience; he had bought his medical degree but certainly felt he had earned the title of physician. In the case of the apparent breakthrough in inoculation, his scientist's curiosity had overcome his professional snobbery. Knowing that transformational improvements 'are sometimes stumbled upon by men of more confined abilities', he wrote, he had done all he could to learn about the new techniques without stealing them for profit, as others had done, from 'those who are entitled to our gratitude for assisting us in this important process'.[14] From 1765, he had been testing them out for himself.

The Present Method paid its backhanded tribute to the developers of the improved inoculation method, but it did not name them. Politeness aside, there was no need to: the practitioners involved, though forgotten today, were already famous, not only in Britain but among some of the most elevated families of Europe. They were the Suttons: a family of doctors from an East Anglian village whose revolutionary influence had started to transform inoculation.

Robert Sutton, a country surgeon from Kenton, Suffolk, had begun experimenting with the inoculation process in 1756 after his eldest son, aged twenty-four, almost died from the procedure. Sutton recognised the needless complication and risk introduced through the use of inch-long incisions and dried pus-infused threads, which exposed patients to the danger of infection and lengthened recovery time. He tried a new approach, using fluid smallpox matter taken directly from a patient with the disease and administered via a minute superficial pinprick. Sure enough, his subjects experienced milder symptoms, suffered fewer pustules and recovered faster. The revolutionary 'new method' of inoculation was born. After more than thirty years of experimentation, an English doctor had returned to a technique remarkably similar to that used by old women in Turkey.

In 1757, Sutton rented 'a large and commodious house' suitable for residential patients and took out an advertisement in his local newspaper, the *Ipswich Journal*, offering his services as an inoculator. 'Gentlemen and Ladies,' it announced,

> will be prepared, inoculated, boarded and nursed and allowed tea, wine, fish and fowl at seven guineas each, for one month, Farmers at five pounds, to be allowed tea, veal, mutton, lamb. And for the benefit of the meaner sort, he will take them at three guineas a month, if they are not fit to be discharged sooner; and those that can board and nurse themselves, he will inoculate them for half a guinea each.[15]

Business boomed. The combination of comfort, prices for all pockets and a promise of 'no incision' inoculation brought patients flocking from around the county. Sutton opened two more inoculation houses within a year, then expanded further to offer cheaper no-frills procedures while also treating the affluent Suffolk gentry in their own homes. By 1762, now certain of the effectiveness of his light-touch technique – backed up with a specially developed secret medicine – he reported inoculating 365 patients in nine months, 'several of whom were hard drinkers for many years, and not one has been confined in bed two days'.[16]

To meet increasing demand, Robert Sutton recruited six of his sons to the family business. The third eldest, Daniel, had no formal medical qualifications but inherited his father's curiosity and entrepreneurial spirit. Daniel experimented further with new approaches and found that patients' preparation time could safely be reduced from a month to eight or ten days. Once inoculated, he discovered, they recovered far more quickly if, instead of being confined to bed in a hot and airless room, they walked outdoors as much as possible. Both innovations made the procedure not only safer but simpler, quicker and more affordable, dramatically increasing the potential client base.

When his father rejected his new methods as rash and danger-ous, Daniel moved to the next county and set up on his own. In 1763, aged just twenty-nine, he opened two 'neat and elegant' inoc-ulation houses close to the small town of Ingatestone, Essex, a bustling coaching stop on the busy Great East Road linking London, Colchester and the port of Harwich.[17] There, beyond the jurisdic-tion of the Royal College of Physicians in London, he could practise without a licence and attract travellers heading to the continent or to the smallpox-infested capital. Advertising his unique method with the same confidence as his father, Daniel focused on the free-dom given to his patients to walk outside and the comparative brev-ity of the treatment. It was all over in around three weeks, allowing a quicker return to work. In a bid to target women, he stressed that his patients suffered no more than twenty pustules each: 'Worthy of the attention of the public, particularly the fair sex, as by this method the face is effectually prevented from being disfigured.'[18]

The response was immediate, and remarkable. By the end of his first full year in business, the younger Sutton had inoculated 1,629 people and earned 2,000 guineas – around half the annual salary of the Prime Minister. In 1765, he treated 4,347 people and amassed £6,300, one of the highest incomes in the country.[19]

The residents of Ingatestone were far from enthused by Daniel Sutton's success. Fearing the spread of infection from his patients, they published notices warning his trade would be 'a detriment to the public' and threatening legal action. The young doctor, well aware there was no law against inoculation, ignored them. Through relentless promotion of his 'Suttonian method', he continued to expand his business and his wealth. His reputation grew, and patients of all ages and classes flocked to his door, prompting him to set up more inoculation houses to ensure the highest payers were not disturbed by the boisterous rabble on cut-price rates who shared rooms and even beds.

Sutton Junior kept the details of his method and medications secret, recognising from the outset the commercial value of exclu-sivity, but word of his technique spread as past patients related their experiences. The Essex lawyer and politician Bamber Gascoyne gave a rare written account in letters to a friend, the landowner

John Strutt. With smallpox widespread in the county in spring 1766, Gascoyne decided to have his three young sons inoculated, summoning Sutton to treat the boys and his servant, Moor. He recorded the preparatory vegetarian diet prescribed by the doctor, featuring 'asparagus, spinnage, cucumbers and puddings with plumbs, pruens or gooseberries . . . cold water and cyder . . . and sometimes milk and water'. It left one of his sons as thin as 'a gun barrel', while Moor – who was terrified at the prospect of inoculation – looked 'as if he had slip'd the chains from a gibbet'.[20] Sutton did not divulge the make-up of his purging powders, but Gascoyne deduced from their side effects that they contained mercury, antimony and coral or powdered shell: all standard medical ingredients available to any apothecary.

On the day of the inoculation, Sutton arrived in a chaise with a Mrs Wallis, one of his newly inoculated patients, whose light scattering of pocks provided the infected matter for the operation. Gascoyne noted that the doctor took the pus on a lancet and applied the tip so gently under his son's skin 'that he was not sensible of the point's touching him'. All four patients were given foul-smelling purgative tablets and endured a few days' unpleasant sickness but were instructed to walk outside in the fresh air and soon recovered. 'If this is the small pox I would sooner have it than an ague,' the boys' father declared. Sutton, whom he had originally referred to flippantly as 'the pocky doctor', had been 'very punctual in his attendance, and . . . is a most surprising fellow, and hath a most amazing secret in giving and abating the venom of the small pox'.

The famed inoculator was in demand from all levels of society. The First Surgeon to the King of Poland dropped in at Ingatestone to watch him in action, even having a go at inoculating some patients himself under supervision. Sutton's reputation received another boost when in 1766 he conducted a mass inoculation in the Essex town of Maldon at the request of the parish authorities, treating 487 inhabitants in a single day – almost a third of the population – and halting a smallpox outbreak.[21] Seventy of the patients were gentry and tradespeople, who paid for their own treatment, but the inoculation of 417 of the poor was funded by public subscription. The herculean eradication effort saved lives but also the town's economy, allowing tradesmen to return to work and the market to reopen.

Sutton capitalised on the success, offering general inoculations to other towns around south-east England, with the poor treated at low rates or for free. He won a court case accusing him of allowing infectious patients to spread smallpox, and carried on expanding his business.[22] Over three years from 1764 Sutton and his assistants treated almost twenty thousand patients, without a single death linked to the treatment. In 1766 alone, he personally inoculated 7,816 people: an average of twenty-one a day.

It was still not enough for the ambitious entrepreneur. To enhance his respectability and attract devout clients, he built a small chapel in the garden at Ingatestone, then hired a clergyman, Robert Houlton, who doubled up as a public relations spokesman for his business. In 1767, Houlton published *A Sermon . . . in Defence of Inoculation*, in which he batted away potential religious and conscientious objections to inoculation before issuing a guilt-inducing warning to cautious parents: 'If you neglect to have your children inoculated, and they are infected, as they grow up, with the natural Small pox and die, have you not *real cause* to be uneasy, and to accuse yourselves of carelessness and want of natural affection?'[23] Calling on the government to encourage inoculation to help boost the population for labour or war, he turned his promotional pen to the pleasantness of the Sutton inoculation experience. 'With respect to pain, it is not equal to the thousandth part which the prick of a pin gives . . . Here is no confinement, no keeping of bed. All is mirth and all seem happy. In fact, this fortnight visit to Mr Sutton's abounds with real pleasure and satisfaction.'[24] For those able to pay for residential care, inoculation had turned from risky ordeal into something billed as a holiday.

While Houlton advertised his business, the Essex surgeon focused on enhancing his own social status. He moved to a London mansion on a site now occupied by the Albert Hall, and applied to the College of Heralds for his own coat of arms and family crest. The resulting design featured a serpent, symbolising the medical profession, and a dove, hinting at the gentleness of his care, set on an azure background to represent perseverance. With it came a

Latin motto for his business, which translated as 'Safely, Quickly, Pleasantly'. Crueller contemporaries laughed at Sutton's vanity – one anonymous wit described him 'strutting like a frothy mountebank'[25] – but his catchy slogan brought patients flocking.

The overwhelming demand for his services prompted Daniel Sutton to build bridges with his father and brothers and set up a system of local franchises with surgeons around Britain and beyond. By 1768, the extended Sutton family and their authorised partners were inoculating throughout England from Cornwall and the Isle of Wight to Liverpool and Durham, and across Wales. Further afield, there were twelve licensed operators in Ireland and one each in Paris, the Hague and the colonies of Jamaica and Virginia, bringing the total to sixty-four approved practitioners worldwide. The full list of 'artists' was included in *Indisputable Facts relative to the Suttonian Art of Inoculation*, a booklet published by Robert Houlton Junior, son of the pulpit PR man, who had inherited his father's florid prose. Thanks purely to the 'skill and indefatigable labours of the Sutton family', he wrote, 'the practice of inoculation has taken rapid strides towards the summit of perfection; has broken loose from the shackles of ignorance and prejudice, and like the sun, unveiled from a thick cloud, shines, at this moment, in its full splendour.'[26]

Houlton Junior acknowledged there was no way to count precisely the number of individuals inoculated under the new method by the Suttons and their partners, especially as 'several hundreds' of the poor had never been recorded. But he estimated from the family's records that since 1760, in England alone, an astonishing 55,000 people had undergone the operation. A mere six had died, four of which he put down to other disorders and two to breach of doctor's instructions. The inoculation mortality rate calculated by James Jurin for the Royal Society forty years previously had been one in fifty; now it was less than one in nine thousand.

The scale of Daniel Sutton's business made his name a byword for inoculation in Britain, where the surge in take-up prompted nationalistic comparisons with less progressive neighbours. In continental Europe, the practice was generally confined to elite families, and even they did not always put their faith in its preventative powers. In October 1767, as the Habsburg royal family in Vienna was devastated by a smallpox outbreak, the writer Horace Walpole – himself inoculated as a small boy when the practice first came to Britain – wrote to a friend:

> I wonder all the princes of Europe are not frightened into their wits – why, they die every day! And might avoid it, most of them, by being inoculated. Mr Sutton would ensure them at twelve-pence a head. He inoculates whole counties, and it does not cause the least interruption to their business. They work in the fields, or go up to their middles in water, as usual. It is silly to die of such an old-fashioned distemper![27]

The poet Henry Jones went further, depicting Daniel Sutton in his 1768 poem *Inoculation; or Beauty's Triumph* as an inoculation superhero, holding back the tyrant Death and fending off the 'hideous apparition' of Superstition. Even Columbus's conquests were trumped by Sutton's 'nobler and unmatch'd Discovery':

> What's America and all her vast Domain,
> Another Hemisphere and Stars unknown
> Before, . . .
> If once compar'd with precious human Life
> Preserv'd secure against its deadliest Foe,
> And Millions rescu'd from th' untimely Grave?[28]

Daniel Sutton was making more money, treating more patients and enjoying a higher profile than any inoculator in history. It was no wonder that members of the medical establishment wanted to know the secret of Suttonian inoculation, while simultaneously discrediting its inventor. With his aggressive advertising campaign and his smelly pills and 'punch' drink whose formulae he would not disclose, Sutton was painted by some as an 'empiric', hardly different from an unlicensed quack advertising cure-all nostrums to the poor and gullible. It was an unfair charge: he observed his patients with a scientist's eye and conducted sophisticated experiments exploring skin reactions and immune response. But he didn't share his findings or engage in the dynamic globalised debate around inoculation. Sir George Baker, educated at Eton and Cambridge and physician to the Royal Household, sneered in a 1766 treatise on the new method that some of inoculation's 'most valuable improvements have been received from the hands of ignorance and barbarism'.[29]

Attempts by elite practitioners to discredit the upstart Suttons played straight into the family's hands. The snobs could mock, but thousands of satisfied customers proved their method worked, and they could offer inoculation at cheaper prices than the grand physicians with exactly the same result. Robert Houlton Junior was delighted: he could position the Suttons as the people's champions, bringing cutting-edge healthcare to a grateful populace and tweaking the nose of a privileged medical faculty still labouring under 'stubborn theoretical prejudices' and obsessed with protecting its own interests. 'The sluices of malice, envy and detraction were opened against this new mode of inoculation,' he declaimed in *Indisputable Facts* in 1768. 'Old practitioners were alarmed for their practice; and many who had considerable incomes from attending patients under the natural Small-pox, afraid they should have nothing to do.'[30] His language was florid but his point was fair: the Suttons had democratised inoculation.

Thomas, whose treatise had acknowledged his debt to the Suttons but not named the family, was 'a worthy good man' motivated by 'the best intentions', Houlton Junior wrote loftily.[31] But there was no way the physician's research could have revealed the full details of the secret medicines involved, or of the management of patients. 'All that I insist on is that the Suttonian art of inoculation is singular, is confined to themselves and partners, and cannot be attained by *report*.'[32]

Houlton's pamphlet even invited the government to order a public trial, in which a Suttonian practitioner would go head-to-head with a traditional physician to test out their inoculation methods on 'three or four hundred orphans appointed for the purpose'.[33] The offer of an 'inoculation-off' was never taken up, but as curious doctors scrambled to identify the key to the Suttons' revolutionary practice, children at the London Foundling Hospital were co-opted as subjects in a more constructive experiment.

Dr William Watson, a respected physician at the hospital who oversaw the compulsory inoculation of new arrivals, had already adopted the new method of small incisions and fresh air. Now he launched a trial with seventy-four boys and girls to test the benefits of mercury purges and the relative merits of inoculating from new or established pustules, keeping all other aspects of the regimen identical. Counting the children's pocks to measure the severity of each reaction, he concluded from his pioneering controlled trial not only that mercury had no effect but that – despite Houlton's claims – no additions to the simple pinprick and outdoor recovery made much difference at all. All the children recovered well and, crucially, inoculation was less dangerous than natural smallpox no matter how it was conducted: 'practised by any person whatever, in any manner yet devised, and at any time'.[34] Watson paid tribute to the Suttons for their role as popularisers as well as innovators: 'They have deserved well; not only on account of some real improvements they have made in the process, but also for the confidence they have excited in the public, from which vast numbers have been inoculated, who otherwise would not.'

The Suttons had won public trust fundamentally because their method, followed carefully, was safe. Daniel Sutton regularly challenged his detractors to provide verifiable evidence of deaths caused by inoculation at the hands of his family or partners; none came. But the family's significance also lay in stripping back inoculation sufficiently to allow the 'vast numbers' noted by Watson to take advantage of the treatment. By simplifying the method and continuing the process of standardisation under way since the 1750s, the Suttons not only created a spectacularly successful business model but paved the way for affordable mass-scale inoculation. While physicians continued to protest that each individual needed tailored preparation and treatment, which they alone could properly provide, Daniel Sutton's marathon general inoculation sessions proved the opposite. The new one-size-fits-all method did not have to be adapted to the patient: doctors could now focus on fighting the disease itself and begin to protect whole communities. The possibility of inoculation as a public health measure was emerging.

For towns and villages facing outbreaks of smallpox, coordinated general inoculations provided a means of saving lives but also safe-guarding the local economy. From the mid-1760s, coordinated community-wide inoculation became increasingly common, initially in the wealthier south and south-east of England. The impulse was not wholly philanthropic. Nursing and burying the sick poor was expensive, orphaned children had to be cared for, and periods of quarantine damaged trade. Parish authorities saw preventative healthcare as a cost-saving measure. Likewise, untreated sections of the community provided fuel for fresh disease outbreaks that placed everyone at risk. Smallpox could never be beaten back unless the poor were protected.

The fact that inoculated patients were temporarily infectious only strengthened the case for collective treatment, when everyone in a community who chose it could undergo the procedure together. Cities and large towns were too populous for the mass schemes, but in smaller communities it was possible to reach everyone at once, as Daniel Sutton had done at Maldon. Free inoculations for those who could not pay were funded out of parish poor relief or, where greater funds were needed, through charitable donations or a single wealthy benefactor. Surgeons and apothecaries competed for the lucrative contracts, charging the parish an average of five shillings a head, and making extra cash by offering a cheap rate for private clients.

Participation was voluntary, but take-up was generally high. The process was a world away from the relaxing residential experience Sutton advertised at Ingatestone. Deserving paupers were given tickets entitling them to inoculation, queued to receive their jab and purging medicine, and were sent home with instructions to avoid church, markets and other gatherings. Some received a check-up a few days later to be sure the procedure had taken; others were left to their recovery.

Despite the growing acceptance of the new technology, general inoculations were usually prompted by fear of an imminent disease outbreak. Thomas Dimsdale conducted a mass treatment of the poor at Hertford in 1766, halting an epidemic. In January 1768, he made his hazardous journey through deep snow from Bengeo to the village of Little Berkhamsted to attend to George Hodges, the ten-year-old from a poor family suffering with a virulent form of smallpox. The physician could not save the boy's life, but offered to inoculate residents of the parish for free to stop the spread of the disease. With the help of a visiting Dutch doctor, Jan Ingen-Housz, a talented scientist who had studied inoculation under William Watson at the Foundling Hospital, Thomas treated 290 inhabitants of Little Berkhamsted and, at the villagers' request, the neighbouring parish of Bayford. All the patients, aged from five weeks to seventy and including pregnant women, did well, and a note in the parish register paid tribute to Thomas as 'a gentleman of great skill in his profession, and of the most extensive humanity and benevolence'.[35] The experience had a profound impact on the physician too: he became increasingly convinced of the need for state-sponsored inoculation for the poor. The wealthy, he observed, had generally adopted the practice, and tradespeople could now afford to protect their families if they chose. As he carried out 'sundry general inoculations of different parishes in the county of Hertford', he began to consider in earnest how to protect those at the bottom of the social ladder, who 'if neglected, would be the greatest sufferers'.[36]

Thomas saw the public health potential of inoculation, but he shared the fears of other doctors over its risks. The simplicity of the new method prepared the way for wider access to the protective measure, but also opened up the technology to any lay operator with a sharp needle, a plausible manner and no concern for infection. In poor communities living in close proximity, inoculated patients could cause new outbreaks. Just as physicians in the 1750s had tried to protect their business against competition from provincial surgeons and apothecaries, now the medical profession united to fight incursions by amateurs who might not only threaten their livelihoods but bring the safety of inoculation disastrously into doubt. Thomas encountered 'almost endless' instances of 'the mischief arising from the practice of inoculation by the illiterate and ignorant'.[37] Called out to visit a young woman ten miles from Hertford, he found her dying from a botched inoculation by his own former coachman, who had used his connection with Thomas to set himself up as an inoculator and had now run away. A poor schoolmaster who begged for the physician's help after fatally attempting to inoculate his own family also turned out to have taken money to treat his neighbours, who infected and killed others in the town. Furious at the damage unskilled and dishonest operators could cause to the reputation of inoculation, Thomas called in vain for a licensing system for physicians and surgeons specialising in the practice.

While some lay inoculators practised successfully on a small scale in towns and villages, helped by handbooks such as *The Present Method*, most patients still turned to professional medical men, choosing the service that suited their pocket. The innovative, entrepreneurial nature of medicine in eighteenth-century Britain, regulated by the marketplace rather than government, encouraged an explosion in provision as surgeons and apothecaries set up as specialist operators. Competition was so fierce that many towns and villages introduced controls to force practitioners targeting their residents to practise in dedicated houses outside their boundaries to avoid spreading infection. The gentlemen and Overseers of the Poor in Winchester took out newspaper notices in 1767 to warn 'some persons' rumoured to be planning to open an inoculation house in the town would be 'prosecuted with the utmost severity of the law', as would anyone entering the parish to be inoculated.

Operators countered with advertisements highlighting their flawless safety records and suitably isolated premises. In the first four months of 1767 alone, no fewer than twenty-three surgeons offered their services in the *Ipswich Journal*. In Sible Hedingham, Essex, surgeon Baptist Spinluff boasted he had 'never lost a patient', stressing 'the care taken to render every accommodation agreeable' for patients paying five guineas (just over five pounds) a head. Messrs Porter and Perfect, Surgeons, advertised their inoculation house near Campden, Gloucestershire, where they practised 'with every improvement which the new and most successful method is capable of'. The days of selecting only healthy patients were over: 'No objection is made to those of a scorbutic, arthritic, or serophulous habit; to the old, the corpulent or the hard-drinking.'[38]

The Suttons, watching copycat newcomers profit from their innovation, tirelessly promoted their brand. In May 1768, just as the Empress of Russia was forming her inoculation plan, Daniel

Sutton advertised yet another new partnership, this time with surgeons in York, combining home visits for the wealthy with no-frills free treatment of the poor. His notice in the *Leeds Intelligencer* pronounced that inoculation had won out against 'the prejudices of ignorance and the cavils of malice'. He could not resist reminding readers of where credit lay for the revolutionary new method, and whom he had beaten to the discovery.

> What has rendered the practice of late so universal in this king-
> dom, has been the success of the Suttonian method: a success,
> which indeed has ever been most earnestly wished for, by every
> honest practitioner in physic; but which after many laborious
> researches and repeated experiments, the most learned of the
> faculty had despaired of attaining to.[39]

When the advisors to Catherine II came to choose a physician for the imperial inoculations, there was no question where to start the search. Britain had been the first European country to adopt inoculation, first to grant the practice official medical approval, and was now leading the way in developing and implementing a revolutionary new method. The man behind the improved technique, Daniel Sutton, had international fame, a near-flawless safety record and an inoculation empire stretching as far as the American colonies. Yet the invitation to travel to St Petersburg to treat Catherine and her son did not, in the end, go to the pioneer of Suttonian inoculation. Instead, it went to the man who wrote about it: Thomas Dimsdale.

In terms of medical practice, whatever the claims of Robert Houlton, there was little difference between the two men. But Sutton's get-rich-quick approach had reputational costs among wealthier patients. Joseph Cockfield and his friend and fellow Quaker John Scott, the poet whose parents had kept him at home for years to avoid smallpox, chose Thomas for their inoculation in 1766 out of fear at the consequences of Sutton's cheap rates. Cockfield wrote: 'The terms are so moderate that men in mean circumstances, men of low education and dissolute life, repair to his house, which is so confused and disorderly a place that one would admire one tenth part of his patients do not perish by their irregularities.'[40]

Rowdy clients were not Sutton's only problem. As more operators picked up his method, pushing down prices, he devoted ever more time and money to a hopeless effort to protect his brand. While Thomas was meeting the Russian ambassador in London in July 1768, Sutton and his brother William were placing yet another newspaper advertisement denouncing an inoculator who falsely claimed to have trained with them. 'We take this opportunity to inform the public that every person instructed by us, or any of our family in the Suttonian Art, have a certificate, and those that pretend to that art, and cannot produce such certificate, are imposters.'[41]

It was a losing battle and Sutton, already one of the wealthiest men in Britain, began to look greedy. He still inoculated titled patients, but his industrial-scale franchise operation and obsession with publicity diminished his attraction as the prime purveyor of specialist care. His enormous, newly acquired fortune had bought him a coat of arms and grand house but not social acceptability in the judgemental world of elite Georgian London. His lack of formal medical qualifications had always dogged him; now he was mocked for his gauche ineptitude in refined company. The diarist and patron Hester Thrale recorded a barbed account of her introduction of 'the famous Daniel Sutton' to a party. Overwhelmed in the presence of guests including the writer Samuel Johnson, the surgeon 'grinned and gaped' before clumsily confiding 'I never kept such company before.' He was 'a fellow of very quick parts,' noted Thrale, 'though as ignorant as dirt both with regard to books and the world'.[42]

The ambivalent establishment attitude to the Sutton family's contribution to inoculation was summed up in a report published in February 1768 by doctors at the court of George III in response to an enquiry from the Austrian ambassador in London, Count Seilern. The smallpox epidemic in Vienna had killed the daughter and daughter-in-law of the Habsburg Empress Maria Theresa, who had barely survived an attack herself. She had now lost five of her immediate family to the disease in six years and wanted to recruit a top specialist to introduce inoculation in her empire. The royal physicians and surgeons reported that the success of the practice in Britain could not be overstated, with barely one death in a thousand patients 'even before the time of the Suttons'. The key to the Suttons' 'great success' was exposing patients to the open air, a method they were sure would be as successful in Vienna. The report's conclusion denied the family any real credit for the transformation in inoculation in Britain: 'The Suttons are undoubtedly in some respects improvers in the art of inoculation, but by applying their rules too generally, and by their not making a proper allowance for the difference of constitutions, have frequently done harm. All their improvements have been adopted by other inoculators, and in the hands of these the art seems to be carried to a very great perfection.'[43]

With such a qualified – and unjust – review it was not surprising the Austrians did not invite Daniel Sutton to Vienna. The inoculator chosen instead was Jan Ingen-Housz, the Dutch physician and scientist who earlier that year had perfected his skills with Thomas Dimsdale, helping him with general inoculations in Hertfordshire. Ingen-Housz successfully treated the royal children and was rewarded with an appointment as Maria Theresa's court physician and a handsome pension.

The Russians, too, passed over Sutton. According to one rumour, published anonymously a year later, he had been invited to the embassy in London to discuss the role but had been turned down after asking for a £4,000 advance.[44] More likely, particularly given his patronising treatment by the royal doctors, he never got his foot in the door. There were too many reasons to choose Thomas Dimsdale. By 1768, with his treatise already in its fourth edition, Thomas was the leading global authority on the new method of inoculation (his title, *The Present Method of Inoculating for the Small-Pox*, had subtly helped detach the technique from Suttonian branding). His book had made its way to Russia: Baron Cherkasov, head of the St Petersburg Medical College and a key figure in arranging the imperial inoculations, owned a copy.[45]

With his hospital training and thirty-five years' experience running a successful country practice, Thomas had a quiet professional confidence in his abilities that resonated with patients. Twenty-three years older than Sutton, he offered attentive, personalised care. Charles Blackstone of Winchester wrote to a friend in 1767 of his wife's positive experience after undergoing inoculation in Hertford along with her two maids. She had recovered well with

J. INGENHOUSZ. C. ET ARCHIAT. CÆS.
OB CAESAREAM PROLEM
INSITIONE VARIOLARUM SERVATAM

Dr Jan Ingen-Housz.

only six pocks on her face, Blackstone reported. 'Dr Dimsdale has everything to recommend him as an operator: sagacity, tenderness, diligence, and genteel behaviour.'[46]

In a practice requiring a deliberate exposure to risk, a trusted physician was priceless, and Thomas could charge accordingly. His lifestyle remained less ostentatious than Sutton's, but he was a wealthy man, with properties and land around Hertford, a home in London and money to provide for his large family. He was no longer insecure about money, but he knew his value. Shortly before his visit to the embassy, Thomas charged £50 – over £7,000 in modern terms – to inoculate the Quaker merchant and philanthropist Osgood Hanbury, a governor of the London Smallpox Hospital.[47]

The Quaker network, with its web of free-thinking, well-educated men, often determined to improve society, remained central to Thomas's life. He was no longer a practising member of the Friends, but his upbringing had moulded him permanently, and his list of patients included many prominent Quakers. The reforming values of the sect would drive his campaign to bring mass inoculation safely to the poor. His faith underpinned his lifelong bond with Fothergill, whose influence had brought him the invitation to Russia.

The most important reason Thomas Dimsdale eclipsed Daniel Sutton had nothing to do with status or connections. It came down to openness. The Sutton family had never made their inoculation 'secrets' public: their entire business depended on keeping the information to themselves. Daniel promised to put his method in the public domain but did not do so until 1798 – the year Edward Jenner published his revolutionary findings on inoculating with cowpox. Where Sutton was an early biotech entrepreneur, Thomas was a scientist and reformer. He heard of the family's breakthrough, researched and tested the method and within two years made his findings public for all to share. He concluded *The Present Method* with an assurance that he had held nothing back: 'It will, I hope, be needless to tell the reader, that I have disclosed the whole of what I know with certainty relative to this process . . . according to the best of my judgement and experience.'[48]

The surgeon Richard Lambert, a campaigner for improved healthcare among the poor of north-east England, was one of many admirers. Where the Suttons had advanced inoculation through 'accidental merit', he wrote in 1768, the greatest boost had come from the 'disinterested, spirited, open, accurate, and full explanations of the present new manner, in all its different modes, published by the worthy Dr Dimsdale'.[49]

The Empress's advisors agreed. Thomas accepted his invitation, and the court of George III was alerted to the mission. By Monday 18 July, in true scurrilous style, an English newspaper had got hold of the story. In a column of court and political gossip, the *Salisbury and Winchester Journal* revealed: 'His Excellency, the Russian ambassador, we hear, has engaged Dr Dimsdale, an eminent physician at Hertford, to go over and inoculate the Empress and the Great Duke: 'tis said this gentleman will set out for Petersburgh in about a fortnight.'[50] How the provincial paper heard the news so fast is a mystery, but in Britain, at least, the secret of the imperial inoculations was already out.

On Thursday 28 July, Thomas and Nathaniel took the stagecoach from Stratford, Essex to Harwich, where they boarded the packet ship for Holland. Despite the risks of the project, the doctor was in upbeat mood. 'It is considered by most people a very hazardous enterprise,' wrote Thomas's former patient Joseph Cockfield. 'It is there said the small-pox is extremely epidemic in the city, and there is great hazard of their Majesties' taking the natural disease ere he can arrive.' Nevertheless, 'he went away with great cheerfulness and gaiety.'[51]

From Amsterdam, the Dimsdales travelled by private chaise, a closed carriage designed for swift long-distance travel which transported them day and night with only occasional stops. Thomas was highly impressed, writing home to his friend Henry Nicols: 'I really believe I could travel in the same manner for a year together without going into a bed for the chaise was so convenient that we slept as much as necessary and both agreed in being quite brisk and well.' The stopovers, where they were treated to good food and drink, proved more exhausting than the road. They passed quickly through Hanover ('there is nothing in the city worth seeing'), then to Berlin and Potsdam where they stayed for two days ('to see the things, palaces, picture gallery etc', scribbled the doctor) and were entertained first by the English ambassador and then the Russian, who treated them 'with great civility and politeness'.[52] Reaching the Baltic coast at Danzig,[53] the travellers pressed on to the port city of Riga, gateway to the Russian empire.

Now with a military escort, they sped through the Russian dominions, arriving in St Petersburg exactly a month after setting out from Amsterdam and before the house being prepared for them was ready. The chaise drew up instead outside a grand apartment building on Millionnaya, the most impressive street in the capital, a stone's throw from the Winter Palace and the sparkling waters of the River Neva. In four weeks, they had left Hertford and reached a new world. But as their journey ended, the greatest challenge of their lives was just beginning.

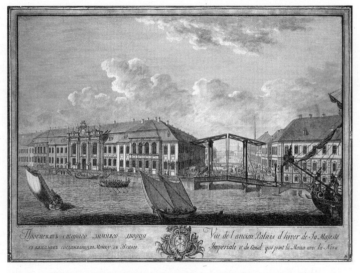

View of the Old Winter Palace, St Petersburg, 1753.
Painted by Yefim Vinogradov and Ivan Sokolov.

5

The Preparations

'The most important employment'

Count Nikita Panin[1]

The Dimsdales woke the next morning in their elegant apartment, opened their windows and breathed in the late summer warmth of St Petersburg. After weeks of changing landscapes and the jolting rhythm of the chaise, father and son were happy to be still at last. Like Western travellers before and after them, they were awestruck by the city's magnificence and unfamiliar, fairy-tale beauty. Just a few weeks previously, William Richardson, tutor to the children of the new British ambassador, Lord Cathcart, had arrived in the city by sea, and described the view from the water. 'The country around St Petersburg is very woody: so that in approaching it, the steeples and spires, which are covered with tin and brass, and some of them gilt, seemed as if they arose from the midst of a forest.'[2]

Another English visitor wrote: 'The views upon the banks of the Neva exhibit the most grand and lively scenes I ever beheld. That river is in many places as broad as the Thames in London: it is also deep, rapid and as transparent as crystal; and its banks are lined on each side with a continued range of handsome buildings.'[3]

From their new lodgings, the Dimsdales could see the Winter Palace, the imposing imperial residence dominating the Neva embankment. In the opposite direction along the Millionnaya, set in gardens on the bank of the Fontanka river, lay the more modest, two-storey Summer Palace, home to the Grand Duke Paul. Through the open casements of the apartment came sounds of building work as the Small Hermitage, commissioned by Catherine as a personal retreat and art gallery, neared completion. A coach and four, provided by the Empress for the doctors' personal use, waited on the street outside.

Thomas and Nathaniel had little time to relax and explore the wonders of the city. A notice from Count Panin, chief advisor to Catherine and in charge of the inoculation plan, summoned them to a meeting at his apartments in the Summer Palace the following afternoon.

Catherine's loyal minister, almost fifty and studiedly old-fashioned in a wig with three ties at the back and fastidious dress, received the visitors with formality and 'remarkable politeness'.[4] He made sure the two doctors were left in no doubt of the enormous political significance of the task ahead. Leaning towards Thomas, Panin declared:

> You are now called, Sir, to the most important employment that perhaps any gentleman was ever entrusted with. To your skill and integrity will probably be submitted, no less than the precious lives of two of the greatest personages in the world; with whose safety the tranquillity and happiness of this great empire are so intimately connected, that should an accident deprive us of either, the blessings we now enjoy might be turned to the utmost state of misery and confusion. May God avert such unspeakable calamities.

The message was clear: Thomas Dimsdale held two royal lives in his hands and the fate of all Russia too. The warning was so stark that the doctor recorded it in full in notes of the inoculation he made and later published at the Empress's instruction. Panin, whose own fiancée had died of smallpox only months before, explained that the threat of the disease was so great that the Russians had had no choice but to turn to inoculation. Russia had 'physicians of great learning and abilities in their profession', he stressed, not mentioning that – as Catherine had discovered – there were far too few doctors for the size of the country and most of them had been imported from abroad. The local lack of experience in inoculation had prompted the Empress to order her ministers to recruit a leading foreign expert in the procedure, he explained, and England was the obvious place to look. He told Thomas: 'You come to us well recommended in these essential points, I shall therefore repose the utmost confidence in you, and have only to request that you will act without the least reserve.'

The Empress would explain her own plans herself, Panin added, but her thirteen-year-old son Paul, who had spent the spring and summer in countryside palaces with his mother escaping a smallpox epidemic, had already made up his mind to be inoculated after being given the choice. 'It has been submitted to his own consideration; he approves, and even wishes it.' Now it was up to Thomas to confirm whether the often-sickly Grand Duke was healthy enough to withstand the operation. Panin, tutor to the young prince and in daily charge of his routine, urged the physician to observe the boy and reach his own conclusions. 'Be with him as much as possible; see him at his table, and at his amusements; make your observations, and, in short, study his constitution.'⁵ He told Thomas to be honest. If he decided the procedure was too risky for her heir, the Empress would be equally obliged to him and the 'acknowledgements' – the payment the doctor had declined to name – would be unaffected.

Thomas was facing the medical decision of his life. Swallowing down his anxiety, he reassured Panin he would produce a 'just report'. His first chance to assess the Grand Duke came the following day, when the two doctors were invited to dinner at the palace. The teenager received the visitors 'with the utmost politeness and affability', extending an open invitation to 'come at all hours without reserve' to eat with him and spend time at his court as often as they wished.⁶

While the Englishmen dined with her son that evening, Catherine II and her entourage returned to St Petersburg from Peterhof, the spectacular 'Russian Versailles' overlooking the Gulf of Finland some twenty miles west of the capital. The following morning at ten o'clock, in the more intimate surroundings of the Summer Palace, the Empress and the doctor finally met.

Only Panin and Baron Cherkasov, the English-speaking President of the Medical College who acted as interpreter, were present when physician and patient were introduced. The Empress saw a

56-year-old Englishman with a strong, open face, a firmly set mouth with a hint of stubbornness, and softer brown eyes revealing intelligence but not calculation. The doctor, in turn, bowed before a pleasantly smiling woman a little taller than average and of comfortable build, her fair complexion accented by her trademark rouge. Her blue-eyed gaze conveyed warmth and acute perception. When they began to talk, Catherine in French and her visitor in English, the connection was immediate. Thomas recorded: 'Though I was prepared to expect very much from the excellent understanding and politeness of her Majesty, yet her extreme penetration, and the propriety of the questions she asked, relative to the practice and success of inoculation, greatly surprised me.'[7]

Just as she had when overhauling her country's laws or reforming its health system, the 39-year-old Empress had researched with care. Her informed curiosity, combined with her fabled charm, worked their magic on Thomas. In a private letter to his friend Henry Nicols at Old South Sea House in the City of London, the measured tone of his medical treatise was replaced by breathless superlatives. 'I assure you that she is of all that ever I saw of her sex, taking all things together, the most engaging. Her affability and good sense is amazing.'[8]

THE OLD SOUTH SEA HOUSE (*see page 538*). *From a Print of the Period.*

Old South Sea House, Threadneedle Street, London –
home of Thomas Dimsdale's friend Henry Nicols.

Those first impressions were reinforced at a dinner with the Empress and a dozen court nobles the same evening. Thomas, used to an English seasonal diet, marvelled at the variety of dishes served 'after the French manner' in tureens and on platters for diners to serve themselves. A rich selection of meat and river fish was followed by 'the finest fruits and sweetmeats' he was surprised to find in a northern climate. The long table, headed by Catherine, was laden with watermelons and grapes from Astrakhan, melons from Moscow and apples and pears from Ukraine. There was even a small but tasty home-grown pineapple, the spiky status symbol found only on the wealthiest eighteenth-century tables, though he noted the fruit was usually imported to Russia from the hothouses of England. The luxurious menu, however, was less impressive to the English visitor than the 'most unaffected ease and affability of the Empress herself'. The most powerful woman in the world chatted informally, paying attention to each guest 'with a freedom and chearfulness to be expected rather from persons of the same rank, than from subjects admitted to the honour of their sovereign's company'.[9]

While Thomas was observing the Empress, she was watching him. If the fruit-filled banquet was a test, he passed it, and the following day he was summoned for another audience. She had made up her mind, Catherine told him, 'to submit to be inoculated as soon as possible'. Brushing away his suggestion that he explain his proposed preparation and treatment to her court physicians, she told him: 'You come well recommended to me; the conversation I have had with you on this subject has been very satisfactory, and my confidence in you is increased; I have not the least doubt of your abilities and knowledge in this practice.'[10] Her own doctors had no experience of inoculation and – particularly as her good health meant she had barely consulted them – would offer no useful help, Catherine insisted. In fact, as Thomas would discover later, she barely trusted them, and often joked about their incompetence. She told her English physician he could gain all the information he needed about her health and constitution by asking her directly, meeting as often as necessary. He would measure her pulse, but standard procedure required no physical examination. For the

Empress, inoculation was a personal act to be conducted as she chose. She told her doctor: 'My life is my own, and I shall with the utmost chearfulness and confidence rely on your care alone.'[11]

Thomas was on his own, dependent solely on his medical experience and judgement. Even discussing the procedure informally with others was out of the question. Catherine informed him she wished to be inoculated before her son, adding, 'at the same time, I desire that this may remain a secret business, and I enjoin you to let it be supposed that, for the present, all thoughts of my own inoculation are laid aside.'[12] Thomas was to use the Grand Duke's inoculation as pretext for visiting the Winter Palace to prepare the Empress for the procedure.

Catherine's terms could not be challenged; the doctor promised absolute secrecy. In his quest for personal reassurance, he tried one last request: would the Empress allow him to experiment by first inoculating some women of similar age and habits to herself? He did not take such precautions in England, but the status of his patient and his uncertainty over the nature of the virus in Russia prompted caution. Catherine refused. She had read up on the procedure, weighed up the statistics and made up her mind. If inoculation had been new, she told her physician, or if 'the least doubt of the general success had remained', such a precaution might have been necessary. Since neither was the case, 'there would be no occasion for delay on any account.'[13]

At home in England, despite the surge in enthusiasm for inoculation thanks to the simplified new method, Thomas was still used to rebutting sceptics. In *The Present Method of Inoculating for the Small-Pox*, published the previous year, he had written wearily: 'Discoveries in physic, as in every other science, are in their infancy liable to censure and opposition . . . It would be tedious to enter into a detail of the many false and ridiculous reports that have been spread against it.' Now, for the first time, he faced the opposite problem. The monumental pressure of the task, combined with his scientist's desire to test and prove, argued for extreme caution, yet his royal patient wanted her inoculation as fast as possible.

Whatever the doctor's worries, the plan was now fixed. The Empress's orders were given, and the imperial machine cranked into action, beginning preparations for the introduction of inoculation across the Russian empire. As a first step, Catherine purchased a grand two-storey house, the baroque 'dacha' or summer residence once owned by the late Baron Jacob Wolff, to be used as an isolation hospital for inoculees. Wolff, a banker and former British consul-general renowned for his skilled oversight of the flourishing British merchant community in St Petersburg, had built up a successful business exporting Russian products including hemp, potash and rhubarb – a prized wonder drug in huge demand across eighteenth-century Europe – and importing English woollen cloth.[14] Wolff House was situated across the Neva on the less developed Petrograd side, far from the royal palaces and surrounded by extensive gardens leading down to the Bolshaya Nevka river, making it a perfect location for infectious inoculated patients. Following an inspection visit by Thomas and Nathaniel, work got under way to equip the house as a hospital. Dr Schulenius, the physician who had introduced inoculation in the western Russian province of Livonia, was appointed as resident supervisor, assisted by Dr Strenge, a court counsellor.

Wolff House, St Petersburg.

While Wolff House was fitted out, Thomas followed Catherine's instructions to take advantage of her hospitality as he prepared for the inoculations. The arrangements were reported to London by Lord Cathcart, newly installed as British ambassador. The former soldier, nicknamed Patch Cathcart after the black silk patch he wore on his right cheek to cover a bullet scar, found himself confronted just days after taking up his post with a diplomatic matter of the utmost delicacy and risk.[15] In a despatch on 29 August to Viscount Weymouth, the British government member responsible for relations with northern European states, he sent upbeat word of the Dimsdales' arrival.[16] 'The Empress will certainly be inoculated and afterwards the Grand Duke. It is a secret which everybody knows and which does not seem to occasion much speculation.'[17] The newly arrived diplomat's breezy assurance was premature: delays in arranging the inoculation soon dampened any suggestion that the Empress was the intended patient. Her frequent meetings with Thomas could be passed off as discussions on Paul's operation. The physician, still hoping to inoculate 'forty or fifty people' before treating Catherine, had received a warm welcome, Cathcart reported.

> Things have been so managed that the Doctor is upon as free and easy a footing in the imperial palace as he could be in the house of any nobleman in England. He is a very worthy and respectable man and of great prudence; he speaks hardly any French, but understands it. The Empress, I have heard, understands a little English and will have no interpreter.

Thomas was less sanguine about his woeful language skills. He wrote to his friend Henry, an adept linguist who had lived in Budapest, heartily wishing he could have joined him in St Petersburg as an interpreter. At the invitation of the Grand Duke Paul, 'a very handsome fine young gentleman, quick, lively and of very good parts as far as I can judge', he and Nathaniel had joined the teenager for dinner or supper almost every day.[18] He was flattered, but the experience was embarrassing.

He is extremely familiar and good natured and tries me on several subjects in French but my mind has been so anxiously engaged that I have not been able to improve myself worth mentioning in the language, which is an inexpressible vexation to me as it is by no means pleasant to converse with difficulty.[19]

Communication challenges and increasing anxiety over his mission in St Petersburg did not prevent the physician appreciating the splendour of the city and its entertainments. 'The brilliancy of this Court and the magnificence of the palaces are amazing,' he enthused to Henry. The Winter Palace contained its own 600-seat theatre 'as big as Covent Garden' hosting plays in French and Russian and concerts with 190 performers at which 'the music is the most excellent I ever heard'. It was all paid for by the Empress, who attended each night with Paul. The autumn season would see the start of masquerades featuring 'dancing, card-playing, wine, sweetmeats', also at Catherine's expense, and he had attended a magnificent ball. 'I suppose there is not so gay [a] court in Europe.'

The simple life of his early Quaker forebears was long behind Thomas, but the high-octane revelry and indulgent diet at Court were a dramatic change from his moderate routine back in Hertford, where his only vice was a fondness for the occasional malt whisky.[20] 'We have lived a luxurious life by which and want of exercise I am afraid my health may suffer,' he fretted. 'I have not been on horseback since I left England, only twice with the Grand Duke, and then we didn't ride fast or far.' The doctor worried, too, about a social slip-up amid the complex protocols and hierarchies of Russian Court life. He was somewhat out of his depth, he confided to Henry. 'I have not repented of my journey but several times have been amazed to find myself here and frequently am within an inch of committing an enormous blunder, which you will easily believe from so careless a person as you know me to be and upon a stage so entirely different from anything I have ever been accustomed to.'

Thomas need not have worried. He never detailed any actual blunders in his letters to Henry, and in any case, his intelligence and integrity were more important than any social nicety to Catherine. Her trust in her physician was so complete that she invited him away from the pressured public sphere of the court into her private apartments in the Imperial Palace. 'He is an ingenious, plain, free man whose open manner I was sure would obtain a freedom with the great lady,' wrote John Thomson, a Scottish merchant in St Petersburg who claimed to have witnessed the daily meetings of doctor and patient.[21] Thomas, the Quaker-born medic used to polite home visits in rural Hertfordshire or London drawing rooms, found himself discussing the forthcoming inoculation with the Empress of Russia while sitting on her bed, sometimes with her lover beside them.

'[Dimsdale] had free access every morning to her bedchamber,' Thomson recorded.

They conversed for an hour or two together according to the time she could spare and he was not alter'd by sitting tête à tête on the canopy with her, nobody disturbed them [except] Count Orlov who often made a third on the canopy. She made the doctor speak to her in English what she could not comprehend in French and she comprehended it justly. She accustomed herself to treat him like an old man and an intimate friend and bid him go away when her time came to prepare to see others . . . She was charmed with the simplicity of her doctor and she determined to be inoculated.

Catherine was an expert in the power of public display but she also relished its opposite: playful familiarity. Just as she collected vast quantities of art to boost Russia's reputation as a civilised nation, so she delighted in collecting people. Thomas, an expert in his field, direct in manner if a little clumsy, courteous but not fawning, pleased her enormously. The doctor dealt in scientific laws, rationality and the calm weighing of evidence: precisely the enlightened values she hoped to impose on a nation she felt was held back by superstition. Not only that, he came from England, a nation whose culture she admired and whose political friendship Russia enjoyed and sought to strengthen. A commercial treaty with the British, renewed just two years previously, had further boosted the flourishing trade between the two states and expanded the lively British community of merchants, diplomats, doctors, gardeners, tutors and even circus performers living and working in St Petersburg.[22] A whole section of the Neva embankment, packed with grand merchants' houses, was known as the English Line, and the fashionable Russian nobility flaunted their love of English products, from cloth and ceramics to carriages, hunting dogs and Burton ale.[23] Catherine, though she never visited England, often boasted of her 'Anglomania', declaring that she felt 'at home' among English people.[24] Ambassador Cathcart, already bewitched by the Empress just a few weeks after arriving in St Petersburg, wrote to Weymouth: 'Russia to my predecessors, as their correspondence shows, appeared under French influence, from inclination, custom and education. Russia is now, by the Empress's firm, determined and declared opinions, and will be more so by all her institutions, decidedly English.'

At court, Thomas was known as 'the English doctor', he reported to Henry. 'I am most certainly treated with very great respect by everyone but particularly by the Empress from whom I have as they tell me received greater favours than ever was conferred on a foreigner.' By not setting terms for his work, the physician discovered he had unwittingly transformed himself in Catherine's eyes from contractor to 'a gentleman who pays me a visit'.[25] But Catherine's offer of access to her presence at any time had not turned his head, he assured his friend hastily. 'These civilities I have not abused by impertinent visits but have occasionally waited on Her Majesty as I thought it my duty.'

Doctor and patient were forging a remarkable bond of mutual respect and affection, but Catherine remained keen to press on swiftly with the inoculation. Though the precarious early years of her reign had passed, her illegitimate accession to the throne still required her to reinforce her credibility and authority as a ruler. The woman whose symbol was a bee got up before dawn and was always busy. There was work to do on her Legislative Commission and other domestic reforms in health, education and agriculture, and her cultural stimulation programme. Scientists and explorers fanned out to chart remote corners of the Russian empire; Catherine sought updates on expeditions to observe the Transit of Venus across the sun the following year. 'She is at the head of every work and looks into every detail herself, and all her conversation turns upon subjects of improvement,' Cathcart reported admiringly. Abroad, more alarming challenges were emerging. Tensions were running high in Poland with rebellions by anti-Russian patriots, prompting the Empress to move more forces into the country. Now the French were bribing Turkey to challenge Russian arrogance, and a violent raid on Ottoman territory by Russian Cossacks pursuing Polish rebels had pushed the Turks further towards war. Diplomatic despatches from London to St Petersburg spoke of British unease at renewed instability in Europe, just five years after the end of the devastating Seven Years' War.

Catherine's capacity for work was legendary, but she was testing herself to her limit. Her inoculation meant sacrificing valuable time while she recovered. The burden of responsibility began to weigh heavily on her physician, isolated without medical colleagues in an overwhelming world whose manners and language he did not understand. 'I have gone on tolerably well but many corroding cares disturb me and embitter all this greatness and indeed I am not able to enjoy as many would,' he admitted to Henry. 'I heartily wish you had been with me.'

Thomas prepared for the world's most high-profile inoculation just as he did with all his paying patients: with a medical questionnaire. Even though his own experience increasingly showed that any healthy individual could safely be inoculated with little or no preparation, he was old-school enough to investigate patients' medical history, constitution and current state of health before pressing ahead with the procedure. Royal expectation, and his own personal reassurance, depended on traditional personalised care.

The doctor listed his questions for Catherine, who jotted them down in French and provided detailed answers. The woman whose body would be written into history as a symbol of voracious sexual appetite revealed herself to be generally abstemious, health-conscious and prone to the physical symptoms of overwork. A typical day's menu, she reported, consisted of coffee and green tea for breakfast, sometimes with biscuits, then a dinner of soup followed by meat or, in summer, vegetables. It sounded like a menu at a modern yoga retreat, but Catherine admitted that her self-control sometimes slipped. 'There are times when I am very moderate, but others where I eat whatever is to be had,' she confided. She ate only a light supper, having discovered it helped her sleep better, and drank a maximum of two glasses of burgundy diluted with plenty of water, with no food or drink between meals except lime juice in hot weather. 'One's good digestion for better or worse, depends on one's diet, I think,' the Empress wrote. 'I don't remember being constipated three times in my life.'[26]

After the pleurisy she had suffered at fifteen, for which she had been bled sixteen times in under a month, she had been made to drink asses' milk and mineral water for years to ward off a recurrence, she revealed. She had no time for such faddy diets and concluded it was horse riding that had settled her stomach. Now, she suffered only occasional colic which she put down to eating too much fruit, or to the piles that plagued the inhabitants of St Petersburg. Her other ailments, Catherine told her doctor, were self-inflicted, prompted by the intense work she had done when writing her landmark legal reform blueprint, the *Nakaz*. Count Orlov had wisely warned her that sitting too long at her desk, which gave her eye strain, was bad for her health. 'For two years I have started to feel sometimes unbearable headaches which I attribute to overwork and because I got up for three years consecutively between four or five in the morning. However, I have found myself relieved of these headaches since this summer because I get up later, which is to say between six and seven o'clock.'[27]

The Empress's responses, showing fierce discipline combined with occasional indulgence, provided insights to her character, but there was nothing to trouble her doctor. A report Thomas had requested from the physicians to the Grand Duke Paul was more concerning. Both men, Dr Cruse and Monsieur Foussadier, refused to be personally involved in the inoculation, claiming they knew nothing about the process and could not give an opinion. Thomas turned to Dr North Vigor, the aptly named Scottish doctor to Paul's maids of honour, whom he hoped, as a fellow Briton, would support him; he too excused himself on the grounds that the matter was too important for him to engage in. Everyone had ducked out and again, Thomas was taking full responsibility alone. Worse, Foussadier's written report on Paul's health since birth claimed the boy had been effectively the subject of a tug of war between his western European physicians, with their purges and drugs, and his elderly Russian nurses. According to Foussadier, the women's traditional child-rearing methods saw Paul overfed, overheated by thick cradle coverings and hot rooms and carried so badly that his knees began to turn inwards. The late Empress Elizabeth, who had taken the baby from Catherine to bring up herself as the future heir to the throne, had ignored his doctors' recommendations of a plain diet and allowed the boy to be given any food he liked, washed down with beer. The teenager, unsurprisingly, suffered from indigestion and constipation, having survived fevers, swollen glands and worms – one of them 'half a foot long'.[28]

Thomas was 'extremely disappointed' at the doctors' refusal to help him, and astonished at the 'injudicious and extraordinary' management of the Grand Duke's health. His anxiety increased when he heard that a respected figure at Court had remarked that they wished him success but that inoculating either the Empress or her son would be 'more than any man that knows Russia would do'. It would be wise, Thomas decided, to record the situation and his recommendations in writing in a report to the Empress. Although Paul was of a 'delicate and tender constitution', he wrote, his own observations of the boy at their many shared mealtimes had shown him to be 'perfectly well-formed, active and free from any natural infirmity'. He was lively with a keen appetite and, though thin, seemed to be surprisingly strong and able to exercise without fatigue. In England, Thomas would certainly have considered the teenager a suitable inoculation candidate, but, left with no medical back-up, he was still worried. Russia's different climate might be less favourable, he speculated, and it might affect patients' recovery. He suggested a trial inoculation of some boys of 'inferior rank' of the same age and constitution as Paul, giving him the chance to reassure himself his methods were as effective against smallpox in St Petersburg as in the villages of Hertfordshire.

Catherine granted the request. Two fourteen-year-old army cadets, named Basoff and Swieten, were chosen for the experiment.

Neither were thought to have had smallpox, though the physician was surprised to find that the nature and symptoms of the disease were so little known in Russia. Few people seemed to be sure whether they had had it or not as children, and there was no public collection of data on causes of death. To allow Thomas the freedom to remain at Court without risk of transferring infection, Panin proposed Nathaniel should inoculate the boys at Wolff House. He sent his father twice-daily reports which were translated for the Empress.

The news arriving from across the Neva was concerning from the start. Even obtaining matter for the inoculation revealed how fiercely families clung to dangerous home treatments. Nathaniel took pus from a local child with a bad case of smallpox who seemed to be recovering safely but was kept by his impoverished parents in a cramped and overheated room. Despite the young medic's pleas that they open the window, the parents insisted 'it was impossible to keep the patient too hot', Nathaniel reported, and the child died a few days later.

The inoculation of the two cadets brought Thomas yet more cause for alarm. On the second day, Basoff suffered severe sickness and fever, and admitted he had, against orders, stuffed down a stomach-full of dried fruit. 'My son's accounts were clear and I could depend on his judgement, but unfortunately the fever continued,' the physician wrote.[29] The two young soldiers had bravely accepted their inoculation but, it emerged, they were actually terrified, believing themselves to be 'victims to a dangerous experiment'.

By day six, the news of the cadets was still bleak, and Thomas made up his mind to go to Wolff House to care for them himself. Before leaving, he was summoned by the Empress. 'I do not like to see you so unhappy; tell me what is the matter,' Catherine said. The physician explained his concern, but, when she questioned him closely, acknowledged he was certain Basoff's fever had started too soon and was too unusual to be linked to the inoculation. 'Then dismiss your fears,' the Empress declared. 'I make no doubt, with the blessing of God, he will be carried safe through his complaint, and all will end well.'[30] Her own trust in the procedure and in her doctor remained unshakeable, but she recognised the implications of a bad outcome for her mission to promote inoculation to a sceptical population. 'I must own it is an unhappy circumstance, for if any accident should happen, though from a different cause, it will be impossible to convince the vulgar that it was not owing to inoculation, which would increase their prejudices at the beginning of this practice, and render my project of introducing the practice into my dominions, very difficult.'[31]

The power of example, applied to inoculation, worked both ways: a successful result for the Empress could boost public confidence in the procedure, but even the appearance of a failure, no matter how unrepresentative, could shatter that confidence overnight. Catherine saw the risks, but urged optimism. 'Be in good spirits,' she told Thomas, 'We can but do what is right; events must be left to providence. I am well satisfied with your conduct, and you may depend on my protection and support, and whatever may be the event with this boy, it shall not alter my resolution.'[32] Providing her doctor decided she was suitably healthy, their plan should continue. 'You shall perform the operation on me, and my example will tend to re-establish the reputation of the practice.' Where others were apprehensive or fearful at the prospect of inoculation, the Empress was positively excited: 'I even long for the happy day.'[33]

Catherine advised Thomas to hold off his move to the inoculation hospital until evening to await the latest health report from Nathaniel. To his great relief, it brought better news: Basoff's fever had dropped and both boys appeared completely out of danger. Basoff had just two or three pustules while Swieten had none and seemed likely to have had smallpox before. For a few more warm, late September days, Thomas could remain at court, visiting the Empress once or even twice daily to make final checks on her health and joining in the celebrations for the Grand Duke's fourteenth birthday. The veil of secrecy was still in place: all public focus was on Paul as a decoy for Catherine's personal inoculation plans, and the official court calendar made no mention of the arrangements.

Finally, with an October date set for the procedure, Thomas crossed the Neva to join Nathaniel and the doctors Schulenius and Strenge at Wolff House. With the first two cadets completely recovered, four more were chosen for inoculation, together with a fifteen-year-old servant girl, Eleonora, who was unsure whether or not she had had smallpox. It was only now, away from the glitter of the city, that Thomas encountered the impact of the deadly disease on the Russian people. Visiting a village in search of current smallpox cases to provide matter for inoculation, he was amazed at the death toll: out of thirty-seven people infected, only two had survived. It was impossible to estimate the wider mortality rate with any certainty, but local reports and his own observations indicated the disease was 'exceedingly fatal here', killing a far higher proportion of sufferers than in Britain. He wrote: 'Though I cannot confirm this assertion by proofs, yet from some conversation with the learned I am credibly informed, that of those who have the smallpox in the natural way half die, including the rich and poor.'[34] Extrapolating the figures, he concluded that Russia lost 'two millions of souls' annually out of a population of around 28 million. He would later accept the estimate was probably too high but it was indicative of the brutal effects he had witnessed first-hand.[35]

Diseases affecting those in old age were 'not hurtful to the state', he pointed out, but smallpox spread destruction among the young and active. The tragic loss of life was also an economic disaster. Russia's population – the bedrock of its wealth – was diminished and 'the disappointment and loss incurred is of course neither to be calculated nor conceived'.[36] Only inoculation could save lives for the state.

The search for infected matter for the second batch of trial inoculations took Thomas and Nathaniel and four of their five new patients to the outskirts of St Petersburg, where a German surgeon was appointed by the court to treat poor families afflicted with smallpox. On the evening of Friday 26 September, the doctors were shown into a cramped, dark house, instantly noticing that everyone inside looked at them 'with a kind of horror'. A child with a moderate case of the disease lay on a bed, gasping for breath in the intense heat of the candlelit room. As Thomas approached to take pus from the boy, his mother prostrated herself at his feet, pressing her forehead to the ground, throwing her arms over her head and plaintively begging for mercy. According to Russian belief, the surgeon explained, inoculation might save the person treated, 'yet it produces certain death to the person from whom the matter is taken'.[37] The weeping mother was desperate to save her child.

Shocked at the thought of being considered a murderer, Thomas tried to reassure the woman, explaining via his interpreter that he would never take an innocent child's life. He promised his actions would not be in the least dangerous, but if she did not believe him, he would 'instantly retire and relieve her from all apprehensions'. After a long conversation with her husband, the mother appeared to be persuaded, and Thomas inoculated the waiting cadets and maidservant and took pus to treat the remaining cadet at Wolff House. He could see that the woman seemed still to be in deep distress. Increasingly concerned for the child, the physician begged the family to open the window to give him fresh air, eventually persuading them only by bribing them with a rouble coin.

Thomas quickly gave up any thoughts that his reasoned arguments had prevailed. He questioned the surgeon later and learned that the desperate mother had agreed to allow inoculation from her son's body only because her husband had insisted they must obey the Empress's orders. The man had told her, 'If her Majesty had commanded the hand or feet of our child to be cut off, which would be worse than death, we must have submitted.'[38] The story caused the doctor real alarm. Fear of inoculation in Russia ran very deep, and prejudice would strengthen even further if the donor child did not recover. All hope of enacting the Empress's plan to introduce empire-wide inoculation would be destroyed. He quickly sent back Nathaniel, who found that the boy had fallen into a sound sleep and seemed better, but that the apartment window had been shut up again as tightly as before. To Thomas's great frustration, the family again defied the surgeon's advice and took the boy to the banya, the Russian bathhouse, worsening his health. Thomas prescribed fresh air and Peruvian bark, a widely used medicine containing quinine, and – in another stroke of luck for Catherine's mission – the child finally recovered.

Now the physician turned his attention back to his five newly inoculated patients, only to find that, yet again, things were not progressing as he expected. At the place where his lancet had pierced the skin, normally surrounded after a few days by many small pustules as the body's immune system fought the unfamiliar virus, each had only one large pus-filled blister. A week after the inoculation, when the pocks and fever would usually appear, none showed any symptoms or illness. Thomas was baffled, mortified at his inability to understand the results of his own trials, and increasingly afraid for himself and his royal patients. 'You must suppose this series of ill success must distress me,' he wrote to Henry. 'In short I knew not what to do and then wanted the advice of a friend but had none except Nat, who as far as I could expect has been of great use.' Helpful as Nathaniel was thanks to his father's training and his medical studies, Thomas longed for more experienced support than a twenty-year-old university student. 'I saw and felt the disappointment in its full force, and my utmost endeavours were excited to investigate the cause.'[39]

As Thomas struggled to make sense of the experiments, Cathcart's updates to London reflected the mounting strain. On 7 October he wrote: 'Dr Dymsdale is at his hospital. It has been next to impossible to find sufficient matter for infection. Those who have been inoculated have so few eruptions of smallpox that it has not been thought proper to inoculate from them, at least a person of consequence, which causes great delay.' The planned operation was far from being simply a medical matter: with the life of a head of state in the hands of a foreign doctor, it took on acute diplomatic significance. Relations with Russia were close in trade terms, but there was no formal alliance with Catherine's rising empire. Panin hoped for British involvement in a new 'Northern System' – a union of northern European powers designed to protect Russia's Baltic interests and suppress France and Austria. Britain, though always keen to outmanoeuvre the French, resisted, wary of being drawn into Russian conflicts in Poland and the Ottoman Empire. Now, to growing concern from London, the Empress was poised to risk her life just as war with Turkey seemed inevitable.

Cathcart, still starstruck by Catherine, suggested he pass on to the Empress the concerns of King George III for her son and for herself, though her inoculation was still 'not spoken of here' and therefore not officially known in London. The English doctor had only strengthened ties between the two countries and would even be a good source of inside information about the Russian Court, he wrote to Weymouth. 'No man ever gave or received more satisfaction than Dr Dymsdale in his intercourse with the Empress and Grand Duke and Mr Panin, and as he has lived much with them, when he returns, will be very well worth your lordship's talking with.' Thomas's unique access to his patient had entangled him in politics as Britain tried to get the measure of Catherine six years after the coup that had brought her the crown. Cathcart, sent to Russia with instructions to explore the possibilities of signing a new treaty of alliance, was confident that her grip on power was complete. 'The Empress exteriorly has more dignity than can be expressed, a dignity superior to all form: is cheerful, calm and of an attention and benevolence that extends to all . . . I may venture to assure your lordship that everything here promises the greatest stability.'

The ambassador, a veteran of the War of the Austrian Succession and of Culloden, was not easily troubled. Thomas had formally assured him both patients were entirely suitable for the imminent operation. Even so, he admitted as he concluded his despatch, the waiting was unsettling. 'I wish the inoculation well over.'

He was not alone. A missive from London made plain the concern of George III himself. Weymouth wrote: 'The King has, from motives of humanity, ever been a friend to the practice of inoculation, and it gives His Majesty great pleasure to find, that it is to be introduced into the Empress of Russia's dominions.' Royal commitment was genuine: the two eldest sons of George and Queen Charlotte, Princes George and Frederick, had already been inoculated, and their younger siblings William and Charlotte were due to undergo the operation in December. But the secret inoculation of a reigning monarch was another matter. 'Though under the direction of so able and experienced a physician as Dr Dymsdale there can be scarce any hazard, yet the King cannot avoid feeling great anxiety from the reports of Her Imperial Majesty's intentions to submit to the operation,' Weymouth told Cathcart. 'Your Lordship will therefore be particularly attentive to the progress of the disorder, whenever the operation has been performed: and I am to desire Your

Excellency will send me regular accounts of it for His Majesty's information.' Beneath the veneer of diplomatic language, there was real alarm at Court.

Back at Wolff House, Thomas tried to master his growing trepidation. The hospital and its grounds were now protected, at his request, by a detachment of guards to ensure secrecy and prevent the spread of infection to the nearby city. As the soldiers paced beyond the gates, the physician reviewed all the daily updates he had sent to Cherkasov to pass on to the Empress. He summoned all his reason and judgement, and wrote up a full report for Catherine on the trial so far. Everything had been carried out according to his own directions, he acknowledged, the autumn weather had been favourable, and there were no indications why anything should have gone wrong. Since he was convinced 'by numberless facts and long experience' that inoculation always produced smallpox in those who had never had it before, his only conclusion could be that all his patients had unknowingly had the disease already and that the experiment was therefore useless. To confirm this, he proposed inoculating all five again using the old method, still practised by Dr Schulenius, in which lint moistened with pus was placed in a long incision and bandaged. The suggestion showed his rising panic: he had rejected the old technique in his own treatise the year before. All the patients would also be deliberately exposed to those sick with the worst natural smallpox, he told the Empress. If they all stayed well, it proved his theory that they were all immune already.

Catherine approved the proposal, and the four cadets and Eleonora were inoculated a second time. Again, they showed no early symptoms of infection. But now, far from the closed world of the isolation hospital, dramatic new developments demanded the Empress's attention: Turkey had declared war on Russia. To manage the crisis, she would need to get rid of distractions. She had already made up her mind to be inoculated; now she sent orders to Thomas that the operation must go ahead without any further delay. 'I could scarce believe my eyes,' he wrote, 'for it seemed absolutely improbable to the last degree that her resolution would continue.'[40] He could only obey her commands.

*   *   *

The Empress's inoculation was planned for 12 October. Eight days beforehand, she began a preparatory diet according to Thomas's detailed instructions. She was permitted chicken or veal for lunch, boiled rather than roasted, and with salt added for flavour but no spices. For dinner, he recommended blood sausage, soup, vegetables and fruit pastries but no butter or eggs and no turnips, which could also overheat the body.[41] Meanwhile, the physician selected and inoculated three children 'of good constitutions' to ensure a supply of infected matter at the right time for the operation. All were taken to Wolff House by the doctor, accompanied by police officers, despite their parents' fears that donating pus for inoculation would kill them. One of the three was six-year-old Alexander Danilovich Markov, the eldest child of a warrant officer and already studying in the cadet corps. The boy had a character to match his place in history: Catherine described him as lively, cheeky, full of questions and 'small as a bug'.[42]

Thomas could do nothing more to prepare. He wrote to Henry, thanking him for some help given to his son Joseph and promising to pay him back, adding a line that must have alarmed his friend: 'I hope to be with you and thank you in person . . . but should anything happen this will serve as an acknowledgement of the debt.'

The Empress also recognised the risk for her doctor should the inoculation go wrong. Her death, especially at the hands of a foreigner, would instantly spark conspiracy theories and undoubtedly provoke revenge attacks targeted at the two doctors and, perhaps, their home nation. Even before the dangerous power struggle that would overtake Russia in the event of a second untimely royal death in less than a decade, Thomas and Nathaniel would never leave Tsarskoe Selo alive once the news leaked out. Despite her conviction that all would go well, Catherine made plans. On her orders, a yacht was stationed in the Gulf of Finland, ready to convey the Dimsdales to safety in England.[43] If she did not survive the procedure, a coach and horses stationed outside the palace would rush the doctors to board the vessel before the news became known.

Cathcart too had contemplated the disastrous consequences if the Empress or Grand Duke did not survive the inoculations. He updated ministers in London, passing on Thomas's considered opinion that the operations would be successful and adding, 'which is very fortunate as the loss of either would plunge this empire into confusions of which it would be very difficult to see the end'.[44]

On Saturday 11 October, according to the preparatory timetable, Catherine took five grains of the mercurial powder prescribed by Thomas. The calomel, crabs' claws and antimony purged her system; she was ready for the operation.

At nine o'clock the following evening, as arranged, an express coach arrived at Wolff House. The other doctors and patients at the hospital were unaware of the plan; the Dimsdales played along, giving no sign they knew the reason for their summons. Alexander, the child chosen to provide infected matter for the Empress, was already asleep. He was wrapped in a fur and carried by Nathaniel as the doctors hurried to the coach and set off into the night. Crossing the Neva, they were driven straight to a back gate of the Winter Palace which Thomas had been shown when he left for Wolff House. 'We were conducted up a flight of back stairs, and were met by Baron Cherkasov, who accompanied us to the Empress,' the doctor wrote.[45] Catherine waited in a small room, alone. Thomas took out his silver surgical instrument case and withdrew one of the three knives slotted inside, spinning the blade free of its mother-of-pearl casing. There was no need to wake the little boy: the doctor gently dipped the lancet point into one of the blisters emerging on his body. Then he pierced the skin surface on each of Catherine's upper arms, creating barely visible wounds he now touched with each side of the moistened lancet. The operation, planned over so many weeks, was over in seconds. The Empress of Russia had been inoculated with smallpox.

Thomas and Nathaniel scooped up Alexander and hurried out of the palace. Nathaniel took the boy back to Wolff House, explaining to anxious colleagues his father had inoculated the child of a nobleman. Thomas stayed at the Millionnaya apartment, spending a restless night replaying the evening's events. Catherine's operation was finally over, but, with the deadly virus now in her body, the most dangerous time was only just beginning.

Catherine II before a Mirror, Vigilius Eriksen, 1762.

6

The Inoculations

'A feverish heat & a general uneasiness & the pulse considerably quickened'

Thomas Dimsdale[1]

On the morning of 13 October, an ornate carriage drawn by eight horses and attended by three postillions passed out of the gates of the Winter Palace, with blinds pulled down over its windows. Inside, concealed from view, were Thomas Dimsdale and his interpreter Baron Cherkasov, travelling out of St Petersburg to the royal estate at Tsarskoe Selo fifteen miles south of the city.

The Empress had set out on the same journey several hours before, having passed a restless night punctuated by pains shifting through her body, as if she was succumbing to a cold. As the inoculation took effect, her pulse was racing. She had instructed her doctor to follow her to her country palace, leaving Nathaniel at Wolff House. Her son Paul also stayed behind, beginning the dietary preparations for his own inoculation for which she hoped to use infected matter from her own body. The plan was strategic, not maternal: she aimed to counter the superstition that the process caused the death of the donor. Courtiers were told she was making a brief visit to supervise building work – a plausible excuse given her mania for reconstruction and improvement. Count Orlov, her strongman favourite, was away hunting; no one thought she would undergo inoculation without him at her side. For now, the real nature of her trip remained entirely secret.

Tsarskoe Selo, one of the estates where Catherine and Paul had fled the St Petersburg smallpox epidemic earlier in the year, stunned the English visitor as his carriage drove through the gates. The baroque palace, built in the reign of Elizabeth and almost immediately reconstructed by the Italian architect Francesco Bartolomeo Rastrelli, was an ornate fairy-tale confection in pale azure and snow white. Its 325-metre facade, topped with glittering onion domes, gleamed with gilded stucco and sculpture. Thomas, overwhelmed by the scale of the 'extremely magnificent' building, was accommodated in one of forty state apartments. The rest remained empty apart from servants thanks to Catherine's subterfuge.

Less than twenty-four hours after the procedure, the Empress was feeling the effects of the minute drop of infected matter inserted in each arm. 'She seemed to be in low spirits,' Thomas noted.[2]

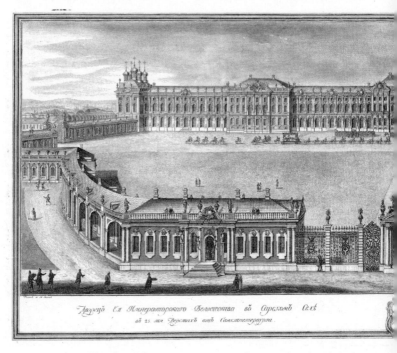

Tsarskoe Selo. Line engraving and watercolour by Prokofy

Following her doctor's instructions, she ate plainly, dining in the afternoon on weak soup, boiled chicken and vegetables. After dinner, she slept for nearly an hour and woke feeling greatly refreshed. 'In the evening she was very easy and chearful [sic],' recorded Thomas.[3] His detailed patient observations helped keep in check his bouts of extreme anxiety.

The following morning, after a 'tolerable' night, Catherine had begun to develop signs of infection, reporting pain on the inside of her arms opposite the lancet punctures. Even so, she was feeling more cheerful and reported to her doctor, as she would every day, on the state of her bowels. 'Upon enquiry I was told her Majesty had two stools on the 13th, being what she was accustomed to in health,' wrote Thomas in his personal medical notes with their irregular looping hand, ink spots and crossings out. For Panin, waiting anxiously for news back at the Winter Palace, he prepared a briefer

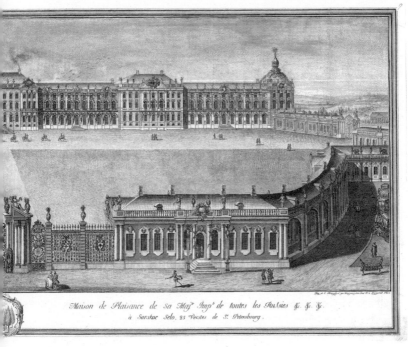

Maison de Plaisance de sa Maj.ᵉ Imp.ᵉ de toutes les Russies &. &. &.
à Sarskoe Selo. 25 Verstes de S.ᵗ Petersbourg.

Artemyev, Yekim Vnukov and Nikita Chelnakov, 1756–1761.

and less intimate daily update. 'Her Majesty has rested very well and is in good health and spirits.'

Wrapping herself in a cloak against temperatures below seven degrees Celsius, the Empress walked for two or three hours outdoors, benefiting from the fresh air seen as central to the new method of inoculation.[4] The long strolls, prescribed each day between the operation and the appearance of the first smallpox pustules, took her through the formal Dutch-style garden immediately in front of the palace and out into the park beyond, with its hermitage, grotto and lake fed by a nearby spring. From an artificial hill beside the lake, the world's first roller coaster – commissioned by Elizabeth as a year-round version of Russian winter ice slides and constructed by Rastrelli – undulated on a steep 300-metre track across the water on to an island, its carriages drawn back to the top of the slope by a horse-powered gin. When guests joined her at the palace, Catherine loved nothing better than to descend the 'flying mountains' at breakneck speed, terrifying her companions with her fearless thrill-seeking. Once, a wheel of her cart jumped from its grooved track, forcing Orlov – riding on the back – to use all his considerable strength to haul it back to safety.

Alone in the autumnal garden, the last leaves falling around her, the restless Empress diverted herself from the risks of her inoculation by planning a transformation of the park in the informal English style. 'I have a profound disdain for straight lines and parallel paths; I hate fountains that torture water to make it run against its nature . . . In a word, Anglomania holds sway in my plantomania,' she explained to Voltaire.[5] Inspired by engravings of the grand English parks at Stowe, Prior Park and Wilton with their lakes, rolling contours and carefully nurtured 'natural' vistas, she had already ordered her gardeners to stop clipping back the regimented hedges and bushes at Tsarskoe Selo. Now her walks gave her time to contemplate a fundamental reshaping of her garden, just as she planned ambitious improvements across her empire. 'I could never live in a place where I could not plant or build,' she wrote, 'otherwise even the most beautiful place in the world bores me. I am here for that very purpose: I often drive my gardeners mad.'[6]

On the evening of the second day after her inoculation, Catherine complained her apartments were too hot, though they were no warmer than their usual cool seventeen degrees Celsius. Dizziness, too, disturbed her. 'Her Majesty complained that her head turned around and felt giddy in a manner according to her idea like drunkenness,' noted Thomas, prescribing a wine glass of cold water and a walk in a cold room. The double chill brought relief, and the doctor placed his fingers on the Empress's upturned wrist. 'Her pulse good but rather low and not quite so good as usual, the degree of warmth on the skin very temperate.'

After a plain supper of gruel, soup and semolina porridge, his patient found diversion in the works of Voltaire. The writer had recently sent her a package of his books, and she had the stories read to her daily during her recuperation by 25-year-old Count Andrei Shuvalov, the son of a statesman in Elizabeth's court and a connoisseur of Western culture. A lifelong lover of reading aloud thanks to her beloved governess, Babet Cardel, the Empress could mull over the philosophe's satirical novella *Candide*, with its caustic critique of optimistic thinking and assault on corruption and brutality. Lampooning the complacent philosophy of Candide's tutor Pangloss that 'all is for the best in this best of all possible worlds', the work reaches the pragmatic conclusion that, to achieve happiness, 'we must cultivate our garden.' The message was not lost on the practical Empress, who sent Voltaire cedar nuts from her beloved Tsarskoe Selo to plant in his own garden, while teasingly comparing herself with the novel's Baroness of Thunder-ten-Tronckh, who 'thought her castle to be the most beautiful of all possible castles'.[7]

Over the following days, Catherine maintained her plain diet, managing a 'heaviness' in her head and body with cool drinks and walks in her palace's unheated Great Hall. As 'someone who loves to move about and who mortally hates being in bed', she was well suited to Thomas's regimen of fresh air and exercise.[8] The physician checked his patient daily, quizzing her on her symptoms and checking for the regular bowel movements he interpreted as healthy signs of her body fighting the virus. 'The appearance on [sic] the inoculated punctures is such as it ought to be at this time and I am certain that her Majesty will have the small pox,' he noted with relief.[9] After the disaster of the cadet trials, it seemed things were finally going to plan. He wrote to Panin, proposing Paul's inoculation for the following week, when his mother's pustules would be ready to provide infected matter for the procedure. When his patchy French failed, the obliging Cherkasov helped out. The round-faced Baron, ever-present aside from a short time laid up with gout, was a 'worthy and good man', Thomas wrote to Henry Nicols, but he heartily wished for his multilingual friend's company and moral support.

Catherine, deeply sceptical of the abilities of her court doctors and modern medicine after her past traumatic experiences of treatment, preferred where possible to rely on the power of nature as a restorative. In middle age, as she watched some of her closest companions die, she lashed out at 'bovine' medics, complaining that 'there was scarcely a doctor who knew how to cure even the bite of a bed-bug.' Only her dog seemed to be well, she pointed out: 'he who has no use for any doctor'.[10] Mocking physicians' reliance on ancient theories and dubious concoctions, she aimed to manage her own health through diet, rest, moderate exercise and a combination of fresh air and steam baths. She turned to the traditional techniques of bloodletting and purges only when her symptoms persisted and interfered with her work.

In Thomas, an advocate of close patient observation but light-touch intervention, Catherine found a doctor she could respect and trust. When, on the evening of the fourth day after the inoculation, he prescribed four grains of his trademark laxative blend of calomel, crab claw and tartar emetic, she asked to use the small supply of the medicine he had brought from home rather than the version made by her chemist. 'Let me take your own powder – I prefer it to any other,' the Empress begged, finding a direct way to her physician's heart. 'Does it not tell a little romantick?' he wrote self-mockingly to Henry.

Daily health consultations with Thomas gave Catherine the chance to develop her plan to introduce inoculation generally across the Russian empire. She pressed the doctor for information, quizzing him on the relative risks of natural smallpox and inoculation, his recommendations for the best age and preparation for the operation, and his ideas for managing mass inoculations without spreading infection. She was pleased with his responses and ordered him to write up his arguments, as well as recording in detail the progress of her own inoculation and her son's. One statistic in particular stayed with her. Thomas estimated he had inoculated some six thousand patients with just one death – a three-year-old child who, he believed, had died for other reasons than the procedure.

The Empress's curiosity did not stop at Thomas's medical expertise. His Quaker identity, albeit more cultural than practised, fascinated her, allowing her to probe details of the dissenting faith she had encountered in the writings of Voltaire or the pages of the *Encyclopédie*. Catherine was full of questions. She asked her physician whether he ever did any preaching, since Quakerism, with its rejection of the priesthood, permitted any virtuous person, of either sex, to do so. Thomas, always uncomfortable with public speaking, confessed he had not 'received that influence or inspiration of the Divine Spirit'. The pragmatic Empress was more interested in any case to learn that the Friends routinely expelled any members who evaded customs duties or dealt in smuggled goods. Honesty was a religious trait she could do business with, she told him. 'As to the inspiration of the spirit, I do not understand it, but from the principle of not dealing in goods suspected to have been run, I wish my sea coasts were lined with Quakers.'[11]

The quiet days after the inoculation were short-lived. When Catherine did not return swiftly to St Petersburg from her supposed building work inspection, nobles of the court left the city and headed to Tsarskoe Selo to join her. To Thomas's surprise, despite his frequent meetings with the Empress and his arrival from the infection hotspot of Wolff House, none of the new arrivals questioned him or seemed at all inquisitive over his presence. Even more remarkably, his patient, despite suffering increasing inoculation side effects, entertained her guests as if nothing had happened. Every afternoon, she left her private apartments and joined the visiting nobles until eight in the evening. Thomas marvelled: 'The Empress, during this interval, took part in every amusement with her usual affability, without shewing the least token of uneasiness or concern; constantly dined at the same table with the nobility, and enlivened the whole court with those peculiar graces of conversation, for which she is not less distinguished, than for her rank and high station.'[12] When not fulfilling her social obligations, she was contemplating her next move in the imminent war with Turkey, writing daily to Panin to update him on her health and her thoughts on the crisis. Thomas pressed her to avoid tiring herself; she took no notice. If anything, she felt happier and healthier than usual. His private notes recorded: 'She informed me that in the night her arms and hands felt hot so that it was more pleasing to put them out of bed but upon the whole she was exceedingly brisk and well insomuch that her Majesty asked me whether the gaiety of heart she felt was not too much.'[13]

Catherine had been happy to socialise in the first days after the inoculation without revealing she had undergone the operation, but she asked her doctor to alert her as soon as the dangerous infectious period of her recovery approached. 'Though I could wish to keep my inoculation a secret,' she told him, 'yet far be it from me to conceal it a moment when it may become hazardous to others.'[14] For most patients, the eruptive fever that signalled infectiousness appeared on day seven or eight after the inoculation, but Thomas was taking no chances. On Friday 17 October, the fifth day after her operation, he urged the Empress to isolate herself from anyone who had not had smallpox, and news of the inoculation was finally revealed at Tsarskoe Selo. The announcement reached Cathcart at the embassy in St Petersburg, who swiftly relayed it to Weymouth in London in the cypher used to encrypt the most sensitive diplomatic despatches: 'I think I may venture to assure your lordship that the Empress was inoculated in the night between Sunday and Monday last. The secret is not known.'

Catherine was now in the critical stage of inoculation, when symptoms worsened but the pustules that indicated the operation had 'taken' properly had yet to appear. Thomas's medical notes tracked her experience minutely. On Friday evening, she complained of a pain in her head and numbness in her hands and shoulders. She ate little, drinking only 'two dishes of green tea without milk or cream', and wanted to sleep. Thomas examined the inoculation site with a magnifying glass and found some reassurance: small pimples were emerging around the puncture wounds – a sign of a healthy reaction.

The following day, the virus had strengthened its assault on the Empress's body. She sent Count Vladimir Orlov, younger brother of her lover Grigory, to fetch Thomas to her side, complaining of bouts of shivering and fever, and 'uneasiness all over her body' that had forced her to rest on her bed. She had not been able to sleep and had got up, but had not eaten and 'was likewise affected with heaviness and giddiness of her head, pain and numbness under her arms and pain in her back'. Her resting pulse, usually no higher than forty beats per half a minute, was now raised to forty-six: not dangerous, but unpleasant. Drawing on all his long experience to quell his anxiety, Thomas advised against lying down, and again recommended cool water and a walk in the unheated Great Hall. 'Her Majesty observed this advice and found herself relieved by it insomuch that she appeared in the public room in the evening and played at cards a little,' he wrote.[15] Public appearances provided vital reassurance for visiting nobles during her convalescence, Catherine knew. Only visibility could counter vulnerability.

Her caution was justified. That evening, she received a message from Panin warning her that the secret of her inoculation was out in St Petersburg and the city's inhabitants were 'unquiet' with anxiety for their Empress. There was now a risk that, if the Grand Duke Paul was also brought to Tsarskoe Selo to be inoculated before his mother was sufficiently recovered to show herself in public, the 'uneasiness' at the apparent power vacuum could increase. Cherkasov and Vladimir Orlov called Thomas to a private meeting to discuss a new plan: inoculating Paul from one of the young cadets so that he could stay in the Winter Palace and calm public nerves. The doctor, fully responsible for the life of the Empress of Russia, could do no more than await events as the inoculation took its course. Panin's warning on his arrival of the significance of his task weighed heavily on him, and the carriage stationed outside ready to rush him from the Russian dominions seemed a laughably inadequate guarantee of his safety.

On Sunday, a week after the inoculation, Catherine rose at her usual early hour and walked in the cold once more to ease her heaviness and fever. The incision sites on her arms were now fully inflamed, and she went to bed early, consuming nothing but tea,

watery gruel and water in which apples had been boiled. The following morning, Thomas prescribed half an ounce of Glauber's salts, a
laxative, and the throbbing in her head eased, though her back and
feet remained painful all day. Around now, too, her period started,
adding a further physical challenge in addition to the symptoms of
smallpox. The event was duly noted by her doctor since she would
not be purged again until the bleeding finished.[16]

By the evening, to Thomas's enormous relief, pustules appeared
round the incisions, together with two on her wrist and one on her
face. Her pulse had slowed, and the fever was almost gone. Catherine
still had no appetite, but her physician began to grow in confidence
that the worst was over.

Despite a troubled night, the Empress woke the next morning
free of pain for the first time in the nine days since the inoculation.
'The fever was entirely gone,' Thomas noted. 'She ate boiled chicken
with a good appetite, and upon the whole passed the day very well.'[17]
While Catherine's safe recovery was not yet guaranteed, she had
passed the most dangerous point in the passage of the inoculated
disease. After weeks of failed experiments and fears he would not
be able to obtain effective inoculum for a patient of such power and
prominence, her physician could finally feel a little of the momentous weight of responsibility lift from his shoulders. Alexander, the
cheeky 'little bug' who had provided the infected material for the
Empress, had proved a perfect donor.

Panin, the orchestrator of the inoculation and as wracked with
anxiety as Thomas, received the good news by letter from Catherine
and passed it straight to the British ambassador, warning him it
remained 'a very great secret' to be kept until the Grand Duke's
inoculation was also safely over. Cathcart shared his relief. He wrote
to London: 'It is with great pleasure that I have the honour to
acquaint Your Lordship that the Empress, who has only had the
slightest indisposition, and has never been confined to her apartments since the operation, had yesterday a very favourable eruption
of small pox, very few in number, and of a quality entirely to Dr
Dymsdale's satisfaction.' Catherine's inoculation messaging was
already at work, portraying her as a robust figurehead, barely
affected by the procedure and always fully in command. Her

recovery was not only a question of her personal health: it was a matter of state, with international significance. Cathcart played his role of go-between, writing:

> I assured [Panin] the news will give the King the greatest satis-faction, as His Majesty expected from Dr Dymsdale's going abroad that the resolution was taken and would, I knew, be under anxiety till all was happily over . . . Having been the author and conductor of the whole affair, [Panin] is peculiarly happy in the success of the event, upon which so much depended.

The following day, after a peaceful night for the Empress, Thomas felt confident enough to travel back to the Winter Palace in St Petersburg, where the Grand Duke was suffering from a mild case of chickenpox. Although the teenager was not seriously unwell, his operation would have to be postponed until he had fully recov-ered. That meant he could not now be inoculated from his mother, as her pustules would have cleared up by the new date. Thomas prescribed two doses of light medication for Paul, leaving him 'in high spirits and eager for the experiment' after his years avoiding smallpox. The English doctor collected Nathaniel from Wolff House and returned to Tsarskoe Selo.

Though she could not provide inoculum for her son, Catherine ensured others were inoculated from her own infected matter, deter-mined to prove the safety of donation. She also took the first small steps in her campaign to introduce inoculation across her empire, personally encouraging some poor villagers living near the grand palace to undergo the procedure. In a footnote to a treatise he wrote later on general inoculation in Britain, Thomas recorded the auto-crat Empress's telling reflection during the visit on the relationship between her inoculation mission and her wider attitude to power. 'I remember the Empress said to me, with that vivacity and liberality of sentiment for which she is remarkably distinguished, "If I was to order the poor of this neighbourhood to be inoculated, it would be complied with, and be beneficial to them; but I love to use persua-sive means, rather than authority." '[18] Persuasion, in this case, meant cash bribes, even though Catherine recognised the tactic was open to abuse and quickly led to an inoculation bidding war. 'I have advanced a rouble . . . to each that would consent, and several have accepted it and recovered; but I find they now talk of raising the price to two roubles, which I must consent to as a further encouragement, for I wish the practice may be advanced by the mildest methods.'[19] Coming soon after the publication of her *Nakaz*, and with her Legislative Commission still theoretically in operation, the experience neatly demonstrated both Catherine's self-consciously enlightened instincts and the challenges of living by them.

The Empress's recovery continued, interrupted only by an extreme sore throat as the smallpox blisters spread to her tonsils, treated by Thomas with a gargle of blackcurrant jelly. On 27 October, two weeks and a day after the inoculation, he finally allowed himself to break the news of his experiences in his third letter to Henry in London, his relief at the outcome bursting from the page. 'She has had the smallpox in the most desirable manner – a moderate number of pustules and complete maturation which now thank God is over and I find an inexpressible load of concern removed from my breast.' Repeatedly stressing the need for secrecy, the doctor poured out the whole story: the many meetings with Catherine, the sick cadets, the carriage ride to the Winter Palace under cover of darkness. He told his friend: 'Many things have happened to me here that have given both anxiety and pleasure in such extremes that I found it very difficult to support my character properly. However upon the whole all has gone well, my happiness is like to be permanent and I hope the painful part is over.'

Thomas's worries over the Empress's health were subsiding, but he could not stop himself returning to his concerns over money, pushed aside in the extremity of the inoculation. He had already been absent from England for over three months, with considerable loss of income from his medical practice, and the Grand Duke's delayed inoculation would now keep him in Russia for longer than expected. His uncertainty over his own reward was heightened with news from his friend Jan Ingen-Housz, the Dutch doctor he had mentored during parish-wide inoculations back home in Hertford. Recommended to the Austrian court in preference to the upstart Daniel Sutton by George III's doctors, Ingen-Housz had arrived in

Vienna in May. He had conducted inoculation trials on groups of poor children, overseen by the Empress Maria Theresa and her son, Emperor Joseph II. Finally, in September – just a few weeks previously – he had successfully inoculated Maria Theresa's two youngest sons, Ferdinand and Maximilian, and Joseph's daughter Theresa. The Austrian Empress had celebrated by holding a dinner in the Schönbrunn Palace for sixty-five of the first children inoculated there, waiting on them herself with the help of her own family.

Now inoculation was the height of fashion in Vienna, and Ingen-Housz told Thomas he had been appointed a royal physician on a vast retainer of £550 a year, with no obligations to work except in emergencies. He had also received a pension for his future wife if he married, lodgings in the court, a valuable diamond ring and a 'most magnificent snuffbox with a portrait of the Emperor'.[20] Soon, he would inoculate more of the Imperial family, including Maria Theresa's daughter Archduchess Marie-Antoinette, future Queen of France. After the highly publicised devastation that smallpox had wreaked on the court the previous year, the Habsburg inoculations were the talk of Europe.

The Empress of Austria had set the reward bar high. 'What is to be my compliment I know not nor think much about,' Thomas assured Henry, not entirely convincingly, 'though I am of the opinion it will be very genteel.' There was no question that the Empress of Russia had the resources to please and used them strategically. With her recovery well on the way and her infectious period over, court life at Tsarskoe Selo returned to its usual round of lively entertainments. 'This place is all joy, music, billiards, cards and other diversions all day long,' wrote Thomas. Freed from the worst of his anxiety, he was even developing a taste for exotic delicacies. 'We all dine at one great table luxuriously; among other things we have always fine water melons from Astrakhan which I am now fond of, though at first they were not very pleasing.' The constant socialising with visiting nobles was exhausting for Catherine during her convalescence, but her desire 'to give everyone satisfaction' pushed her to continue without complaint, he reported. Spending more time with the Empress had only deepened his admiration for her. 'Of all the men or women I ever saw, she has most the way of pleasing without appearing to have any art.'

As her symptoms died away, Catherine set out in her coach each day to take the air. Her recovery was now assured, and she began her campaign to publicise her inoculation on her own terms. She wrote first to the governor of Moscow, Count Petr Saltykov, praising Thomas's 'faultless skill in this art' – proof of her own headhunting talent. She took care to stress that she had not only remained up and about throughout but had experienced no more than minor discomfort from the procedure. 'I tell you this happy outcome so that you can counter any erroneous rumours,' she concluded, keen to establish her narrative before the secret reached the gossip mills of the old capital.[21]

Next to receive the good news direct from the Empress was her regular correspondent Étienne Falconet, the French sculptor she had recently commissioned to create a monumental equestrian statue of her predecessor Peter the Great. Falconet had teasingly reproved his patron for defying the Sorbonne, whose Faculty of Medicine had never quite recommended lifting the Paris Parlément's 1763 ban on inoculation. Catherine made clear she had passed safely through the procedure, and cheerfully claimed it was the Parisian university's resistance that had decided her in favour of it. 'I do not see anything infallible in the establishment of Robert Sorbon,' she wrote, archly advising Sorbonne members to have themselves inoculated without delay.[22] She took the opportunity to launch a swipe at the Conservative French medical establishment, simultaneously goading a rival nation and aligning inoculation firmly with progressive independence of thought: 'They often decide in favour of absurdities, which in my opinion should have discredited them long ago; after all, the human species are no longer goslings.'

A letter from Catherine's politically connected confidante Johanna Bielke in Hamburg brought news that gossip about the inoculation had already filtered across Europe. Who was the mysterious English doctor, with his strange religious faith and mystifying regular presence in the Empress's company? Catherine, who often used her friend as a drawing-room spin doctor, moved fast to extinguish the rumours. On 1 November, she replied, sharing the news of her operation and reassuring her friend that her physician 'is neither a charlatan nor a Quaker'. Her praise for Thomas was boundless: he was not only a skilled physician, but a man defined by his moral qualities. 'In less than three weeks here I am recovered, thanks be to God. He is a prudent, wise, selfless man and extremely righteous; his parents were Quakers and he too, but he left and retained only the moral excellence. I will be eternally grateful to this man.'[23]

Catherine had more information she hoped the influential Madame Bielke would spread across her networks. Her fundamental intention had always been to use the power of her own example to encourage others to follow in her footsteps: now the plan was moving into action. She had started with the military strongmen of the court: already Field Marshal Count Kirill Razumovsky had been inoculated by Thomas, followed by her lover Grigory Orlov, unsure like so many of his countrymen whether he had ever had smallpox. Orlov – in her words, 'a hero like the ancient Romans of the golden age of the Republic, who has both their courage and their magnanimity' – had been so unaffected by the procedure he had gone hunting in a fierce snowstorm the next day. Where risk and novelty were involved, the power of emulation was stronger than reasoned argument. 'All Petersburg wants to be inoculated and those that have been are well,' she boasted.

Sealing the last letter, the Empress left Tsarskoe Selo on the afternoon of Saturday 1 November, two weeks and five days after her arrival from the capital. 'She returned to St Petersburg in perfect health, to the great joy of the whole city,' Thomas recorded.[24] Entering the city, she stopped at the Kazan Cathedral, where she kissed the sacred icons and prayed. At five in the afternoon, she returned at last to the Winter Palace, where she was reunited with Paul, waiting in the billiard room to kiss her hand. That evening, Catherine appeared at court, publicly demonstrating her full recovery and receiving the congratulations of 'an infinite number' of the nobility and gentry. The following day a formal *Te Deum* was held in the chapel at the Winter Palace, led by Archbishop Gavriil, to give thanks for the Empress's safe recovery. Worshippers knelt as the Empress and her son kissed the holy cross to the sound of 101 cannon shots fired from the St Petersburg Fortress and the Admiralty.[25]

For her doctor, the return to the capital meant a debrief with Cathcart, who was keen to capitalise on the inoculation success story in the delicate diplomatic courtship between Britain and Russia. Throughout the autumn, each nation had assured the other of goodwill, treading carefully as Panin's scheme for a Northern System of alliances took on new significance in the context of a likely war with Turkey. The latest letter from London brought an official welcome from George III of Catherine's confirmation of her friendship towards him, her 'just ideas' on the common interests of the two states, and 'of her salutary views for the stability of the North'. Whether he liked it or not, Thomas's inoculation project was wholly interwoven with Britain's wider interests, and Cathcart had no compunction about using the doctor as an unofficial political source who could shed light on Catherine's true character. His next despatch to Weymouth in London read:

> Your Lordship remembers a great man's observation, that there were few heroes in the eyes of their valet de chambres. I assure your Lordship she is a heroine and a tender mother in the eyes of her physician, and from the reports I have received from a very discerning and a very sincere man who has had the greatest opportunity of observing at moments when few are on their guard, who might conceal but who would not flatter, I have in every respect the opinion of the Empress's temper and dispositions which by her exterior she wishes to express.[26]

Thomas, closer to Catherine than any other Englishman, had found himself at the nexus between two of the world's greatest powers, and had tried to balance his loyalties with honour.

Other ambassadors were just as eager to relay news of the inoculation. Count Solms, the powerful Prussian representative in St Petersburg, sent word to Catherine's ally Frederick the Great of the procedure's 'most happy success' after a briefing from Panin. His update read:

> The eruption took place without causing a very violent fever, Her Majesty was affected by it for two days, for which she was

obliged to take to her bed. She had a few pustules on her face, a hundred over her body of which the majority were on her arms; they are already beginning to peel and so, as far as one can humanly predict, she has no more danger to fear.[27]

Panin had ensured word was out that Catherine was back in full command, but requested no publicity for her inoculation abroad until after the Grand Duke's delayed operation.

As the court celebrated the Empress's recovery, Thomas went back to work. Paul had recovered from chickenpox and had taken three grains of the doctor's mercurial powder to purge his system. At ten o'clock in the morning on Sunday 2 November, the day of the *Te Deum*, Thomas inoculated the Grand Duke using fresh fluid matter from the younger son of Mr Briscorn, apothecary to the court. He made the puncture in the right arm only, concerned that treating the other risked causing a flare-up of a glandular condition suffered by the boy on the left side of his throat several years before.

Paul's doctors had made clear their reluctance to have any direct involvement in the procedure. Again Thomas was taking full responsibility alone. Although the boy was young, which usually meant milder inoculation symptoms, his chequered medical history brought its own concerns. Thomas's personal notes, irregular and patched with blots and deletions, once more charted every detail of his patient's progress and bodily functions. On the evening of the operation, Paul took three more grains of the powder and the next day 'had two good stools neither costive or purging and remained the whole day very brisk and well'. That evening, he swallowed three spoonfuls of a 'decoction of bark' – the Peruvian bark concentrate widely used to treat fevers, for which Thomas had managed to gain authorisation from the reluctant Dr Cruse.

By the third day, the teenager began to feel the uncomfortable but reassuringly typical effects of his inoculation. The incision wound was red and painful, showing the infection had taken, and he went to bed complaining of shivering and pain in his arm. The next morning, his pulse was 'considerably accelerated' to ninety-six beats per minute, but his fever diminished by noon and he was able to eat a dinner of weak soup, vegetables and chicken. The following day, five days after the operation, his pulse raced to 104 beats per minute, but his complaints of giddiness and drowsiness were soon eased with Thomas's favoured remedy: a walk in a cool room. On Sunday 9 November, exactly a week after the inoculation, a pustule appeared on his chin and three more on his back, signalling a successful eruption that would bring an end to his fever.

More pustules broke out and Paul began to take exercise, only to be struck down again with a sore throat so painful he could not swallow and spat out frothy saliva. Gargling with blackcurrant jelly dissolved in warm water temporarily soothed the pain, but within a few days a large pustule had swollen the roof of his mouth above his throat and his pulse rose dramatically to 118 beats per minute. Complaining of weakness, he rested on his bed for the only time during his convalescence.

By 14 November, the inflammation had died down. Thomas wrote: 'From this time he was quite free from pain; the pustules, which together did not exceed forty, maturated kindly, soon dried up, and the illness terminated very happily.'

A relieved Cathcart wrote immediately to the Earl of Rochford, the capable statesman who had taken over from Viscount Weymouth as the British government's northern secretary. He updated the secretary of state on the boy's health, comparing Thomas's results favourably with his famous inoculation rival, Daniel Sutton.

He was yesterday without fever and continues so today, so that I hope I may venture to assure Your Lordship, as Doctor Dymsdale's patients have suffered less and made lighter of the small pox even than those of Mr Sutton in England, that the danger is entirely over and this empire at the eve of a very general and very sincere occasion of publick joy.[28]

There was no higher praise. The Empress, meanwhile, was 'in perfect health' and felt her decision to be inoculated ahead of her son had been vindicated. She had personally told him that 'she suffered so little that she is quite easy about the Grand Duke, which she could not have been had she not previously satisfy'd herself by making the experiment on her own person'.[29]

Rochford passed the good news on to the King, who, he told Cathcart, had suffered great anxiety over the inoculations and felt for the young Grand Duke in particular 'most sensibly'. George III was delighted at the outcome, 'not only from His personal regard and esteem for so accomplished a princess and so promising a successor, but as it will secure the internal happiness and stability of the Russian Empire'.[30] Thomas's lancet had protected two individuals from smallpox, but it had also strengthened Russia itself.

As Paul's recovery progressed, the two daunting challenges of Thomas's mission to St Petersburg were almost completed, yet the physician barely had time to draw breath. Catherine's determination to lead the way on inoculation had already prompted a queue of would-be inoculees among the nobles of the court, and Thomas hurried, lancet in hand, from one grand home to the next as the new fashion took off. Cathcart, having seen the Empress 'perfectly recovered and with few marks', reported: 'The numbers daily inoculated, partly from compliment to the great example they have had and partly owing to the danger of infection, is beyond description, and the very favourable manner in which all have had it, is very encouraging. Dr Dymsdale has given during the whole course of his residence the greatest satisfaction.'[31]

On the day of Paul's inoculation alone, Thomas's list of patients, carefully recorded in his notebook with approximations of Russian spellings, featured not only members of the nobility but court servants. It read: 'His Imperial Highness, the Grand Duke; Prince Alexander Kurakin; the Count and Countess Czerimeteff; A.N. Others; a valet, Calmuck; a girl of Czerimeteff's, also called Calmuck; a dwarf; and Simon, a negro.'[32] Simon was the first recorded person of African heritage to be inoculated in Russia.

Squeezing in time for another letter to Henry, the weary doctor admitted he could barely keep up with demand. 'Every one here are mad to be inoculated and in spite of all remonstrances I can make it will be impossible for me to avoid being involved in more business than I can execute properly. At present my patients consist of the first nobility of which I have about 40 inoculated . . . I cannot tell the names of all my patients, but all the families of the Narishkins, Cherbatoffs, Galitzins, Woranzoffs, Butterlins,

Stroganoffs and many others are of the number and all go on well.'[33] Even Nathaniel, his sole assistant, was no longer able to share the burden. He had been sent at Panin's request to stay with Count Sheremetev, whose daughter, the minister's fiancée, had died of smallpox earlier in the year. The Count's surviving son and daughter, aged eighteen and seventeen, had been inoculated in the same wave as the Grand Duke, and Nathaniel was overseeing their recovery. 'The old Count is so fond of these children that he has unnecessarily kept my son much confined while I have been slaving all day,' Thomas grumbled.

His own exhaustion aside, the success of his efforts was beyond anything he had dared hope. Even before the news had officially broken, everyone he met was thrilled at the recovery of the Empress and her heir. 'It is impossible to express the universal joy that prevails here, which I can plainly perceive will within a few days break out in some extraordinary manner for the nation in general adore the Empress and the Grand Duke.' Thomas himself was being overwhelmed with praise which he insisted – as much to himself as to Henry – he would not allow to go to his head. 'I shall say nothing of the compliments and civilities that I receive but they are sufficient to make anyone distracted that did not know that they are owing to the intemperance of others. I thank God that I have sense enough to know that my consequence is like the fly on the chariot's wheel.'

After three months in Russia, most of it spent at court, the English doctor had long got over his fears of committing an embarrassing social blunder. He had spent so much time in palaces and got to know those living and working there so well that he found himself 'quite at ease and go about the apartments as if at home'. The courteous welcome at Court had greatly impressed Thomas, and he had also found ordinary Russians treated him kindly and with intelligence when he ventured out for walks in St Petersburg and often got hopelessly lost. The English typically believed that the Russian aristocracy 'preserve vestiges of barbarism in their midst'; his own experience, however limited, showed no such thing.[34] He wrote to Henry:

Whatever others may have said, if gentility consists in freedom, kindness and an obliging behaviour to inferiors I have reason to think this Court extremely polite but more particularly the Empress who is the very perfection of goodness mixed with greatness at the same time. The Grand Duke also with whom I have now lived a long time is so very good to me that you would wonder at it.

Even Panin, a more impenetrable character, had shown warmth. 'If he was my own brother he could not show me more kindness.'

Thomas had more than fulfilled his obligations, but one uncertainty remained: the question of his payment had still not been touched on. By now he was more confident of reimbursement for his efforts, but time was ticking towards his departure. His old obsession with building up his wealth had never quite gone away. He confessed to Henry: 'I should be glad to come home richer, and surely it is impossible but it should be so for everyone says there is great generosity in her Majesty's soul. I have reason to think my behaviour has been satisfactory.' Despite the charms of Russia, and the comfort of his stove-warmed apartment in icy weather, his thoughts were turning to his beloved Hertford. Tentatively, he hoped to leave in early January, when the snow would allow fast travel by sledge. 'The place is very agreeable but home and the happiness of seeing old friends is still more so.'

As Thomas wrote to Henry, Catherine was also back at her desk. Restored to full health, she returned to the matter of war with the Ottoman Empire. Her period of reflection at Tsarskoe Selo had convinced her that Russia should not bow to Turkish demands. 'She is resolved immediately to draw the sword, and to send a proper force to her frontiers, either to defend her own territories or to demand satisfaction in those of the enemy,' Cathcart informed ministers in London.[35] Now, the Empress combined her two preoccupations in a letter to her stern ally Frederick II of Prussia, who disapproved of both her inoculation and her planned conflict. Had she only known of his opposition to her operation, it would have influenced her decision, she claimed, adding playfully that 'this time my temerity had turned out well.' Now, she implied, the same bold spirit was guiding her into war. 'Until now I have tried to do good. At the moment I am being forced to do evil – for that is what all wars are, or so the philosophers tell us. The only one that can be tolerated, I believe, is the one I shall go ahead and wage. I have been attacked, and I am defending myself.'[36] Fresh from her victory over the smallpox virus, Catherine felt herself invincible.

When General George Browne, the Irish-born Governor of Livonia, congratulated her on her courage in undergoing the operation, she lapped up his praise. 'I suppose I must believe that this is the case, although I had hitherto thought that every street boy in England possessed sufficient courage for this purpose. The honest and capable Dr Dimsdale, your countryman, makes everybody here brave.'[37]

The intertwining of her twin obsessions was clear in her letter to Count Ivan Chernyshëv, the new Russian ambassador who had replaced Count Pushkin in London. 'Now we have only two subjects to discuss,' the Empress began, 'first, the war, and second, inoculation. Starting with me and my son, who is also recovering, there is not an aristocratic household where one cannot find several inoculated persons; many complain that they had smallpox naturally and so cannot follow the latest fashion.'[38] She named a string of nobles who had 'handed themselves over to Mr Dimsdale', including an array of beautiful princesses and many others who had previously refused to accept the operation. She had set a trend, and was determined to take full credit. 'See what setting an example can do! Three months ago nobody wanted to hear about it, and yet now they look on it as salvation!'

Just weeks after her inoculation, Catherine had not only protected herself and her heir but had launched news of her bold step across Europe. At home, she had won admiration and emulation, and introduced a new technology that would benefit her country. It was thrilling, but it was far from enough. Her plan to build on her achievement had barely begun.

Bronze medal reading 'She herself set an example', commissioned by
Catherine to commemorate her inoculation. Engraved by Timofei Ivanov.

7

The New Fashion

'See what setting an example can do'

Catherine the Great[1]

In the Grand Church of the Winter Palace, smoke from wax tapers and the resinous blur of incense rose and mingled in the gilded dome high above the iconostasis.[2] Below, dwarfed by the scale of the great hall with its Ionic columns and golden rococo ornamentation, worshippers gathered for a divine service to celebrate the safe recovery of the Empress of Russia and the Grand Duke from inoculated smallpox.

It was soon after noon on 22 November 1768, forty days since Catherine's secret inoculation and not quite three weeks since Paul's operation. Both were back to full health, and the Empress was wasting no time in her campaign to elevate the piercing of her arm from personal medical procedure to powerful political symbol. For her domestic audience, as religious as she herself was instinctively secular, the first step was to demonstrate her actions had the unequivocal blessing of the Orthodox Church.

The date chosen for the thanksgiving for the inoculations fell on the Afterfeast of the Entry of the Mother of God into the Temple, one of the twelve Great Feasts of the Orthodox year.[3] Nobles and foreign dignitaries crowded into the palace church, designed by Francesco Rastrelli with the same baroque splendour he had deployed at Tsarskoe Selo. Ambassador Cathcart was among the guests, accompanied by his wife and all his children, brought along at the Empress's personal invitation. Alongside them was Thomas

Dimsdale, a better scientist and doctor than commentator on royal occasions. 'The nobility and gentry expressed their satisfaction and joy in a manner to be expected from loyal subjects attached to their sovereign,' he noted succinctly at the conclusion of his report of Paul's inoculation.

Luckily another British observer, William Richardson – the erudite tutor to the Cathcart children, who had arrived in Russia just days before Thomas – recorded the 'solemn and magnificent' ceremony in all its multi-sensory detail.[4]

> On the inside of a rail which extended across the room, and close by the pillar which was next the altar, on the south side, stood the Empress and her son: and also on the inside of the rail, and on each side of the altar, was a choir of musicians. All the rest who witnessed, or took part in the solemnity, excepting the priest, stood on the outside of the rail.[5]

After choral singing and prayers, two folding doors by the altar were swung open from the inside, revealing to onlookers the most holy part of the church. Richardson wrote:

> Opposite to us was a large picture of the taking down from the cross: on each side, a row of gilt Ionic pillars; and in the middle, a table covered with cloth of gold; and upon the table were placed, a crucifix, a candlestick with burning tapers, and chalices with holy water. A number of venerable priests, with grey hair, flowing beards, mitres, and costly robes, stood in solemn array on each side of this magnificent sanctuary. The whole suggested an idea of the Temple of Jerusalem.

From the sanctuary came a priest bearing a lighted taper, followed by a second who recited prayers and carried a censer smoking with incense. 'Advancing towards her Majesty, he three times waved the censer before her; she all the while bowing, and very gracefully crossing her breast. He was succeeded by another priest, who carried the Gospel; out of which having read some part, he presented it to the Empress, who kissed it.' The service continued as priests

administered the bread and wine of the Eucharist, accompanied by
'deep-toned and sublime' choral music. When the doors of the
sanctuary opened a third time, Richardson and his fellow worshippers watched as Metropolitan Bishop Platon climbed to a pulpit
opposite the Empress and delivered an address celebrating her
'fortitude and magnanimity' and thanking God for bestowing
goodwill upon Russia. One remark in particular struck the Scottish
tutor: that 'the Russians had borrowed assistance from Britain, that
island of wisdom, courage and virtue.'

Finally, Catherine and Paul knelt as Archbishop Gavriil of
St Petersburg led bishops from across the empire in a prayer for
their health before mother and son kissed the cross to the sound of
cannon fire from the Admiralty fortress directly across the Neva.
The roar echoed round the city: fifty-one cannons for the Empress
followed by thirty-one for the Grand Duke.[6]

The candlelit ceremony brilliantly harnessed the theatricality of
traditional Orthodox worship to reframe cutting-edge science.
Amid the swaying censers and transcendent singing, the Empress's
inoculation was represented as a sacred act. Catherine's acute
understanding of the power of Russian religious display, honed at
her own extravagant coronation, had associated the most physical
of processes, with its purges, pustules and fevers, with holy mystery.
She had even thrown in a sprinkling of incense diplomacy for the
British attendees at the ceremony who, even if they were baffled by
icons, understood praise for their country.

The thanksgiving service was just the beginning. Afterwards,
guests moved to the public reception rooms of the palace, where
Catherine stood before representatives of the Senate, Russia's prin-
cipal governing body, members of the Holy Synod representing the
Church, and deputies of her Legislative Commission, drawn from
across the empire under her drive for legal reform. Archbishop
Gavriil congratulated the Empress and her heir on their inoculation
in the name of the Synod, and Count Kirill Razumovsky, himself
newly inoculated by Thomas following Catherine's example, offered
thanks on behalf of the Senate. Russia's 'loving mother' had
protected all generations of her subjects since taking the throne,
capped by her selflessness in putting herself and her son in danger

for the sake of her people and their descendants. 'Now all ages and both sexes embrace your feet and praise in you the image of our God the healer,' he proclaimed.[7]

The depiction of Catherine's inoculation as a religious act was now explicit. She had not simply protected her own body and her son's: her action had endowed her with a version of divine power to heal all her people. Her insistence on the use of her infected matter to inoculate others had been well publicised as she tried to combat the superstitious belief that doing so killed the donor. Thomas had noted: 'Both the Empress and the Grand Duke were pleased to permit several persons to be inoculated from them; and by this condescension, the prejudice which had reigned among the inferior ranks of people, that the party would suffer from whom the infection was taken, was most effectually destroyed.'[8] In practice, Catherine could not possibly hope to change attitudes overnight: she had to keep campaigning. Now she added another layer of symbolism to her gesture: she had given her body for her people just as Christ had symbolically offered his when, at the Last Supper, he broke bread, gave it to his disciples and commanded, 'do this in remembrance of me.' Inoculation, in Russia, had become a sacrament.

Catherine's response to the Senate pursued the biblical theme. 'My object was by my own example to save from death my numerous loyal subjects, who, not knowing the benefits of this method, and fearing it, remained in danger. By this I have fulfilled part of the duty of my title; for, according to the Gospel, a good shepherd lays down his life for his sheep.'[9] The message was clear: in taking the personal risk of inoculation, the courageous Empress had shown herself to be the saviour of her heir but also of the Russian people, protecting them as Christ had sacrificed himself for humanity. She had revealed the miracle of inoculation, and by trusting in her example her nation would be led from danger to safety. 'You may be sure that now I will intensify my effort and care for the wellbeing of all my loyal subjects generally and of each and every individual. I give you this as a sign of my benevolence,' she concluded. In promoting the medical procedure that would save her people, Catherine was simultaneously promoting herself.

Now inoculation had been imbued with mystical meaning, it was time to amplify the good news of her own operation and recovery. On her orders, churches in the capital performed liturgies and delivered celebratory sermons, followed by a night vigil for the health of the Empress and her son. Outside in the snowy streets of St Petersburg, there was a festival atmosphere.[10] All workers had been given the day off to participate in the celebrations, which were to be repeated in cities across the empire as soon as each received the news. Church bells rang constantly all over the capital and its houses and twin fortresses were brightly illuminated for three days, bringing light to the winter darkness. Inside the Winter Palace, nobles and foreign dignitaries drank vodka toasts to the Empress, accompanied by more cannon fire, and in the evening attended a celebratory ball. The festivities were recorded in the official court journal, which had ended its blackout of references to the royal inoculations following Catherine's recovery.[11]

The Empress decided to keep the party going. Empire-wide inoculation would be a long campaign, requiring regular prompts to maintain momentum – and remind Russians of her own pioneering contribution. What better way than by giving everyone a day off? A Senate decree proclaimed 21 November an annual national holiday to mark the recovery of the Empress and her son from their inoculation against smallpox. The celebration, to be marked in every city of the empire, was one of sixty-three court and church festivals observed each year in Russia, but the first to mark a medical event and only the fifth to honour Catherine herself. Inoculation was afforded the same recognition as her birthday, her name day, her accession to the throne and her coronation.[12] The new public holiday, the Senate decreed, would be both secular and spiritual, opening with a night-long vigil and divine liturgies for health. A mandatory day of 'freedom from public affairs' would be celebrated with fireworks (lasting a full three days in the capital and one day elsewhere) and accompanied by the sound of bell ringing from every Orthodox church across Russia. The Empress's inoculation was firmly embedded in the national calendar: it would be commemorated every year at Court until 1795.[13]

On 24 November, the St Catherine's Day holiday, the moment Thomas had been waiting for so anxiously finally arrived. The

Empress, dressed in Guards' uniform and a small crown with the star of the Order of St Catherine pinned to her breast, attended divine liturgy to celebrate her name day with prayers, speeches and cannon fire.[14] Afterwards, leaving the palace church to the sound of music and military drum rolls, she received the congratulations of her courtiers. Then, at last, she announced the rewards her physician would receive for completing the task Panin had called 'the most important employment that perhaps any gentleman was ever entrusted with'.[15] Her gifts were fittingly exceptional.[16] Thomas Dimsdale, she proclaimed, would be made a Baron of the Russian Empire, a hereditary title that would pass down the male line of his family in perpetuity. The baronetcy was the first Catherine had created in her six-year reign, and only the twelfth since Peter the Great had granted the title to his powerful Vice Chancellor Peter Shafirov in 1710.[17] Nathaniel, too, was made a baron, again with the right to pass on the title to his heirs. With the double baronetcy came the right to augment the Dimsdale coat of arms with a wing of the Russian Imperial eagle on a shield in the centre. It was a great honour, despite the awkward fact that the Quaker family had no such arms to which the wing might be attached, and had to create one for the purpose.[18]

The Empress had not forgotten the third visitor who had joined Thomas and Nathaniel on their secret mission to the Winter Palace for her inoculation. Alexander Markov, the mischievous six-year-old whose pustules had provided the matter for her own inoculation, was also ennobled, taking the new surname Ospenniy – 'smallpoxy' – from óspa, the Russian for smallpox. Little 'Lord Smallpox' had suffered only the mildest case of the virus after his own inoculation and had fully recovered, adding to the proof that donating pus was safe. He was awarded three thousand roubles and a coat of arms featuring a child's flexed bare arm with its sleeve rolled up to reveal a single pock, the hand holding a pink rose.

Thomas's financial rewards were as remarkable as his honours. Catherine presented him with a one-off gift of ten thousand pounds – the equivalent of around twenty million pounds in income today – together with two thousand pounds in expenses to cover his journeys to and from Russia and a pension of five hundred pounds a year for life.[19] The sums were vast, and word swiftly spread across

Дворянскій гербъ

Александра Оспеннаго

Coat of Arms created for Alexander Ospenniy.

Europe. Thomas's decision not to name his price for his work, whatever his degree of calculation, had brought him wealth beyond any fee he might have dared charge. The English doctor was also appointed Body Physician to the Empress and Counsellor of State, a title with the rank of Major General in Russia's highly formalised system of military, civil and court positions. Recompensed beyond his wildest imaginings, Thomas kissed the Empress's hands.[20] Far from his Hertford home in an unfamiliar land, free of anxiety at last, the 56-year-old physician was overwhelmed. The Grand Duke, kept in the dark over the reward to allow him to enjoy the surprise, almost wept at the gratitude shown to the doctor he had grown to love. Ambassador Cathcart, attending a celebratory ball and dinner for 120 guests, was touched by the father-less boy's emotion. 'The Grand Duke . . . did me the honour to tell me in the evening, almost with tears in his eyes, that it was impossible for him to express the satisfaction he'd felt, and gave me a very strong proof of that sensibility of heart which is natural to him and which has been cultivated with great care.'

The baronetcy announcement was not a complete surprise, Thomas confessed in his latest letter to Henry. Panin had privately requested his consent beforehand, informing him that Catherine 'had the highest sense of my service and was desirous that the name of Dimsdale might remain respectable as long as Russia existed and for that purpose had determined to create me a Baron of the Empire'. The doctor had consulted Cathcart, nervous of a diplomatic upset and concerned he should not adopt the elevated foreign title until his own monarch had approved it. The King would wish him to accept rather than await royal permission, the ambassador quickly assured him; it was not worth offending a major ally at a sensitive political moment over a small matter of timing. Thomas wrote: 'I could only say that though unworthy of the honour I should submit to her Majesty's pleasure.'

News of Catherine's gifts quickly made its way to London, as she had expected. Cathcart's report could not have been more favour-able if the Empress had written it herself. 'By these circumstances Your Lordship may judge of the magnificence and generosity of Her Imperial Majesty,' he wrote admiringly to Rochford. 'Such emolu-ments, great as they are, have a determined value, but the manner in which they have been conferred, the satisfaction of the Grand Duke, and the applause of the whole nation, are an addition which I am persuaded in the eyes of Mr Dymsdale is inestimable.'

Catherine had not finished yet. She had more gifts for Thomas that would not only show her heartfelt gratitude for his care but promote her desired image of a civilised, cultured Russia capable of producing beautiful luxury goods to match any in Europe. Since taking the throne, she had encouraged foreign artisans of all kinds to bring their skills to St Petersburg, developing the capital as a centre of jewellery-making, porcelain, gold- and silverwork, medals and coins. Often adorned with her own – carefully controlled – image, the exquisitely manufactured items acted as public relations merchandise for her country and her own leadership.

Her physician received at least four examples of one of Catherine's trademark promotional pieces: snuffboxes intricately set with diamonds and featuring a miniature portrait of herself in enamel. Valuable as they were, the jewelled boxes were routinely given to important visitors as advertisements for Russian craftsmanship and wealth. A more personalised gift was a travelling tea and coffee service specially designed by the Imperial Porcelain Factory, its gilded pots, lidded cups and spoons decorated with allegorical images and Thomas's monogram and set in a wooden case covered in Morocco leather and lined in pink satin.[21] A collection of sixty-two silver commemorative medals and a diamond ring added to the haul.

Nathaniel, thrown in at the inoculation deep end, received gifts of his own. Paul, only six years his junior and now as close to the young medical student as he was to his father, presented him with a snuffbox in four colours of gold encrusted with diamonds. Count Sheremetev, whose son and daughter Nathaniel had cared for after their inoculation, also gave him a snuffbox, together with an ostentatious cash reward. Thomas wrote to Henry: 'The old Count is exceedingly happy. He is very rich and generous. On Friday he gave me something so heavy that I went limping out of his house – on examining the contents I found £500 in gold coin.'

With the royal inoculations over and the rewards presented, Catherine's hospitality continued. Over the weeks and months in her company at St Petersburg and Tsarskoe Selo, Thomas had become far more than a hired medical specialist: he was now a trusted friend. Even with the tense days of her recovery long gone, she enjoyed his company and the Dimsdales remained favoured fixtures at court. One winter's day she invited him to join her shooting party, hunting black grouse against a white sky in the snow-covered countryside outside the city.[22] Thomas shot four birds to the Empress's nine, while two accompanying noblemen killed another four between them. Catherine was a passionate hunter who loved to pursue game birds and hares with guns or falcons, but it was not a good idea to outshoot her. Afterwards, she presented him with a set of arms, a gun belt and powder flask from her own collection, telling him she had shot with the pistols herself and proved them to be good ones. She had a silver cartridge box engraved in English: 'To Thomas Dimsdale, Baron and State Councellor Actuel'.

Thomas described the gifts in a letter to his cousin's son John Dimsdale, a surgeon, and urged him to consider bringing his medical skills to Russia or Poland ('if you have the spirit to undertake the journey').[23] A lack of native doctors meant opportunities for adventurous Englishmen. He reassured John his own 'difficulties and uncertainty' were now behind him. 'Having happily got over all my troubles at this time everything smiles. The very noble manner in which I have been rewarded you have already heard. Beside this, I am happy in continually receiving marks of favour from the Empress, the Grand Duke and the whole court.' A note at the end of the letter requested any reply be addressed to 'Monsieur Le Baron Dimsdale à Moscou, Russia'. Already, the man whose Quaker forebears refused all titles on principle was relishing his new status.

Quakers, with their commitment to plainness and simplicity, had also traditionally rejected the vanity of portraiture. Thomas had no such reservations. For Catherine, expert in the influencing power of art, it was essential the royal inoculator and his son should be painted as part of her publicity campaign for the new technology and her own courageous early adoption. The two newly created barons duly sat for the court painter Carl-Ludwig Christine. Thomas stared seriously from the frame in an uncharacteristically vivid scarlet velvet coat and matching waistcoat, while Nathaniel was more relaxed in a Continental-style blue velvet dress coat with fashionable shirt ruffles of fine white lace. The portraits, together with others of the Grand Duke, Panin, Cherkasov, Vladimir Orlov and several of Catherine herself, were presented to Thomas as part of the growing pile of gifts from the Empress.

The list of presents from Catherine and others he had inoculated was now so long it was hard to keep up. Thomas used a notebook to record his patients and their gifts: four snuffboxes, a pearl necklace, another necklace and bracelets. With a recipe for ink and notes on addressing Russian nobles and pronouncing their unfamiliar names, he jotted down commissions from patients following the latest fashions from England, promising to source a book on bees, assorted hunting hounds and china pheasants.[24]

With so many wealthy families to attend to, there was scope to boost his haul even further, but thoughts of home were growing stronger. 'Many of the first nobility have been already inoculated and many more remain desirous of it,' he wrote to Henry on 25 November, the day after the Senate ceremony. 'If money was my aim I could in all probability make a great sum in a short time but I am content.'

In the eyes of official British opinion, Thomas had nothing left to prove. Cathcart, settling into his new posting and relieved that the risky inoculation project had only enhanced British–Russian relations when it could have destroyed them, could not praise the politically judicious doctor highly enough. He wrote to London:

As for Baron Dimsdale, he is exactly what Dr Dimsdale was when he left Stratford. The manly simplicity of his behaviour, and his firmness and prudence in a course of very delicate and nice circumstances have done honour to his country as well as made his own fortune. He has never forgot the honour he has of being the King's subject, and has ever communicated with me on matters which the duty of his situation did not render improper for him to talk upon.

Thomas had walked a fine political line, providing useful insights without betraying confidences. He had impressed as much with his character as his medical skills.

The tense negotiations over British support for Russia's war with Turkey were beginning to frustrate the ambassador, but his admiration for the German-born Empress remained stronger than ever. 'The Russians in general are men of no education or principles of knowledge of any sort, though not without quickness of parts,' he reported dismissively later in Thomas's stay. The ex-soldier found Catherine easier to understand. 'The Empress has a quickness of thought and discernment, an attention to business and a desire to fill her throne with dignity and with utility even to the lowest of her subjects, and to the rising and future as well as present generation, which without seeing her it is difficult to imagine.'[25]

As the hubbub of church bells and cannons resounded over St Petersburg, Catherine ratcheted up her inoculation publicity drive. The mighty Orthodox Church had blessed her actions; now she turned to the promotional power of the arts. On 28 November, the court theatre in the Winter Palace staged an allegorical ballet, *Prejudice Defeated*, dramatising the Empress's battle with medical prejudice as she fought to save her stricken people. Choreographed by the Italian ballet master Gasparo Angiolini and performed by young pupils of the dance school at the St Petersburg Foundling Hospital, the performance depicted a tearful Ruthenia (Russia) protected by the Spirit of Knowledge but threatened by Superstition, Ignorance and an army led by Chimera, the fire-breathing monster of Greek mythology, symbolising smallpox. A Russian Minerva, representing Catherine, helped Russia and Knowledge defeat Chimera, freeing the common people from the grip of Ignorance and allowing Ruthenia to present her son Alcid – a version of Hercules, standing in for Paul – for inoculation. In the unlikely case that the audience missed the message, the drama ended with the erection by Russia of an obelisk inscribed to 'our All Merciful Monarch . . . a redeemer of human kind'.[26]

The fawning production was not intended to be subtle. Catherine's representation as Minerva, Roman goddess of military prowess, wisdom and patronage of the arts, was already well established. Voltaire called her 'The Minerva of the North' and she regularly appeared in the guise of the armoured warrior deity in portraits and poetry. Now, her introduction of the new science of inoculation was also given a mythical heroic spin, rooting her actions in classical legend as much as modern medicine. For an audience used to seeing allegorical representations on anything from coins to dinner plates, the symbolism was easy to interpret.

The mythological theme continued in *Triumphant Parnassus*, a five-act theatrical spectacular by the poet Vasily Maikov which also celebrated the recovery of the Empress and Grand Duke.[27] Opening with Apollo and the Muses seated on Mount Parnassus with St Petersburg enveloped in storm clouds in the background, the performance depicted smallpox as a venom-spewing dragon. 'The monster flies through the air,' the Chorus cried, 'And infects everyone with its poisonous breath, striking everyone in its rage, sparing not by age or sex . . . The odious monster piles up the bodies. Many have lost friends, brides and children.' Only Catherine, 'the Russian Pallas' – Minerva's Greek counterpart – dared to challenge the monster, slaying it with her sword, extracting its deadly poison and saving 'her people, herself and her son from this danger'. As the clouds parted over St Petersburg, and the court theatre was symbolically illuminated, Apollo exclaimed: 'She challenged the serpentine evil, and the grand deeds of this monarch are hailed as glorious throughout the country. Let Russia blossom like this forever.'[28]

With her defeat of a venomous serpent, Catherine was now presented as a gender-defying superhero, likened not only to Minerva but to Hercules slaying the Lernaean Hydra in the second of his twelve labours. 'Wouldn't it be proper that the whole universe should be subordinate to her only?' the Chorus asked. There was no need to answer the question. The play concluded with a leap to contemporary politics and a warning to Turkey, now squaring up for war: 'The monarch here was able to quash evil, And Asia will know about those tempestuous days, When she ignites from Russia's spark . . . Turkey will know what it means to respect Russia.'[29] The implication was clear: having conquered smallpox, the Empress was ready to destroy any other enemy threatening her Christian people.

Poetry marking the inoculation drew on the same classical themes with equally hyperbolic praise. An ode by Mikhail Kheraskov, a leading figure of the Russian Enlightenment, echoed the image of Catherine fearlessly beheading the hydra, replacing darkness with light. The 'poison' she had allowed to enter her blood had infected all of the Russian people, who had suffered alongside her and looked to her for salvation, he declared. 'You are considered a deity on earth, You are the saviour of our Fatherland, And a consolation to loyal Russians.' Maikov, creator of the Parnassus production, penned a *Sonnet on the Day of Celebration of a Happy*

Recovery from Inoculation against Smallpox of her Imperial Majesty and His Imperial Highness. Urging the wintry natural world to flower and 'Pay respects to the Minerva of the Russian people, The saviour of all and our goddess,' it combined the rhetoric of salvation with the triumph of science:

Twice all Russia was saved by her,
She sent vice and Hydra to hell,
Here mortals have been saved from danger by her,
Sciences and laws have been upheld.

The poet and translator Vasily Ruban, in an ode also responding to the celebrations of 22 November, likened Catherine to the bronze serpent hung on a tree by Moses to heal his Israelite followers after they were bitten by fiery snakes as punishment for their lack of faith. The biblical analogy, with its images of poisoning and miraculous healing, identified the Empress with a symbol of Christ on the cross, recalling her depiction of herself as the Good Shepherd in her address to the Senate.

Through performances and poetry, with their mix of classical and Christian associations, Catherine aimed to set the tone early for interpretations of her inoculation in Russia, while simultaneously using the act to define and promote her own wider identity as a leader. In a country with little print culture and limited literacy even at court, the hagiographical Russian-language accounts could become the first draft of history. In Britain, the introduction of inoculation over forty years before had prompted vociferous and widespread debate in newspapers, pamphlets and periodicals, even when the royal family themselves adopted the procedure. The experiments on the Newgate prisoners and orphans and eventual inoculation of the daughters of the Prince and Princess of Wales had all been reported, often with incredulity at the medical novelty. There was no scope for such public arguments in autocratic Russia where, the British tutor William Richardson observed:

no intelligence of a political nature, but such as the court chooses to communicate; no views of men and manners, and no anecdotes of incidents in domestic life, can be collected from the newspapers. How unlike England! that land enlightened by the radiance of Chronicles, Advertisers and Gazeteers. The half of Russia may be destroyed, and the other half know nothing about the matter.[30]

The report of Catherine's inoculation in the officially sanctioned *Saint Petersburg News* was as on-message as the court productions and poems. It was full of praise for Thomas's skill and courage in saving the Empress, her son and subjects from danger, and hoped his rewards would inspire others in Russia and beyond 'to practise similar endeavours and scientific research for the benefit of mankind'.[31] Catherine had sought by her inoculation to set an example 'not only to the whole of Russia, but to the entire human race', the newspaper declared. Her example was 'stronger than all other images in introducing a much-needed case [for inoculation] in our country'.

Even if criticism had been permitted, support for inoculation in Russia became remarkably strong, according to Richardson's fellow Briton William Tooke, chaplain to the English merchants in St Petersburg. In 1799, he wrote:

> The great nobles of the empire, the inhabitants of the residence, all ranks and classes of people, seemed to vie with each other in following so illustrious an example. Not a single physician, not one ecclesiastic made any public opposition to inoculation; almost all of the former adopted it in their practice, and several among the latter recommended it even from the pulpit.[32]

For Catherine, constantly fashioning and reframing her own political narrative, the mythologised inoculation offered the perfect opportunity to symbolise multiple facets of her leadership at once. The heroic battle against the poisonous serpent recalled the masculine warrior queen, riding astride in military uniform as she led her troops to claim the throne and propel Russia to greatness. At the same time, comparisons with the benevolent Good Shepherd offered a gentler, feminised image, portraying the Empress as 'Matushka', the Little Mother of the Russian fatherland, and obscuring darker memories of the coup and violent death of her husband that had brought her to the throne. Catherine the benevolent despot would use her absolute authority to protect and save her people, literally through the introduction of the life-saving procedure across the empire and metaphorically through her firm but enlightened rule. The Empress's gender-flexing quality, often noted by foreign observers as they tried to make sense of her female power, found perfect expression in the mix of strength and love embodied by her inoculation. 'I take the liberty to assert on my own behalf that I was an honest and loyal knight, whose mind was infinitely more male than female. But for all that, I was anything but mannish, and in me others found, joined to the mind and character of a man, the charms of a very attractive woman,' she wrote in her memoirs.[33] Her woman's body, purged, bled and rubbed with saliva, its headaches, fevers and menstrual blood tracked in minute detail by her doctor, had fought off one of the most feared diseases in history so that her people might live.

The complex messages of the artistic representation of Catherine's inoculation were distilled down to a three-word Russian slogan on a commemorative bronze medal she commissioned from the engraver Timofei Ivanov. 'She herself set an example' was imprinted above an image of the Empress holding her son's hand and reaching out to a grateful mother and children, symbolising Russia and her people. Behind her, the Hydra of prejudice lay dead, while in the background a temple, depicted in classical style, represented faith.

While her court watched allegorical performances featuring gods and dragons, the Empress was already providing a very different narrative for consumption outside Russia. Her early letters from Tsarskoe Selo had emphasised her safe recovery. Now she wanted to give her inoculation wider resonance as the action of an enlightened European leader. On 5 December, she wrote again to Frederick the Great of Prussia, answering his criticism of her 'rash' decision and representing her motives as a mix of justifiable emotion and rational judgement.[34] 'As a child I was brought up to have a horrible fear of smallpox; at a more reasonable age, I have had a thousand difficulties in mastering that fear: if the least malaise came over me, I thought it was the aforementioned illness.' Forced the previous spring and summer to flee 'from house to house' with her son to escape the disease, she had 'considered it a weakness not to seek to escape it. I was advised to have my son inoculated. "But," said I, "how would I have the nerve to do it if I did not start with myself, and how would I introduce inoculation if I did not preach by example?" ' After researching the subject, she claimed to Frederick, she had turned the decision into a model of enlightened thinking, coolly weighing the balance of risk.

> The following reflections made up my mind: 'Any reasonable man, on seeing two dangerous paths before him, chooses the one that is the least so, all things being otherwise equal.' It would be cowardice not to follow the same rule in things of the greatest importance: 'To remain for one's whole life in real danger, along with several thousand men; or to prefer a lesser danger that lasts only a short time and to save many people?' I thought that I was choosing the safest option.

The inoculation itself, depicted as a messianic sacrifice in Russia, was brushed off in a sentence. 'To tell the truth I found that the mountain had given birth to a mouse and that it was a peril not worth speaking of. One could not say the same of the natural smallpox.'[35] Catherine urged Frederick to follow her example, recommending Thomas's skills and safe track record. 'One is ill as pleasurably as can be.'

The Empress used the same fable to make light of her operation in a letter to Voltaire, her correspondent since 1763 and an important conduit to disseminate news of her actions in Europe.[36] Writing with the jaunty flirtatiousness typical of their exchanges, she presented her decision as a thank you present to the inoculation-supporting philosophe in return for his recent gift of copies of his books and a porcelain bust of himself.

> My line of reasoning was as follows. A poorly scribbled bit of paper covered with bad French is a pointless thank you for such a man. I must pay him my compliments by some action that he might like . . . In the end, I thought it best to make of myself an

example that might be useful to mankind. I remembered that, happily, I had not yet had the smallpox. I sent to England for an inoculator; the famous Doctor Dimsdale was bold enough to come to Russia.

On the Winter Palace theatre stage, inoculation was a heroic conquest; in Catherine's letter, it became a playful gesture to please a friend. There was no mention of the racing pulse, sweat and fevers charted in Thomas's medical notes. For a Western audience, the Empress presented herself as briskly unaffected by the procedure. 'I did not keep to my bed for a single second, and I saw people daily.' Voltaire's own books, she flattered, had helped her recovery, read aloud by Count Shuvalov.

I added to the small or non-existent quantity of medicine that is given during the inoculation three or four excellent remedies that I advise any man of good sense not to forget on such an occasion. It is to have *The Scotswoman*, *Candide*, *The Artless Man*, *The Man with Forty Crowns*, and *The Princess of Babylon* read to one. It is impossible to feel the least pain after that.

She and the philosopher were on the right side of history: united against the 'shouters', including the French establishment, who still opposed inoculation. 'Let us pay no mind to those overgrown children, who do not know what they are saying and talk just for the sake of talking.' Updating her letter a few weeks after beginning it, she boasted of the trend set by her example, competitively claiming more impact than the Habsburg Empress Maria Theresa had achieved with her inoculation campaign. 'I can tell you, Sir, that just about everyone wants to be inoculated, that there is a bishop who is going to undergo the operation, and that we have inoculated more people in a month than were inoculated in Vienna in eight.'

The bishop would be inoculated by Thomas, who shrewdly recognised the plan as another strategy by Catherine to fend off popular opposition to the procedure. He wrote to his friend Henry: 'This is one further mark of the extraordinary abilities of her Majesty for I dare say it is intended to strike at the root of all religious scruples which this instance will do more effectively than all the writings or preachings of the whole clergy.'[37]

Parcelling up yet another of her personalised snuffboxes, a fur wrap and a copy of the new French translation of her *Great Instruction* for Voltaire's perusal, the Empress despatched her letter. The philosopher's congratulations were swift and refreshingly direct. 'Oh, Madam, what a lesson your Majesty is giving to us petty Frenchmen, to our ridiculous Sorbonne and to the argumentative charlatans in our medical schools! You have been inoculated with less fuss than a nun taking an enema.'[38]

His native France was, as always, a disappointment – 'I don't know what has happened to our nation, which once set great examples in everything' – but Catherine was showing encouraging signs of enlightened leadership. Her *Instruction* was 'clear, precise, fair, firm and humane', and the woman he dubbed the 'Semiramis of the North' was fighting the barbarian Ottomans when other European nations were reluctant to do so. From distant Ferney, his estate on the French border with Switzerland, he could help the Empress mould herself as the saviour of Europe through the virtual world of correspondence, without ever risking a visit to her faraway empire or the fields of battle. 'I revere the lawmaker, the warrior, the philosopher,' he wrote. 'Defeat the Turks and I shall die happy.'[39]

In her inoculation, Catherine found a ready-made symbol to convey outside Russia her desired image as the enlightened ruler of a civilised nation. Buying up libraries and sponsoring impoverished philosophers had been useful signals, but in offering her body to test an innovative scientific procedure that would protect her people she had physically enacted the values of the enlightenment. She received congratulations from Diderot, the philosophe she had bailed out financially and whose *Encyclopédie* she had offered to publish when it faced opposition in France. The work's seventeen-thousand-word article on Inoculation, written by the physician Théodore Tronchin but leaning heavily on the arguments of the campaigner Charles-Marie de La Condamine, had presented support for the practice as a touchstone of enlightened thought. France had failed that test.

In this century so polite, so full of enlightenment that we call it the Century of Philosophy, we do not perceive that our ignorance, our prejudices, our indifference to the well-being of humanity consigns stupidly to death every year in France alone twenty-five thousand subjects who would depend only on us to preserve for the state. Let us agree that we are neither philosophers nor citizens.[40]

Catherine's stated rationale for her decision to inoculate not only herself but her son aligned perfectly with the 'enlightened love' La Condamine had urged parents to show in protecting their children. As she had written to Frederick the Great, her action was prompted only partly by the coolly rational weighing up of competing risks. She had also been motivated by emotion: her own childhood fears and her desire to shield her son from danger. The combination of sentiment and reason had driven her to act.

The risk to Paul might have prompted the Empress to turn to inoculation, but the boy played only a supporting role in her promotional campaign after the event. Early in her reign, Panin and others at Court had assumed she would rule as regent until the Grand Duke reached his majority, but that had never been Catherine's plan. The only inoculation she described to her correspondents was her own, and the image she projected at home was more Matushka to all her people than mother to her son. It was no accident that the commemorative medals represented Paul, aged seventeen by the time the coins were struck in 1772, as a young child holding his mother's hand as she turned away from him, reaching out to the grateful Russian people. Rather than use her inoculation to present herself as protector of the next emperor, she hoped to deploy it to help banish her image as a foreign usurper and reinforce her own legitimacy as ruler, at home and abroad. Her repeatedly rewritten memoirs shaped and reshaped her life history to create a sense of destiny; in the same way she could frame her fight against smallpox as a metaphor for benevolent female leadership.

Catherine's messaging travelled quickly. On 1 December (20 November by the Russian calendar), news of her inoculation was reported in Britain, complete with details of Thomas's role and the fact that 'she was not confined one day to her chambers'. The write-up had precisely the angle she wanted. 'We think this ought to be told, to the honour of the Empress, that, in a country where the practice of inoculation was unknown, she suffered the first experiment to be made upon herself: a noble instance of her Majesty's great resolution and firmness of mind, as well as of uncommon attention to the welfare of her people.'[41]

British newspapers also published news from Vienna, where Catherine's inoculation rival Maria Theresa was likewise promoting the procedure. 'A great number of persons of the first distinction, have lately sent their children to the castle of St Veyt to be inoculated,' *The Scots Magazine* reported. The Habsburg empress had not been inoculated herself and lacked Catherine's talent for image-making, but her example in treating her own family had still set a trend. The fashion had spread to Venice, following successful trials on twenty-four poor children in the city's Hospital of Mendicants. 'Inoculation for the small pox, which is so much in vogue in several other states of Europe, begins also now to be introduced into the territories of this republic; and the senate have formally permitted this operation to be performed,' the *Bath Chronicle* reported.[42]

Not every account of Catherine's inoculation was respectful: the waspish Horace Walpole heard the news from the Russian ambassador.

> He treated me the other night with a pompous relation of his sovereign lady's heroism – I never doubted her courage. She sent for Dr Dimsdale; would have no trial made on any person of her own age and corpulence; went into the country with her usual company; swore Dimsdale to secrecy, and you may swear he kept his oath to such a lioness. She was inoculated, dined, supped and walked out in public, and never disappeared but one day; had a few on her face and many on her body, which last I suppose she swore Orloff likewise not to tell. She has now inoculated her son. I wonder she did not, out of magnanimity, try the experiment on him first.[43]

Even the gossipy Walpole, unable to mention Catherine's body without reference to her figure or her sex life, could not hide a note of admiration. Meanwhile, Voltaire had discarded jokes about nuns and enemas and was busy amplifying her triumph in more reverential style. In January 1769 he wrote to the diplomat Prince Dmitry Golitsyn, the middleman in Catherine's purchase of Diderot's library and her art buyer-in-chief: 'The inoculation which the Empress tried in good fortune and her generosity towards her doctor, reverberated across all Europe. I have long admired her courage and her contempt for prejudice.'[44] Again, he linked Catherine's medical triumph to her predicted military victory in Turkey, defining Catherine as both philosopher and warrior queen. If she took Constantinople, he promised, he would settle there with her permission. But he would not move to St Petersburg, 'for there is no way that at seventy-five I would go and face the ice of the Baltic Sea'.

While the Empress focused on promotion, Thomas continued to deal in practicalities. As well as inoculating at Court and in the great houses of St Petersburg, where the nobility flocked to follow Catherine's example, he was called out of the city to Ropsha, the estate of Grigory Orlov thirty miles south-west of the capital. There, the deadly power of smallpox had struck as brutally as ever, raging with such fierceness that thirty-one people in the country village had already been snatched away. With the help of Dr Strenge, assistant to Dr Schulenius at Wolff House, Thomas inoculated everyone showing no signs of the disease, treating 123 inhabitants, 47 of them babies and the rest mainly children. The results were as impressive as his practice at court: all but three of the patients survived, with the young victims all afflicted with other conditions. The first general inoculation in Russia provided another example of the power of the treatment, and allowed Catherine's favourite to present himself as a loyal follower of his mistress and progressive supporter of enlightened medical practice.

The success of the royal inoculations and the mass programme at Ropsha only increased Thomas's concern to preserve the reputation of inoculation in Russia. Catherine's example had encouraged support for the technology, but it was fragile and could be easily reversed by a single high-profile fatality. Thomas treated Count Scheel, the Danish ambassador to Russia, and one of his two young children, but decided the other was not healthy enough to undergo the procedure. While the Count recovered, his wife gave birth to twin sons, one of whom developed severe smallpox. Desperate, the Countess begged Thomas to inoculate the other baby and his sickly older sibling, both of whom had already been exposed to the disease. At home in England, the doctor would have had no hesitation in treating patients who might already have become infected with natural smallpox, thanks to long experience showing inoculation could still work if carried out quickly. But in Russia, he held back: 'I could not avoid expressing some reluctance, lest a prejudice should be formed against the practice, in a country where the introduction of inoculation was so newly attempted, in case of a failure of success.'[45] Both parents implored him to change his mind, and he relented. 'The importunity of the Count and the tears of the Countess, who earnestly entreated me not to put the lives of her children in competition with the reputation of the practice, together with the hopes I entertained of success, induced me to comply.' While Catherine dealt with the symbolism of inoculation, Thomas's kind heart encountered the human reality of distress and fear. His gamble paid off: the baby with smallpox died, but his siblings, inoculated from his little body as he fought the virus, had the disease mildly and survived.

With inoculation under his modern method firmly established in St Petersburg, and his rewards announced, Thomas had initially expected to return directly to England. But his success and the Empress's personal respect for his abilities led to a new invitation, as hard to turn down as the original summons to Russia. As the December cold set in earnest, the two Dimsdale doctors packed up their belongings and gathered furs for the next stage of their journey. The trip would take them deeper into the empire, away from St Petersburg and the now familiar world of the court. They were heading for Moscow.

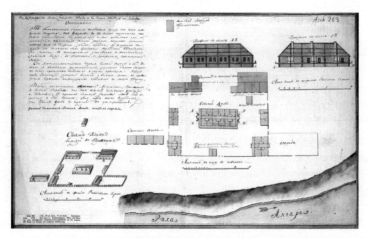

Inoculation hospital on the Angara river, north of Irkutsk, Siberia, founded to treat nomadic people in the region. Drawing by surveyor Anton Losev, 1790.

8

The Impact

'What a lesson your Imperial Majesty has given!'

Voltaire[1]

As the Dimsdales prepared for the five-hundred-mile journey to Russia's old capital, their mission hit an unexpected obstacle. There was, remarkably, not enough smallpox in Moscow. Just as in St Petersburg, strict quarantine was enforced in the city to prevent cases spreading, and though epidemics could break out, the virus was currently under control. 'It was very probable that much time might be lost before the disease could be discovered there, in a proper state for inoculation,' Thomas wrote.[2]

The problem would need to be solved quickly. As news of the Empress's example spread, nobles in Moscow had begun preparing to set out for St Petersburg to have their families inoculated by the famous English doctor. It was pleasing proof of her influence, but Catherine was concerned at the prospect of children travelling long distances in the depths of winter. If the patients could not come to Thomas, he would have to go to them, and somehow secure infected matter for the procedure. The Empress's generous rewards had made it impossible to refuse her request to extend his stay, though she had told him he was free to return to England if he wished. 'It would have been inexcusable in me to hesitate a moment on such an intimation; I therefore offered to set out immediately for Mosco [sic] with my son, and to render all the services we could, to as many as were willing to accept of them.'[3] If all went well, Nathaniel, who had taken enthusiastically to

Russia and made a good impression, would stay on while his father went home to Hertford.[4]

Thomas's instructions were not only to treat the many noble families now clamouring for inoculation. Catherine had also charged him with finding a suitable house near Moscow to convert into an inoculation hospital, on the model of Wolff House on the outskirts of the capital. He had sent details of the necessary design to 'a nobleman of distinction' in the city and planned to inspect potential properties with him. If no satisfactory building was available, he was to decide on an appropriate spot to construct a hospital from scratch.

It would all take time, and experience during his first inoculation trials had shown the doctor the challenges of finding willing donors of infected matter. If he could not track down live cases, there would be more delays. To minimise uncertainty, he took a step he admitted 'was thought pretty extraordinary'.[5] Instead of searching out smallpox sufferers in Moscow, he would inoculate 'one or two children' in St Petersburg and bring them with him on the journey. If he could time things correctly, they would reach their destination just as the youngsters' pustules emerged, allowing him to use the fluid matter at precisely the early stage he preferred for arm-to-arm inoculation.

Even this plan proved harder to execute than anticipated. Thomas's own written account betrayed mild frustration that – for his own purposes – the Empress's enlightened despotism was not quite despotic enough.

It was with some difficulty that two children were procured, for though the idea of arbitrary power conveys with it a presumption that nothing more would be wanting, than an Imperial order for us to fix on the persons we thought most eligible, yet such mildness and benevolence prevails under the government of the Empress, that no such compulsion is ever practised.[6]

Just as she had explained to Thomas at Tsarskoe Selo, Catherine – confident in her power six years after the coup – recognised the political value of persuasion, especially when it came to a fear-inducing new medical procedure.

After a few days' searching, two suitable children were finally found: a boy of about six, the son of a sailor's widow, and a ten-year-old girl, Anoushka, who had already found herself passed between adults like an unwanted parcel.[7] The girl's father, a German officer, had died, and her mother had quickly married again and gone away with her new husband, leaving the child in the care of her grandmother. Miserably poor and unable to support her granddaughter, the woman had effectively pawned her: Anoushka was 'placed . . . in the hands of a gentleman as a pledge for eight roubles'. The sum was repaid to him, and Thomas inoculated both children two days before the date fixed for the departure for Moscow. With the journey expected to take four days, the timing would bring the little group into the city on the sixth day after the inoculation – just ahead of the appearance of pustules and the worst of the fever. Finally, he could begin to look forward to visiting 'that great and ancient city' so very remote from all he knew in England.

In contrast to the single, speed-oriented chaise that had brought them from London, the Dimsdales would now travel in luxurious style. The Empress had loaned them one of her travelling equipages – a spacious coach resembling a miniature wooden cottage on wheels and designed for round-the-clock progress. The seats could be let down to sleep, and the wheels could be switched for runners to convert the vehicle into a sleigh. Accompanying the party in a separate carriage was Sergei Volchkov, an eminent lexicographer and translator who had recently published a foreign language dictionary, to act as interpreter.[8] A small group of other coaches accommodated a retinue of servants, together with the doctors' baggage and provisions for the journey.

Despite – or perhaps because of – the elaborate arrangements, the party found themselves 'retarded by unavoidable disappointments', and did not finally take to the road until four days after the children's inoculation. Worse, the little boy turned out to have scald-head – a ringworm infection, most common among the poor, that produced patches of peeling, inflamed skin on the scalp. The contagious condition meant he had to be left behind, leaving the doctors to rely on Anoushka alone to supply pus for inoculations across Moscow. To be certain of having enough infected matter,

Thomas inoculated the little girl in four places, two on each arm. The blister raised at each incision would contain fluid for the procedure, together with other pustules appearing on her body.

Setting out at last, with Anoushka warmly wrapped up alongside Thomas and Nathaniel, the group encountered yet more difficulties. They were beginning their journey in the deep cold of December, but at the critical point before enough snow had fallen to enable the switch from carriages to sleighs. The roads were pitted with frozen ruts. 'After the frost is sufficiently set in to make the ice on the rivers safe to pass over, a considerable time is necessary before the roads over the snow are sufficiently beaten and level for travelling,' Thomas wrote. 'Our carriages were therefore on wheels when we set out, and we were obliged to travel with a great number of horses and slowly.'[9]

To make matters worse, they were following in the tracks of troops heading south from St Petersburg to fight in Catherine's newly declared war with Turkey. The soldiers, marching to their rendezvous in Kyiv, Ukraine, blocked the road ahead, and commandeered almost all available post horses at stops along the way to transport their baggage and supplies. The hardships of the army's winter journey did not worry the Empress as she promoted Russia's lone assault on the 'barbarian' Ottomans. 'My soldiers go to war against the Turks as though they were going to a wedding,' she wrote to Voltaire.[10]

Stuck behind the military convoy in freezing weather with a rapidly sickening child, Thomas felt all his past anxiety flood back.

I was exceedingly concerned at the delay, on account of our little patient, who began to complain on the eighth (as is usual) and seemed to suffer considerably from the fever preceding the eruption, yet we were under the necessity of travelling on night and day, incessantly, without any stoppages, except what were necessary for the exchange of horses at the several stages.

Anoushka's smallpox pustules appeared while the party was still on the road, easing her fever but increasing the urgency of reaching Moscow.

Despite the efforts of everyone along the route to help them, the medical party did not arrive in the old capital until early on the morning of the seventh day after leaving St Petersburg, the eleventh day after the inoculation. Finally able to escape the jolting carriage, the Dimsdales and Anoushka settled into a grand house near the centre of the city. The following morning, anxious to waste no time, the doctors set to work, travelling from house to house to treat each noble family in turn.

By now, the Russian winter had set in hard. The British embassy tutor William Richardson, also encountering its extremity for the first time, was shaken by the experience. 'Cold! Desperately cold! . . . The wind has blown almost constantly from the north-east. It comes howling and cold from the heights of Siberia, and has brought with it immense quantities of snow . . . In the country, nothing appears but a boundless white desert; and the rivers are almost one crystalline mass.' The 'howling blasts' could lower the spirits on overcast days, Richardson found, but clear skies produced an extraordinary ice phenomenon that he had never seen in Britain. 'In the coldest and brightest weather you see an infinite multitude of little shining darts or spiculæ, flying in all directions through the sky. They seem

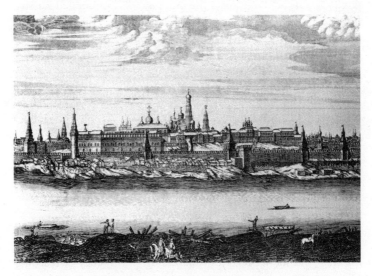

View of the Moscow Kremlin, early eighteenth century.

to be about a quarter of an inch in length; they have not more thickness than the finest hair; and their golden colour, glancing as they shoot through the deep azure sky, has a great deal of beauty.'[11]

Despite its harshness, the icy weather offered a practical advantage. Once the snow on the roads was beaten smooth, and wheels could be swapped for runners to turn carriages into sleighs, travel in Russia was easier than in a muddy English winter. 'The motion of the sledge is very easy and agreeable. It is drawn in this country by horses, and the swiftness with which they go, even upon ice, is astonishing. The horses here are small, but very nimble and beautiful; and the Russians, in general, are excellent horsemen.'

Travelling now by sledge, the English doctors and Anoushka criss-crossed Moscow. Within a few days, they had inoculated over fifty individuals from the girl alone. Thomas, always especially gentle with young patients, worried at first at the risks of taking the sick child out in freezing temperatures, but was reassured by Russian expertise in fending off the cold. 'Our little patient was wrapped up in a fur; in the carriage was a bear skin and the same fur covered the doors; her legs were inside a doubled-over fur. With these precautionary measures there was nothing to fear for her.'[12] As she recovered and regained her appetite, a more nutritious diet than usual was even improving her health.

After the first inoculations, a second wave of would-be inoculees came forward, and – when they were not visiting potential hospital sites – the Dimsdales spent almost two months shuttling between patients often living four or five miles apart in the sprawling city. In their free time, they were tourists. Thomas wrote: 'We spent a wonderful time in Moscow, looking round the city and interesting sights there; there are many of them and they deserve the attention of travellers.'[13] The doctors' enthusiasm was not shared by Catherine, who could barely tolerate the disorder, dirt and Asiatic feel of the former capital compared with modern, Western-oriented St Petersburg. To her efficient, industrious mind, Moscow was a 'seat of idleness'.[14] She recognised the incomparable symbolic power of the Kremlin, holding her coronation there to boost her dubious legitimacy, but shuddered at the superstitions and 'fanatical' religiosity of the people. 'Moscow is a crowd and not a city,' she wrote to Voltaire.[15]

With its 250,000-strong population, around double that of St Petersburg and swollen during the winter months as provincial nobles decamped from the countryside, Moscow was indeed sprawling and chaotic, but it was far from a backwater.[16] Just as in the new capital, the elite embraced inoculation. The Imperial Moscow University welcomed the Empress's recovery with a special celebration, at which Sergei Zybalin, Professor of Anatomy and Surgery at the Medical Faculty, gave a speech on 'The benefits of inoculated smallpox over the natural disease, with moral and physical evidence against wrongthinkers.'[17]

With the principle of inoculation firmly established in the city, and every patient fully recovered, Thomas prepared to return to St Petersburg, only to encounter a new and alarming setback. After months of stress, travel and hard work in an unforgiving climate, he succumbed to pleurisy – a condition serious enough to threaten his life. Suffering 'a very dangerous fever, of the pleuritic kind, which reduced me greatly', he was seized with chest pain and struggled to breathe.[18] The doctor was fortunate in being treated by one of the most prominent physicians in Russia: Baron Georg von Asch, the founding member of the St Petersburg Medical College and head of the army medical service. In his report to Catherine, Thomas went out of his way to praise Asch and his Estonian-born colleague Dr Conrad von Dahl, 'who were so obliging as to attend me, and for whose skill and assiduity my best thanks are due'. News of his perilous condition reached St Petersburg, where Lady Cathcart, wife of the British ambassador, sent updates to his family in England. His wife Ann, deeply distressed, wrote back:

> If it is please God to send him safe to me again, believe nothing would tempt me to consent to another so long separation, for though there is the greatest reason to be satisfied and thankful for the great success and rewards he has met with, yet the anxiety and fears that unavoidably attend so very distant and long an absence are greater than I was aware of or could, I believe, bear again.[19]

Still sick, but out of danger, Thomas was finally able to leave Moscow. The little carriage train regrouped, this time with runners fitted in place of wheels. Nathaniel, unwilling to stay behind and leave his father, travelled with Anoushka, while Thomas was given a sledge to himself, roomy enough to contain his mattress. With the doors closely sealed to maximise warmth, he could lie flat under fur coverings as the sleigh sped along. By day, windows let in light, but at night, when the candle in a small hanging lantern was repeatedly extinguished by the driver's abrupt steering, he lay, feverish, in complete darkness. On roads now glistening with beaten snow, the party made much faster progress than on the outward journey, though the cold of February was even harsher than December. A bottle of Hungarian wine that the Moscow governor Count Petr Saltykov had given the physician as a tonic froze solid just a foot from his head.[20] Finally, on the fourth day of their journey, the relieved travellers arrived in St Petersburg.

Safely back in his apartment on the Millionnaya, Thomas took out pen and paper and completed the case histories requested by Catherine of her own inoculation and her son's, sparing no medical details. Her goal, she told him, was 'that being published they would tend to the removal of prejudices, and to the advancement of a practice she had much at heart to encourage'.[21] At her command, he added his own analysis of the impact of smallpox on the Russian people, and a blueprint for extending inoculation throughout the empire.

The effects of the disease in places unfamiliar with proper treatment and prevention were 'scarcely less general and fatal than those of the plague itself', yet, he warned, they were often underestimated. With no firm statistics to rely on, and no personal experience of Russia beyond the two largest cities, he extrapolated from figures in England, analysing the London Bills of Mortality in exactly the way James Jurin of the Royal Society had done when inoculation had first been introduced in England over forty years before. Compiling more recent numbers, from 1734–67, into tables, Thomas found his new findings tallied exactly with Jurin's observations. After discounting under-twos, who died of so many diseases of infancy, smallpox was responsible for one in eight of all deaths in London. Almost one in five of those who contracted the natural disease died, even in a city with a temperate climate and experienced doctors. In Russia, where the disease was 'exceedingly fatal', he concluded, the proportion could be as high as one death in every two cases, leading him to suggest a fatality rate as high as two million individuals a year. He conceded later the estimate was excessive and influenced by the virulence of cases he witnessed, but the impact of the disease remained devastating. According to a calculation made in 1807, Russia lost 440,000 lives a year to smallpox out of a population of 33 million: about 1.3 percent.[22] Even without precise numbers, the doctor's conclusion was clear. 'The public, I am persuaded, must be sufficiently convinced from fact and demonstration, that inoculation is the only means of preventing the mischief arising from the smallpox.'[23]

For Catherine, the stronger the statistical case for promoting inoculation, the better for her campaign. Alongside a humanitarian desire to save her people from death and suffering were economic imperatives shared across Europe: if a state's population formed the core of its wealth, then that population must be protected and expanded. 'It seems hardly necessary to shew, how much the riches and strength of states depend upon the number of inhabitants,' Thomas wrote. 'But perhaps there is not any country in which the certainty of that position is more indisputable than Russia.'[24] The Empress, overseeing a vast, sparsely populated empire, agreed wholeheartedly. 'Too much encouragement can never be given to the propagation of the human species,' she had written in her *Great Instruction*. Thomas was pushing at an open door: since her accession, Catherine had made improved public health a centrepiece of her social reforms. Ambitious plans were already under way to promote medical care not only of the military but of the civilian population throughout Russia, train more native doctors instead of recruiting from overseas, and establish laboratories and apothecary shops across the empire. Thomas had seen for himself new regulations imposed by the Medical College to control the price of medicines and require all physicians and surgeons to pass an examination before being allowed to practise.[25]

Inoculation itself already had a foothold in Russia, where medical elites, frequently born and educated abroad, were well connected with the scientific networks of western Europe. Dr Schulenius, supervising the hospital at Wolff House, had been inoculating in the progressive Baltic province of Livonia for over twenty years, and other doctors were practising on a small scale in St Petersburg. Now, with the high-profile example of the Empress and her heir, the procedure had finally received the impetus it needed to spread across the empire.

Thomas, writing up his recommendations, could only draw on his own experience. In his 'small treatise . . . an imperfect sketch drawn up in haste', the leafy villages of Hertfordshire served as an example for general inoculations of the poor in Russia.[26] In Little Berkhamsted he had inoculated all willing residents on the same day, taking care to avoid infecting those who could not or would not accept the treatment and encouraging those with fewer symptoms to help the sicker patients to keep costs down. The same could be done in every town or village in Russia every five years, he suggested, adding details of his own small inoculation house at Bengeo as another model of good practice. Only licensed professionals should be permitted to carry out the procedure, 'for the mischief arising from the practice of inoculation by the illiterate and ignorant is beyond conception.'[27] His own treatise setting out his favoured method, published the previous year, was translated into Russian for distribution to practitioners.

Russia's new inoculation drive began at Wolff House, opened under Thomas's direction and established permanently at imperial expense as the St Petersburg Smallpox Hospital. Under the overall oversight of the Scottish doctor Matthew Halliday, another long-standing member of the capital's thriving British community, groups of children of all backgrounds were inoculated and nursed until their recovery. At first, parents were given money to persuade them to bring their infants for treatment, but the English chaplain William Tooke, writing in 1799, reported that the success of the practice soon made the bribes redundant.[28] From 1783, the hospital admitted children twice a year in spring and autumn, treating them for free. Halliday, who also inoculated most of the large family of the Grand Duke Paul, was still in post in 1791, when he advertised in the *St Petersburg News* offering free treatment of smallpox patients every evening from six till eleven.[29]

More inoculation houses were opened in major cities and provincial towns across the country on the same model. Georg von Asch, the doctor who treated Thomas for pleurisy and had studied inoculation techniques at the London Smallpox Hospital, introduced the practice in Kyiv in 1768. The hospital set up by Thomas in Moscow was followed by another in Kazan, on the Volga river, in 1771 and the following year in Irkutsk, Siberia, where 15,580 people were inoculated within five years.[30] 'These institutions have since so greatly increased, that we are not in a capacity to give a complete list of them,' Tooke wrote at the turn of the century. He linked the expansion directly to Catherine's support. 'Russia, in the eighteenth century, appears to have the advantage over most other countries in Europe, that establishments of general utility meet here proportionately with fewer difficulties, and are encouraged with far greater munificence from the throne, and more quickly attain to a generally diffused operation.'[31] More hospitals were built in the countryside and on the estates of the nobility, who had the power to compel their serfs to be treated, just as British colonial plantation owners inoculated their enslaved workers with no thought of consent. To encourage those wary of the new procedure, colourful prints, or lubki, featuring illustrations advertising its power were widely distributed.[32]

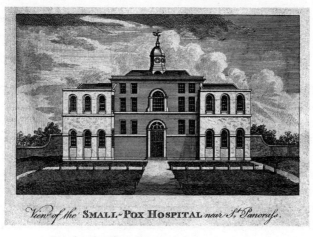

London Smallpox Hospital, St Pancras, 1771.

Despite the Empress's autocratic power and backing of inoculation, there was no general compulsion to undergo the procedure. As in Britain, children at the foundling hospitals were routinely and effectively treated; in the Moscow home founded by Catherine there were only four deaths in twenty years. With a shortage of doctors and a scattered population, Thomas's insistence that only licensed practitioners should inoculate was not practical in Russia. Instead, some communities were taught to perform the operation themselves. In progressive Livonia, the energetic Lutheran pastor Johann Eisen managed to inoculate five hundred individuals in his own home in two years from 1769, before training gardeners and church assistants to help out. Finally, he opened a school of inoculation and taught ninety-nine peasant mothers to conduct the procedure themselves, using minimal preparation and a tiny needle-prick between thumb and forefinger, hoping they would pass the method on to their daughters.[33] His technique, also recommending fresh air and cold water facial spritzes to cool fever, was published in a book promoted by the new Free Economic Society, Russia's first learned society. Three thousand miles east in Siberia, indigenous tribal leaders, fearful of a disease that swept especially brutally through their populations, approached Staff Surgeon Schilling, director of the Irkutsk smallpox hospital, for instruction in inoculation so they too could protect their own people. Schilling, a German military doctor, also tirelessly delivered the treatment himself, inoculating more than eighteen thousand individuals over thirty years, with only 237 deaths.[34] Over four summer months in 1791 he travelled the wild steppe near Lake Baikal, treating 620 nomadic Buryats and reindeer herders and dutifully reporting his work to the Medical College in St Petersburg.[35]

Catherine's efforts to promote inoculation even in the farthest corners of her empire were only increased by the most dramatic single public health tragedy of her reign: a devastating outbreak of bubonic plague in Moscow. The disease reached the city in 1770 via the busy route from the south, probably in cloth imported from the enemy Ottoman Empire. It caused riots and devastation in the teeming metropolis, sending the nobility fleeing to their estates and killing over 100,000 of those left behind. Amid food shortages and a paralysed economy, the Archbishop of Moscow was killed by rioters after he removed an icon to prevent crowds gathering and spreading infection.

The Empress was horrified at the scale of death, but also by the public disorder and evidence of threat to her empire even as she waged a victorious war. The chaos challenged her health reforms, but also her enlightened ideals and promotion of Russia as a civilised modern state. While playing down the calamity to foreign onlookers, she closely tracked the progress of the epidemic, sending Grigory Orlov to take charge in the city and sponsoring strict new controls empowering officials to impose quarantine and hygiene measures. Lessons from the disaster influenced reforms in 1775 which underpinned her drive for more public health institutions across the empire, better medical education and recruitment of more doctors. Each town was to have a physician and a surgeon, plus assistants and pupils, and pay would be higher in the most remote regions.[36] The epidemic, occurring so soon after Catherine's highly publicised smallpox inoculation, even prompted some medical observers to explore the idea of inoculation against plague, despite the fact that the infection could be caught more than once. The concept did not work, but the drive for understanding stimulated epidemiological research that would become a medical specialism in Russia.

The full extent of the spread of inoculation during Catherine's reign was hard to measure accurately, hampered by patchy statistics. In St Petersburg at least the laborious data-gathering of another Lutheran clergyman, the German-born Pastor Joachim Grot, provided a uniquely detailed account of the impact of smallpox in the capital.[37] In printed supplements to sermons on inoculation he preached each year at the wooden Catherine's Church on Vasilievsky Island, across the Neva from the English Embankment, Grot published detailed tables of annual smallpox mortality rates throughout the 1770s. Breaking down the numbers by age, sex and month, he found that epidemic waves flowed over the city in cycles of around four years, wiping out over five hundred people annually at their height – one in eight of those infected. The largest group were babies under one, prompting the pastor to recommend inoculation in infancy. In tribal areas, where native people were far more vulnerable to the disease than those in European states, death rates were significantly worse, he reported, with epidemics scything through populations every ten years, leaving no time for birth rates to recover in the interim.

There was no doubt of the effectiveness of inoculation for those receiving it. Professor Wolfgang Krafft of the Academy of Sciences analysed the impact of the St Petersburg Smallpox Hospital, which treated 1,570 children during the 1780s, with just four deaths. One in seven children in the city who caught natural smallpox died of it, representing a mortality rate fifty-seven times higher than for inoculation, which killed just three in every thousand. Despite the hospital's success rate, only a small minority of children in the capital benefited from the flagship institution in the first decade after the Empress's inoculation. Only one child in forty-nine born in the city was treated there, and Grot found that children of nobles and officers dominated the patient list, followed by those of artisans and of serfs, whose masters made the decision for them.[38]

As Catherine had recognised from the outset, poorer families in Russia were far more likely than the wealthy to resist the alien new procedure, even if their reluctance was not publicly expressed. Superstitions such as the idea that providing pus was fatal to the donor were hard to stamp out; according to some folk beliefs, those who died of smallpox would receive a 'robe of Christ' to wear in heaven.[39] 'The ancient Russ had a great dislike to inoculation,' the British ambassador Cathcart wrote to London while the Empress was recovering from her own treatment. 'Mr Panin says the question might have become serious had not the firmness and address of the Empress and her Minister, got the better of all opposition.'[40] As Thomas saw, Catherine's example quickly influenced the aristocracy – a trend that continued after his departure. Writing to him in Hertford from St Petersburg in July 1771, she boasted: 'Here inoculation has reached a point where there is almost no noble household in which they don't await with impatience the suitable age for inoculating the small children; and as soon as it arrives there is nothing more pressing than submitting them to this salutary remedy.'[41] Even Catherine, always ready to talk up her achievements, acknowledged there was still work to do to persuade the poor, though she could not resist a competitive flash of inoculation nationalism:

As far as the common people are concerned, they do not present themselves with such eagerness; however, one must hope that the example of the nobility will overcome their repugnance and prejudice. Several noblemen are having the children of their peasants inoculated. I believe I can claim without deceiving myself that inoculation has not made faster progress in any country than in Russia, where it only dates from your trip.

Sixteen years later, in 1787, a letter from the Empress to Count Piotr Rumiantsev, Governor General and vice regent of Malorossiya (modern Ukraine) in Kyiv, showed both that some resistance to inoculation continued on the ground within the empire and that, almost two decades after launching her promotional campaign, Catherine remained as determined as ever to pursue it. One of Rumiantsev's most important duties, she wrote, 'should be the introduction of inoculation against smallpox, which, as we know, causes great harm, especially among the ordinary people. Such inoculation should be common everywhere, and it is now all the more convenient, since there are doctors or medical attendants in nearly all districts, and it does not call for huge expenditure'.[42] As ever, her instructions were detailed and practical, calling on Rumiantsev to requisition disused monasteries as isolation hospitals for inoculated patients, and to award underpaid provincial doctors a wage supplement to carry out the procedure.

In 1797, the year after Catherine's death, the Riga-born political economist Heinrich Storch reported that in Russia 'prejudice against inoculation has been entirely destroyed: the conviction of its usefulness has become so general, that there are few parents who do not seek to prevent the danger of this contagious disease through a mild operation, conducted at a young age'.[43] It was an overstatement – even Catherine's influence could not reverse deep-seated resistance so quickly[44] – but it reflected a dramatic shift in attitudes and medical provision in just three decades that had seen Russia speed past most other European states in terms of inoculation acceptance. Powered by the Empress's example and determined promotion, the innovation had spread across the empire as part of a fundamental reform of medicine and public health. Long after memories had faded of the poems and allegorical spectaculars that greeted the first Imperial inoculations, bells were still ringing throughout Russia each year for the national holiday commemorating the event. John Parkinson, an Oxford academic accompanying a wealthy student on the Northern Tour in 1792, took part in a celebratory masquerade featuring card games, Cossack dancing and a bar serving lemonade and sweet almond syrup, packed out by a crowd of some two thousand people.[45]

The tradition of empire-wide celebration was continued by the Grand Duke Paul after his accession as emperor. In 1800, the English traveller and mineralogist Edward Daniel Clarke joined the Don Cossacks in a festival marking the recovery of one of Paul's children from inoculation, attending a solemn Orthodox service followed by a banquet of sturgeon soup, wine and goblets of mead flavoured with fruit juices.[46]

Embedded firmly in Russian culture and facilitated by an expanded network of hospitals and medical practitioners, inoculation saved tens of thousands of lives during Catherine's rule. Its familiarity and widespread acceptance also paved the way for Russia's rapid adoption of the next, still more effective weapon in the fight against smallpox: vaccination.

In his apartment near the Winter Palace, Thomas completed his reports for the Empress. Exhausted by strain and illness after his Moscow trip, he was desperate to go home. It was February 1769, almost seven months since he had left his family, and his work was done – or so he thought. 'Having now finished my business, I made my request to Her Imperial Majesty for permission to return to England; she assured me my time should be my own,' he wrote.[47]

As the court buzzed with carnival celebrations for the opening of the Small Hermitage, the riverside extension to the palace built for informal entertainments, Thomas prepared to leave. He said his goodbyes and received an ornate copy of the Patent of Nobility legally granting his baronetcy. The document, each page shining with gilding, elaborately praised 'Thomas Dimsdale, English Gentleman and Doctor of Physic whose Humanity, Virtue and laudable Concern for the Good of Mankind in General induced him long since to apply all this thoughts and faculties towards improving and perfecting the Inoculation for the Small-pox, as the only Rational Preservation of the Human Species from the destructive Consequences of that Mortal Disease.' The familiar mythological imagery of the Empress's inoculation-themed court spectaculars reappeared as the text praised Thomas's skill in not only treating herself and Paul but converting a sceptical nation: 'while he was thus removing the anxious fears of our faithful subjects for the welfare of US ourselves and of OUR dear son and heir [he] destroyed at the same time that baleful Hydra Prejudice and the dreadful apprehensions of the (hitherto fatal) disease.' The document was bound and covered with shimmering fabric woven of gold and silver thread, and accompanied by a golden seal finished with sequinned tassels.

As a final memento, Thomas was captured in an engraving showing him in a richly draped loose coat adorned with a wide collar and more tassels, his right arm resting on two books and his index finger pointing at sheets of notes as he gazed seriously out at the viewer.

With their piles of gifts and luggage packed into their sleigh, and a mounted officer alongside to ensure speedy passage out of the Russian dominions, Thomas and Nathaniel bade their final farewells to all at Court. The horses stamped in the snowy Millionnaya as the two doctors settled into the vehicle and spread out the furs that would keep them warm. Then, as so often on their long journey, the unexpected happened. A nobleman hurried to the carriage with a message: the Empress was unwell and had asked to see the departing doctor immediately. 'I was much concerned to find her with every symptom of a pleuritic fever,' Thomas wrote, 'and she did me the honour to say, that she should be sorry to stop my journey, but wished to have my assistance.'[48] Without hesitation, he postponed the departure and moved into the Winter Palace to care for Catherine once more.

During the inoculation, the Empress's symptoms, though

uncomfortable and not without risk, had been reassuringly predict-
able. Now, as she suffered the dangerous inflammation of the tissues
around the lungs so recently experienced by Thomas, her condition
worsened, and the cluster of foreign doctors at her bedside were
divided over her treatment. 'Her symptoms increased, and the pulse
became now such, as I was convinced made it necessary she should
be bled,' Thomas recorded. 'The Empress consented, and Monsieur
Rousselin, a very able, ingenious surgeon, in whom she reposes
great confidence, was directed to take away eight ounces of blood.'
Rousselin, trusted as he was by Catherine, refused the instruction.
Humoral medical tradition indicated that removing blood, the
standard treatment for fever in the mid-eighteenth century, would
interrupt the sweating, preventing the Empress's body from expelling the poisons he believed were causing her illness. Thomas vehe-
mently disagreed – and got his way. 'I thought, on the contrary,
there was a necessity for instant bleeding, and she was pleased to
determine on being bled, from which she received an immediate
relief.'[49] Yet again, he had experienced 'the greatest anxiety', and
again Catherine had trusted him with her own life. For three weeks
more, he stayed at her side, watching over her as her condition
improved and insisting she put aside her punishing daily schedule
and rest. The ban on work did not prevent his patient writing to
Madame Bielke, reporting on the doctor's instructions and explaining that her fever had 'kept me in bed for six whole days, something
I found very inconvenient for someone who loves to get a move on
and who mortally detests being in bed'.[50]

Finally, in mid-March, the danger was over and the Dimsdales
could pack up their luggage one more time for the journey home. In
the Empress's eyes, Thomas had proved himself twice over: as a skilled
inoculator and as an experienced bedside physician taking life-saving
decisions in an emergency. The English doctor had won her respect,
but also touched her heart. Lord Cathcart, another admirer, wrote to
Sir Andrew Mitchell, his diplomatic counterpart in Berlin:

No man ever succeeded so completely in a commission which,
all things considered, I may well say was a hazardous one. No
part of his merit has been lost here, nor can anything be stronger

than the expressions of the Empress of her sense of it: she speaks of him to us not only with esteem but with tenderness. When he took his leave, it was not without tears.[51]

Catherine gave Thomas one final parting gift before he and Nathaniel left Russia. As the doctors climbed into their carriage, the Empress passed by in her sleigh. Thinking Thomas looked cold, she threw him her muff of Siberian black sable, the most desirable and expensive fur in the world.[52] Extravagant, playfully delivered and above all useful, it was the perfect present. The doctors added it to their collection of the finest luxuries Russia could provide and set off at last, out of St Petersburg and west across the width of Europe towards England.

With packed snow still blanketing the roads, and runners on their carriage, the Dimsdales made fast progress to Riga, the last outpost in Russian territory. There, they were escorted over the border by their accompanying officer, who ensured they were spared the baggage checks usual for foreigners leaving the empire. They were joined on the journey by a young Irish-born merchant, Stratford Canning, who recorded their onward route in a letter to his father in Dublin.[53] The party passed through Mitau, the capital of the Duchy of Courland, before pushing on across a corner of Poland and into Prussia, where they stopped at the small port town of Memel. En route to Königsberg, where Canning stayed on for business, the travellers made their way along the amber-sprinkled Curish Haff, a sixty-one-mile sand dune spit separating the Curonian Lagoon from the bleak Baltic Sea. The Dimsdales continued to Danzig, and from there on 11 April to Berlin, where the irresistible force of British diplomatic hospitality compelled them reluctantly to break their journey and pass on news of their Russian adventure.[54] Mitchell, the British envoy in the Prussian capital, reported to Cathcart: 'Baron Dimsdale was in so great a hurry to get home, that with the utmost difficulty I prevailed with him to stay two days here.'[55]

Thomas's new fame had run ahead of him: Frederick the Great, who had berated Catherine for risking inoculation, summoned him to an audience. The physician was driven by coach with an English-speaking interpreter to the palace of Sanssouci in nearby Potsdam, where the Prussian king kept him waiting for two hours. Returning at last from a riding trip, Frederick met Thomas at the door of his apartments and said in French, 'Sir, I think you inoculated the Empress and the Prince at Petersburg.' When the visitor politely agreed, he grunted, 'I felicitate you on the occasion, and wish you a good journey,' before turning on his heel and vanishing into his rooms. The brusque encounter, so different from the adulation of St Petersburg, was a shock for the new Baron, now rather used to flattery. 'It seems as if an Englishman was not in fashion there, for upon the whole his Majesty's manner of speaking was far from being gracious,' he wrote to Mitchell as he hurried onward to Magdeburg.[56] The envoy disagreed: the Prussian king's snub was aimed at the Empress of Russia, still trying to lure him into a Northern Alliance against the French. Thomas's reputation might now be great, but he was still a pawn in the power play of Europe's competing monarchs.

There were no more delays, and the Dimsdales took the packet ship from Amsterdam back to Harwich and, in late April, returned home at last to Port Hill House, nine months after they had left it. The snows of St Petersburg were far behind them; in the hedgerows of Hertfordshire, the blackthorn was almost over and the may was blossoming. Thomas was reunited at last with the family he had missed so much: his wife Ann and the six children who had stayed at home, all now demanding to hear stories of Russia from their father and brother.

In the report he had completed before leaving St Petersburg, the doctor had put on the record his opinion of the Empress and of the Russians he encountered during his visit. His praise for Catherine was as unstinting as in his first letter to Henry Nicols not long after arriving in Russia. Highlighting her relentless work ethic, moderate diet and talent for languages, he concluded: 'She adds to her natural charms, courtesy of manner and kindliness and benignity of the highest degree, besides manifesting on every occasion such clearness of judgement as to compel admiration . . . The promotion and encouragement of the liberal arts, the welfare of her subjects, these are the objects to which, in times of peace, she devotes all her splendid talents.'[57] Thomas was far from impartial: Catherine agreed with him on the subject closest to his heart, inoculation, trusted his abilities and had rewarded him with exceptional generosity. But, as his scientific works showed, he was typically an understated, moderate and precise observer, not given to excess. His genuine admiration for the Empress was based on his own experience.

The physician seemed to try to pre-empt accusations of bias or naivety in his description of the Russian aristocracy, being careful to define precisely the parameters of his expertise. He knew his narrative ran contrary to prevailing British perceptions of Russia as a boorish, uncivilised land fuelled by vodka, but he had personally witnessed a very different picture, and he recorded it as honestly as any medical case study.

> Everybody is prejudicial against other countries, and against their manners and customs. Hence many English people, who are surprised at the character of the exalted persons described above [the Empress and Grand Duke], have a different opinion of the aristocracy and the people of Russia, and even believe that they preserve vestiges of barbarism in their midst.
>
> I shall not say anything of what they were before, but beg to observe that I am speaking of the years 1768 and 1769 only; at that period the performance of my medical duties and the frequent invitations to the tables of the nobility gave me an opportunity of becoming acquainted with them and their families, and enabled me to form a more accurate idea of them than can possibly be obtained in the superficial and conventional acquaintanceships made at ordinary social gatherings. I can certify absolutely that persons of rank are polite, high-minded, and honourable, and, what may seem stranger still, extremely moderate in the use of strong drink.[58]

Thomas had moved in the most elevated circles imaginable in Russia, but he was also anxious to share what personal experience he had to correct misapprehensions of the poor.

> It may be easily imagined that I had no frequent intercourse with the lower orders, nevertheless, to the best of my observation, they always seemed ready to render any services in their

power, and during any walks abroad, when I was alone, I had occasion to put their obliging kindliness to the test; frequently did I have to ask my way and make myself understood by signs only, and I always found the poorer classes to be the most intelligent and ready to be of service.[59]

Seven months living in Russia, much of it at court, had given Thomas unparalleled access to a world many judged but few knew. By training, he had observed and recorded it as accurately as he could, and by instinct he had made his findings public. But the experience had also changed him personally, opening his eyes to a new world that would remain close to his heart for the rest of his life, even as he returned with relief to the familiar comforts of home and family.

In July 1769, the Dimsdales' travelling companion Stratford Canning – by now in London – wrote again to his father. He had met up with Thomas in the capital and received a warm invitation to visit the Dimsdale family at home in Hertfordshire. The young merchant summed up the physician's mood, exactly a year after receiving the invitation to St Petersburg he had at first resisted: 'He is wonderfully happy at the recollection of Russia, while he finds himself safe in his native country.'[60]

With his noble title and handsome payment, Thomas could now have retired, enjoying his wealth and his new celebrity status. But his Quaker upbringing and medical training had imprinted themselves too firmly: while smallpox continued to wreak havoc, especially among the poor, he had unfinished business. There were new challenges ahead.

Omai, the South Sea Islander inoculated by Thomas Dimsdale at the request of King George III. Portrait by Joshua Reynolds, c. 1776.

9

The Celebrity

'In fact, I am an advocate for inoculation'

Thomas Dimsdale[1]

On a cold morning in December 1769, two men arrived for breakfast at the elegant London home of Dr John Fothergill in Harpur Street, Bloomsbury. One was Samuel Galton, a wealthy gun maker from Birmingham and a Quaker, like his host.[2] The other, shrugging off his coat after the brief walk from his London residence in Red Lion Square, was Fothergill's old friend Thomas Dimsdale, Baron of the Russian Empire.

Betty Fothergill, the physician's lively seventeen-year-old niece visiting from Warrington for the winter, was thrilled to find herself sharing toast and tea with the celebrity doctor who had inoculated the Empress of Russia. She wrote in her diary:

> I was much pleased, and perhaps my ambition was a little flattered, to be in the company of a man who a few months ago made such a noise in the world, from his receiving so many marks of the favour and friendship of one of the greatest sovereigns in Europe. It was a new thing for me to hear talk of Princes, Counts and Barons in so familiar a style.[3]

While news of Catherine's inoculation ricocheted around Europe, propelled by her personal publicity drive and the acclaim of admiring philosophes, the newly ennobled Baron Dimsdale also found himself a household name. His *Present Method* treatise, published two years before and now in even greater demand, had already brought him professional prominence. His new noble title, which he used everywhere his name was mentioned, ensured no one could forget his links with Russia. It was as 'Baron Dimsdale' that he drew up a bond paying his fifty-two-shilling annual subscription to the Royal Society, to which he was elected on 11 May 1769, shortly after his return from St Petersburg. Fothergill, Quaker networker extraordinaire, was one of three proposers recommending him to the illustrious scientific institution, which had played such a central role in the evaluation and acceptance of inoculation in Britain four decades before.[4]

Thomas's Russian title also added a touch of grandeur to a new private bank he added to his portfolio of interests. Already a member of the partnership Dimsdale, Archer and Byde, he was one of two partners who broke away in 1774 and reformed as Staples, Baron Dimsdale, Son & Co.[5]

Banking never won Thomas's heart. Though the family firm would continue for more than a century, guided by his sons and their descendants, he retired from personal involvement in the new business after only two years. The pillars of his life remained just as they had always been: the practice of medicine, and – driven by the Quaker upbringing that still shaped his character and network of friendships – the quest for social reform. He might be loaded down with Russian gold, but he was soon back at work at his inoculation house beside his Hertford home, and continued to conduct the village-wide general inoculations he had so enthusiastically recommended to Catherine. His experiences, and reports he gathered from fellow physicians inoculating as far afield as Leeds and Chester, fed into a new treatise that would focus less on the practice of safe inoculation and more on how to extend its benefits to the poor without risking lives through infection.

Just as he had done before going to St Petersburg, he combined his concern for the poorest patients with lucrative treatment of the wealthiest. His list of aristocratic clients, keen to be attended by the Empress of Russia's personal physician, grew longer than ever. Even the supremely well-connected Dorothy Bentinck, Duchess of Portland, found Thomas was too busy to inoculate her three children at his countryside hospital. She wrote to her husband William, 3rd Duke of Portland and future Prime Minister: 'Baron Dimsdale was with me yesterday morning, he thought it a very proper time to inoculate the children but had so many engagements in London that it would be out of his power to do it in Hertfordshire as he wished and therefore advised me to let it be done directly, which it was.'[6]

Thomas had celebrity status, but he did not forget the connections that were the source of his fame. As his travelling companion Stratford Canning had observed, he looked back on his time in Russia with true happiness. From the moment he returned to Hertfordshire, he maintained close relationships with Catherine, Paul and others he had met during his visit that would last to the end of his life.

Thomas had built a warm bond with the fatherless Grand Duke in Russia as they shared meals and discussed the boy's health. Both were determined to keep up their connection. In the few months after his homecoming, the physician wrote twice to Paul, and sent him a pack of hounds – coveted by Anglophile Russians – and a fountain. A water feature might have seemed an unusual present for a teenager, but the boy thanked him effusively for both gifts: 'The one and the other have caused me such pleasure, and I send you my thanks.'[7] Paul, kept at arm's length by his mother, felt great affection for the doctor, who had spent so much time in his company before and during his inoculation. 'The two letters that you have written me have given me much satisfaction, since they come from a person whom I esteem and to whom I owe in part of the safety of my life. Also be persuaded that my gratitude is so great that I cannot find suitable terms in which to express it, but my heart is full of it.'

The inoculation had done more than protect him from smallpox: it had 'completely changed' his whole constitution, he told Thomas. 'I have more appetite, I sleep better, I can stand more fatigue and, what to me is of even greater consequence, I no longer have such frequent indispositions.'

Paul's thanks were just as heartfelt over six years later, when he readily agreed to have details of his inoculation published in Thomas's next treatise. 'I am not more certain of anything than that my cure is a proof of your competence and the goodness of your method. I pray you be persuaded that I am never ungrateful of your consideration, and I shall always remember the service that you have rendered me.'[8] He excitedly shared more good news with the physician: his wife, the Grand Duchess Natalia Alexeyevna, was about to be delivered of their first child. Tragically, both mother and baby were to die in childbirth a few weeks afterwards.

The perils of birth and infancy prompted an emotional letter to Thomas from Count Vladimir Orlov, the youngest of the five Orlov brothers and president of the Russian Academy of Sciences, who described his own wife's desperate but unsuccessful attempts to breastfeed their newborn baby. After two weeks, her severe mastitis led to fever and an abscess in the breast, which was cut open on the advice of Dr Cruse – one of the court physicians who had refused to be involved in the Grand Duke's inoculation – to release infected matter and relieve her pain. 'I confess to you that I have been very disturbed,' wrote Orlov. 'I do not know how to describe to you how much she has suffered.'[9] Trusting Thomas far more than doctors at Court after spending time with him at Tsarskoe Selo, he begged for his advice on 'what is done in England by people of commonsense in having their robust children'.

You will oblige me if you can communicate to me what ought to be done for a mother who wishes to feed her babies, to prevent accidents which may befall, but I could wish such regulations had already been practised. Tell me further if my wife will be fit to nourish in future although she has not been able to this time . . . The confidence that I have in your person encourages me to charge you with so many requests.

Thomas's role as long-distance child health specialist for the Orlovs continued. As the couple's family grew, the English doctor provided medical recipes and advised on the best age and time of year to inoculate their children. 'I will not fail, Monsieur, to instruct you of the success of the inoculation as soon as I can,' the young father promised.[10] 'We are filled with your memory, for all the good that we owe you.'[11]

It was Vladimir Orlov who provided Thomas with copies of the papers on inoculation he had written in St Petersburg on Catherine's instruction, published by her in Russian but not yet available in English. The doctor wrote in elaborate French to the Empress, flattering her for her decisive victories over the Turks (but expressing hopes she would now 'grant them peace') and requesting the right to have the tracts translated and to dedicate their English publication 'to Your Imperial Majesty as my very great and generous Patroness and the most illustrious personage of this century'.[12] Within a few weeks, a reply was delivered to Hertford, stamped with the Imperial seal and signed 'Caterine' in a confident hand. Inoculation was flourishing and already embedded among the nobility in Russia, the Empress wrote, adding a warm tribute to her physician: 'I shall never forget the care you gave me, and the anxieties you had during the time following my inoculation and that of my son, from which however all three of us very happily pulled through, by the grace of heaven.'[13] She encouraged Thomas to tell the story: 'Knowing your integrity and your love of veracity, I am persuaded that the book you wish to publish and that you wish to dedicate to me, will be written appropriately . . . As I do not doubt that your observations contribute to the advantage of the public, I encourage you to give them to them.'

Catherine, back to her workaholic habits as she oversaw the long war with Turkey and continuing domestic reform, did not always reply to Thomas in person. Baron Cherkasov sent thanks on her behalf for a gift from the doctor sent not long after his return to England: an Italian greyhound called Sir Thomas Anderson. The miniature dog, with its beseeching, expressive face and need for constant human interaction, was an instant hit with the Empress, becoming an inseparable companion. When Thomas sent a second greyhound, Lady Anderson, in 1776, the pair bred and produced an extended family of 115 descendants, including the mischievous Zemira, the most beloved of all Catherine's dogs, who slept beside her bed and left muddy paw prints on her letters. A 1794 portrait of the Empress by Vladimir Borovikovsky showed her strolling in the park at Tsarskoe Selo with Zemira at her feet, gazing appealingly at his mistress, though the little greyhound had died nine years before.[14]

Her dogs' devotion matched Catherine's love of adoration, but she remained cheerfully unsentimental in her daily dealings with people, especially when preoccupied by war. When Thomas became ill with kidney stones, she sent her best wishes via Dr John Rogerson, a Scottish physician at Court. Rogerson, sending his friend court gossip and a gift of Siberian pine seeds,[15] passed on her bracing comment: 'When he [Thomas] hears of our successes and of the hearty drubbings I have given the Turks I am sure he will rejoice with so much sincerity as it will greatly contribute to the re-establishment of his health.'[16]

The Empress was less sympathetic in her response to the death from smallpox of the French King Louis XV. In France, most people – including the royal family – still resisted inoculation, despite the continued advocacy of Voltaire and many of his fellow intellectuals. In the *Encyclopédie*, Diderot had described the practice as 'the most wonderful discovery yet made in medicine for the conservation of lives', while the article on 'Inoculation' predicted that, despite its central role in the culture war between superstition and reason, it would eventually be accepted in France: 'Let us not degrade ourselves to the point of despairing of the progress of human reason; it proceeds slowly: ignorance, superstition, prejudice, fanaticism, and a lack of regard for the public good will slow its march and they will fight us at every step. But after ages of struggle, we will finally have our moment of triumph.'[17]

French supporters of inoculation hailed Catherine's example. *L'Inoculation*, a heroic poem published in 1773 by the Catholic priest Abbé Roman, was dedicated to the Empress 'whose courage Europe admires', painting her as even braver than the Habsburg empress Maria Theresa in Vienna because she had personally undergone the operation. Reassuring his sensitive readers he had not used the term 'smallpox' in the verse as it was too upsetting, the poet flattered:

No less sensitive than her [Maria Theresa], and much more
  courageous
You did it on yourself, and you repeated it
On this son, the only hope of your vast States.

By this precious gift, you return to your Crown
This crowd of humans that war harvests,
And your happy Subjects will owe you all at once
Day, liberty, all the arts, and laws.[18]

The 64-year-old King of France, always resistant to inoculation, eventually paid the price. In late April 1774, he felt the first headache and fever that would develop into a case of smallpox so brutal his body emitted a fetid stench and his face became swollen and darkened like a bronze mask. His panicking flock of doctors drained off four large basinfuls of blood, which unsurprisingly did not save him. He died at Versailles on 19 May, in the early hours of the morning.[19] Louis was the fifth reigning European monarch killed by smallpox in the eighteenth century.[20] His rotting corpse was hurriedly placed in a double lead coffin, covered with spices, vinegar, lime and wine and transported to the crypt at St Denis.

Fifty people at the French court went on to contract smallpox; ten of them died. The king's grandson and heir, nineteen-year-old Louis XVI, was sent into quarantine for the first nine days of his reign, then again from 18 June when he and his two younger brothers were all successfully inoculated.

Catherine's reaction was uncompromising. 'It is shameful for a King of France living in the eighteenth century to die of smallpox,' she wrote bluntly to the Encyclopédiste Friedrich Grimm, adding that she had sent advice to the new monarch to follow her example and have himself inoculated by Thomas.[21] The King's death gave her a fresh opportunity to express her general contempt for doctors: 'these charlatans always do more harm than good: witness Louis XV who had ten of them around him and who is dead anyway, though I imagine that to die at their hands that was nine too many.'

While the King of France died of smallpox, the King of England followed family tradition and continued to trust inoculation. Unlike Catherine, George III did not actively campaign for widespread adoption of the procedure, but he and Queen Charlotte had already begun having their growing brood of children inoculated. Then, in July 1774, just weeks after the death of Louis XV, the King insisted on it publicly for an individual outside his own family. The circumstances were extraordinary, and the inoculator he chose was the doctor who had recently 'made such a noise in the world': Thomas Dimsdale.

The high-profile patient arrived in England on 14 July aboard HMS *Adventure*, a ship accompanying Captain James Cook of HMS *Resolution* on his second Pacific voyage. The passenger was nicknamed Jack by his shipmates, but his real name was Omai, or Mai.[22] Aged around twenty-two, he had been born on the Polynesian island of Raiatea but had fled to nearby Tahiti after his father was killed and the family's land taken. It was in Tahiti that Cook and Tobias Furneaux, captain of the *Adventure*, agreed to Omai's request to join them on their return journey to Britain, where the young man reportedly hoped to acquire the skills and perhaps the guns to avenge the death of his father.

For the British explorers, on a mission to discover and lay claim to the lands and resources of the South Seas, Omai, with his unfamiliar language, flowing dark hair and tattooed hands and body, represented a living specimen to add to their extensive botanical and animal collections. Their hazardous expeditions were driven by territorial ambitions and scientific curiosity, but also a desire to discover live evidence of the origins of human civilisation: peoples untouched by European progress and Christian faith. They carried with them their embedded cultural assumptions of superiority and the right to dominate, but the voyagers – and those back at home who read and interpreted their accounts – nevertheless wrestled with conflicting perceptions. The people they found were simultaneously primitive 'savages', ignorant of the glories of civilised society, and symbols of an unsullied Arcadian existence, who lived close to nature with none of the complexity and questionable values that same modern society embodied. Jean-Jacques Rousseau, the Genevan political philosopher, argued that individuals in a state of nature embodied peacefulness and equality, while civilisation had made man a slave to unnatural wants. The idealised literary representative of such uncorrupted communities was the Noble Savage, whose 'natural' unspoiled freedom was used by social critics to hold up a satirical mirror to Western manners and vices.[23]

In Omai, as with three previous South Sea Islanders who embarked from Tahiti on the ships of European adventurers, Western observers saw the mythical noble savage brought to life. In 1769, the French explorer Louis Antoine de Bougainville had brought thirty-year-old Aoutourou, brother of a Tahitian chief, to Paris, where his brief novelty among the intellectual elite had quickly worn off when he failed to learn French. He had been sent back home after a year, only to die of smallpox en route on the island of Réunion. Meanwhile the naturalist Joseph Banks,[24] travelling on the first Cook expedition to the Pacific aboard HMS *Endeavour*, had persuaded his reluctant captain to permit him to bring back to Britain two other islanders: Tupia, a priest who had escaped Raiatea with Omai, and his servant boy Tayeto.[25] 'I do not know why I may not keep him as a curiosity,' Banks wrote of Tupia, 'as well as some of my neighbours do lions and tigers at a larger expense than he will ever put me to.'[26] Leaving Tahiti in June 1769, the English crew stopped to repair their ship at Batavia in the Dutch East Indies, a port notorious for its tropical diseases. Again, the stopover proved fatal: Tupia and Tayeto, the two Tahitians who were cheaper to keep than animals, fell ill and died within days of one another.

Omai, disembarking from the *Adventure* at Portsmouth, was the first Pacific Islander to reach British shores safely. He would quickly become a nationwide celebrity. Banks, who had asked Captain Furneaux to bring him another Tahitian to observe, took the new arrival to stay with him at his home in New Burlington Street, London. Omai remembered the naturalist well from the first Cook expedition to Tahiti, and was also reunited with Dr Daniel Solander, the eminent Swedish botanist who had also been on the *Endeavour* voyage. Three days later, on 17 July, the two scientists took him to Kew for an audience with the King and Queen.

The newspapers were fascinated by the visitor from the New World, and reported the encounter in colourful but unreliable detail. Dressed in a maroon velvet coat, grey satin knee breeches and a white silk waistcoat, a fashionable European outfit quickly run up for him in London, Omai was alleged to have followed an elegant low bow with a nervous greeting in his shaky English that approximated George's name: 'Howdo King Tosh!' The King, shy and rather awkward himself, presented his guest with a ceremonial sword, granted him an allowance for the duration of his stay (to be administered by Banks) and promised he would be returned to his home at the end of his visit. Finally, he issued an order: Omai should be taken immediately to Hertford to be inoculated against smallpox by Baron Dimsdale.

George III, familiar with the risks of smallpox and the benefits of inoculation, had good reason to seek to protect the young South Sea Islander. In December 1772, a group of five Inuit had been brought to Britain from Labrador by the naturalist and explorer George Cartwright. The party of two couples, one with a little daughter, Ickeuna, had been presented at Court. They had received regular visits from Banks, Solander and other curious observers, and were put on display to an eager paying public. Then, as they began their voyage home from Plymouth, tragedy struck: all five fell ill of smallpox. Despite efforts to treat them, all but one died.[27] The child, Ickeuna, was wrapped in deer skin and buried with her jewellery and sealskin dress on the shore of Plymouth Sound.[28]

The risks to Omai, unprotected like all aboriginal peoples by any immunity to Western diseases, were clear. The day after the royal audience, Banks, Solander and Thomas Andrews, the *Adventure*'s doctor who spoke Tahitian, brought him to Thomas at Port Hill House.

Numerous accounts of Omai and his appearance and behaviour were written during his stay in Britain, in private letters and diaries and in multiple press reports. Some provided factual details of his activities, recording his dinners with members of the Royal Society, a 'grand oratorio' performed in his honour, and visits to country houses and the University of Cambridge. Others adopted a tone of patronising amusement, claiming the visitor had feared the King would eat him and that, when invited to sit, he had thrown himself down on a sofa. 'It was with some difficulty he could be taught the use of a chair, though he leaned against the back of one gracefully enough,' commented one newspaper. 'In respect to mental qualifications, he seems to possess scarcely any, all his observations leading to immediate corporeal gratifications.'[29]

King George III.

Thomas's version of Omai, drawn from his personal experience and written down apparently for his own records, was very different.[30] While he scrutinised his guest with a scientist's curiosity and reflected on his adaptation to the habits of polite English society, he also tried – perhaps more than anyone else Omai encountered – to see through the eyes of a visitor from a distant, unimaginable land. He quickly discovered that the prospect of inoculation had deeply alarmed the young man. 'He seemed at first much shocked at finding the first welcome on a spot where he was to spend pleasures innumerable was that he must pass through a loathsome dangerous disease.' Reassured that inoculation was 'what all the wise and great submitted to', Omai gave his consent for the procedure. But his fears were heightened when he witnessed the funeral of a child in a nearby churchyard, which also brought back memories of his own father's death. Noticing his apprehension, Thomas tried to ease it, suggesting to Banks, Solander and Andrews that he find some other patients to be inoculated at the same time. Omai jumped at the idea, and the physician recruited three local poor children of sixteen, seven and two to prove all age groups were happy to undergo the procedure.

All four were treated together, and Omai became the first person of colour known to have been inoculated in Britain.[31] He 'very willingly complied with taking all necessary medicines', but once fever set in and the smallpox pustules appeared he became 'much dejected', lying in bed with his face covered by a sheet and predicting he was going to die. He only got up, despite his very real fears, when Solander accused him of breaking his solemn promise to trust his friends. Despite suffering an unusually severe case of the inoculated disease, with some seventy pustules on his face and more in his throat, he soon recovered.

In all, Omai stayed a month with the Dimsdales, building a bond that – like the physician's connection with Catherine – moved beyond the relationship of doctor and patient. Thomas found him 'perpetually amused with the novelty of every thing he saw and unwilling to leave my family, where on account of his singularities and general good behaviour he was a welcome guest'. As he had done with the Empress, the physician described his patient's physique: 'about five feet eleven inches high, genteel in shape being rather thin tho not weakly and on all occasions very active'. He took note of the young man's reactions and listened when he expressed an opinion. Omai was fascinated by farm animals, inventing imaginative ways to name the unfamiliar creatures using his limited English vocabulary, had a great appetite and asked about 'every tree, plant and flower' in the garden at Port Hill House. If he had his own garden, he told his host, he would reject all ornamental plants and grow only those that produced food.

Like many of his contemporaries, Thomas observed Omai as a scientific subject, measuring him against the norms of 'civilised' behaviour. But, just as he had challenged contemporary accounts of Russians, he found his own experience did not tally with common prejudices. He wrote:

> As he came to us immediately after his arrival we had an opportunity of forming an opinion of his natural behaviour and temper, both were very different from any savage I ever read of, for all others have been remarked for a very rude and indelicate manner of conducting themselves, whereas Omiah [sic] who had seen no other persons than the officers and sailors on board the ship from whom one would not expect much improvement, was at once all politeness and civility, which was remarkable in his whole conduct. He entered a room with a good grace, paid a decent attention to everyone, but always addressed himself first to the ladies, if there were any, to whom he was perfectly polite, which I esteem a singular mark of good breeding. In general, during the whole of his visit, his conduct was unexceptionable.

After the inoculation, for which Thomas was paid twenty guineas, Banks and his companions took Omai back to London. Invitations flooded in to attend the fashionable salons and societies of the capital, where the elite could view him at close quarters. Personable, polite and quick to pick up the carefully calibrated manners he was exposed to, Omai was a popular guest. 'Everybody admired at the savage's good breeding,' wrote the society hostess Hester Thrale.[32]

The Man from Otaheite, as the newspapers dubbed him, was painted by Sir Joshua Reynolds, pre-eminent portrait painter of the day, in full-length aristocratic pose wearing flowing robes and a turban. Another painting by William Parry portrayed him under scientific scrutiny by Banks and Solander, his outward gaze at the viewer granting him a dignified humanity. Placing a 'native' on an equal footing to Europeans was beyond contemplation for most, including the writer Samuel Johnson, a critic of Cook's voyages of discovery who insisted 'one set of savages is much like another.'[33] Johnson met Omai and was struck by 'the elegance of his behaviour', an impression he felt forced to justify: 'He had passed his time, while in England, only in the best company, so that all he had acquired of our manners was genteel. As proof of this ... Lord Mulgrave and he dined one day at Streatham; they sat with their backs to the light fronting me, so that I could not see distinctly and there was so little of the savage in Omai, that I was afraid to speak to either lest I should mistake one for the other.'[34]

It was no wonder that when Omai met Thomas again at a Royal Society dinner, he expressed his joy at seeing him and asked to stay with him again at Hertford. By now, the Dimsdales found, he had become proficient in the leisure pursuits of successive affluent hosts: he played cards well and usually won, could 'use a gun dextrously', had taught himself to skate, and was an accomplished and fearless rider who 'took the most dangerous leaps without fear'. He had also improved his skills at chess, a game he had been taught by sailors on the *Adventure* during the long voyage to England. On a visit to the home of Lord Sandwich, first Lord of the Admiralty and co-sponsor, with Banks, of his stay in Britain, Omai's chess abilities were questioned by a sceptical fellow guest. The gentleman was persuaded to pit his own skills against the islander, Thomas recorded, and duly won three games in succession. Pushing aside the board, the man complained: 'It is extraordinary enough that you can have instructed this poor ignorant creature so far that he knows the pieces and the moves, but I am tired with playing with him, you see he knows nothing of the game.' Omai took his sleeve and urged him to play once more. He sat down at the board and easily took four games in a row as onlookers jeered his opponent. 'The superiority of Omai was confessed,' wrote Thomas, 'who then told his antagonist that he only lost the first games to discover his mode of play and now he would beat him as long as he pleased to play.'

Thomas did not set out to idealise Omai or look for signs of 'nobility'; he simply took the trouble to get to know the man he had protected from smallpox. Over his second, six-week-long stay, he recognised that his guest's trouble in pronouncing many English consonants and his rather 'foolish laugh' prejudiced others against him, when in fact he had 'great natural politeness and generosity'. The doctor identified the hypocrisy surrounding the ill-defined experiment on the Man from Otaheite. 'It was rather vexatious to me to hear one wish he had been instructed in agriculture, others in this or that trade, and although perhaps they hardly knew any one thing well themselves, yet it was expected the poor man should acquire a variety in a little time.' Nevertheless, Omai was happy at the Dimsdales', often comparing England so favourably with his home country that Thomas once asked him if he would prefer to stay permanently. The young man said no, explaining poignantly, 'I have relations and friends at Otaheita that love me and there I am somebody. Here I am nobody.'

In June 1776, almost two years after arriving in Britain, Omai set sail for the South Pacific on Cook's third expedition. He arrived the following year at Huahine, not far from his original home island, where his shipmates built him a European-style house and presented him with livestock, poultry, seeds, guns, globes and other items valuable in Britain, together with a haphazard array of gifts including a puppet show, a barrel organ, a suit of armour (which he wore to go ashore) and – from Banks – an electrical machine.[35] For many critics, the absurd collection raised troubling questions over the shortcomings of Britain's culture and its ambitions of imperial dominance. The poet William Cowper, in his 1785 poem *The Task*, imagined Omai stranded between worlds, wistfully longing for news of a corrupted England:

> . . . gentle savage! whom no love of thee
> Or thine, but curiosity perhaps,
> Or else vain-glory, prompted us to draw

Forth from thy native bowers, to show thee here
With what superior skill we can abuse
The gifts of Providence, and squander life.

Cook sailed away on his doomed final voyage, and Omai, the one-man screen on to which the British elite had projected its arrogance and its insecurities, was left among his new possessions to remake his island life after five years' absence.

Omai never recovered the lands stolen from his family on Raiatea. When later sailors dropped anchor at Huahine, they were told he had become ill and died in 1780, still in his twenties.

Thomas had inoculated an Empress and been personally commissioned by the King of England, but at heart he was a reformer. In 1776, he published a new treatise, *Thoughts on General and Partial Inoculations*, setting out proposals to extend smallpox inoculation to the poor, and dedicated it to 'the Legislature of Great Britain'. His campaign would thrust him back into the limelight, but also see him clash with fellow public health advocates over the safest way to give wide access to the preventative treatment.

By now, medical debates over how to perform the procedure were settled. In experienced hands, the revised method developed by the Sutton family and promoted by Thomas was highly reliable, and far safer than risking natural smallpox. The wealthy had been early adopters, and the middle classes and those on modest incomes had followed as the inoculation process became cheaper, less oner-ous and more widely available. In 1772, the winner of the Oxford University poetry prize was William Lipscomb's 'On the Beneficial Effects of Inoculation', which celebrated the technology for protect-ing 'the sacred beauties of Britannia's isle'.[36] The private letters of affluent families routinely contained reports of children's inocula-tions, and the Sutton family and their copycat practitioners contin-ued to turn handsome profits.

For the poor, however, the costs were still too high. Most remained suspicious, at least until an epidemic threatened. Despite the great success of inoculation, wrote the retired Essex doctor Benjamin Pugh in frustration in 1779, 'it is wonderful how it has been neglected by the common people for the last seven or eight years. It seems as much forgot in many parts of this kingdom as though it had never been known, until the natural small-pox comes with its usual train of malignant disorders, and awakens them out of their lethargy.'[37] The extreme infectiousness of smallpox meant no one of any age was safe unless inoculated, Pugh argued, but the full benefit of inoculation would only be felt when the practice was 'made general'. He proposed a law obliging church wardens to oversee the inoculation of all poor children, with hefty sanctions for parents who refused.

> Would not this be a means of diffusing the blessings of this discovery to its full extent? In this law, those who should, through obstinacy, singularity, or, as they might pretend, scruples of conscience, oppose its injunctions, should be made subject to some incapacity such, for instance, as being rendered incapable of voting at elections, or being admitted into provident societies for the benefit of themselves or families.

There would be many advantages besides saving lives, he suggested, including the fact that 'nations abroad would trade with Englishmen with more freedom when the fear of being surprised by this dreadful disease was removed'.

The difficulty of extending inoculation to the poorest in society was compounded by a second problem: contagion. Among informed doctors, old ideas of an 'innate seed' of smallpox within each individual were long gone: Thomas and others were increasingly clear that the disease spread between people through the air or on contaminated surfaces. Newly inoculated individuals could pass on the virus while infectious as easily as those with the natural disease. The philanthropist Jonas Hanway, railing at the 'carelessness' of patients and practitioners who spread infection and compromised the 'blessing' of inoculation, called for government regulation.[38] He proposed a system of official certificates – a form of inoculation passport – confirming an individual had been inoculated or had had natural smallpox, to be required for admission to a workhouse or employment as a servant or apprentice. To reduce the

spread of infection, isolated houses should be set aside for inoculation and medical personnel should have 'changes of garments,
peculiarly devoted to this business'.

Thomas's treatise set out his own proposals to reconcile the
tension between the undoubted benefit of inoculation to individuals and the potential risks posed by contagion to the community. In
small towns and villages, such as those near his own home, general
inoculations in which everyone was treated at once had already
been shown to be highly effective. Even in larger towns, such as
Hertford, his own experience of conducting three community-wide
inoculations a few years apart had meant fewer than six people had
died of smallpox in ten years – an astonishingly low number. He
rejected forcing people to accept inoculation, remembering
Catherine's words on the power of persuasion that had so struck
him at Tsarskoe Selo. Instead, he called for legislation to oblige each
parish to 'offer inoculation to all their poor who should be willing
to admit of it' every five years.[39] To ensure poor patients could
isolate themselves, they and their families should be given financial
support during the infectious period, he proposed, and penny-
pinching parish authorities – often employing amateur inoculators
such as blacksmiths to save money – should be obliged to use qualified practitioners (his favourite theme) and not 'trifle with the lives
of their indigent fellow creatures'.[40]

The benefits of general inoculations in rural communities and
towns were clear, but urban areas – and especially London – were a
different matter. In the sprawling, crowded metropolis of some
750,000 people, there was no possibility of inoculating all the poorest
inhabitants at once, even if their wariness of the procedure could be
overcome.[41] Virtually no residential care was available for those
unable to pay: aside from the Foundling Hospital, the London
Smallpox Hospital, with its very limited capacity and policy of admit-
ting no children under seven, was the only provider of free treatment.
To tackle the problem, reformist physicians – many of them Quakers
and fellow dissenters – proposed an alternative approach: home
inoculation. In 1775, the Quaker physician John Coakley Lettsom,
fresh from emancipating the fifty enslaved men and women he had
inherited on his father's Virgin Islands estate, formed a Society for the

Inoculation of the Poor in their own Homes. Two years later, the organisation established a Dispensary for General Inoculation, offering free outpatient treatment to poor Londoners. Dr John Watkinson, a founder of the society with Lettsom, published a pamphlet promoting the plan to widen access to the procedure on both moral and political grounds: 'As the strength of a nation is, in a great measure, proportionate to the number of its inhabitants, every attempt to increase population by preserving life, has a just claim to regard both of patriotism and humanity.'[42] In the practice of inoculation, Watkinson declared majestically, 'we see human ingenuity opposing itself to the ravages of a dreadful disease, and the medical art triumphing, as it were, over the powers of death.'

Thomas shared the sentiment, if not the dramatic language, but he disagreed fundamentally over the methods. When the organisers of the dispensary invited him to a tavern and asked for his endorsement, he refused to get involved.[43] Home and dispensary inoculation would be dangerously counter-productive, he warned: it would protect a few but expose many to contagion they might have otherwise escaped. In the capital, Thomas wrote, the poor lived 'in close alleys, courts and lanes, generally cold, dirty and in great want of necessaries, even of bedding itself . . . there are frequently several families under one roof.' In such miserable, crowded conditions, where both men and women went out to work to feed their families, there was no hope of inoculated patients isolating themselves. Again, he turned to statistics to prove his point, updating James Jurin's table drawn from the London Bills of Mortality to show that, in the eight years since he had last analysed the figures while in Russia, the proportion of smallpox fatalities had increased from a steady one in eight of all deaths in the capital to one in six. Around two thousand people died from the disease annually in London, and almost four thousand in epidemic years.[44] The rise, he argued, was down to partial inoculations of the poor, which had saved some lives at the expense of many others. 'Inoculation has been on the whole rather hurtful than advantageous to the city of London . . . The loss has fallen principally among those who are not the least useful members of the community, viz. on young persons, the offspring of inferior trades-people, and the labouring poor.'

Dr John Coakley Lettsom.

To try to reconcile the conflicting interests of individuals and community, Thomas had his own proposal. He suggested raising money by subscription to extend the smallpox hospital at St Pancras, walling in its four acres of grounds and inviting poor Londoners to be inoculated there in safe isolation. Acknowledging that 'amongst the lower classes of people in the metropolis, as well as in many other places, the voice of the generality is against inoculation', he proposed offering an inducement: everyone treated would after-wards receive new clothes – 'two new shirts or shifts' – and half a crown. He concluded with an appeal for government backing as an act of patriotism: 'As we are the first European nation who received and encouraged inoculation, we may also have the honour of being the first who have generously diffused the benefit of it to the community at large; and transmitted it to posterity.'

Despite the honourable intentions of both sides, the debate over protecting the urban poor descended into a heated and sometimes abusive public dispute. The Leiden-educated Irish physician William Black, part of the rising new generation of campaigning doctors, was one of many to argue that the mortality tables that had played such an important early role in showing the benefits of inoc-ulation were too crude to take account of more complex factors such as population expansion and the ebb and flow of epidemic disease. He launched a fierce attack on Thomas, ridiculing his grand Russian titles and accusing him of personally contributing to conta-gion by inoculating 'all rich persons in London and its vicinity', who were just as capable of spreading the virus as the poor. He had homed in on Thomas's Achilles heel: his weakness for high-paying clients. Comparing the Baron to a hypocritical clergyman who railed against gambling as a pack of cards fell from his sleeve, Black roared: 'If he is serious in considering partial inoculation as injuri-ous to the community, it is highly criminal in him to be one of the most active instruments in their destruction.'[45]

Painted as a greedy and misguided hypocrite, Thomas stuck firmly to his beliefs, as he had always done. His long career had seen inoculation move from controversial experiment to widely accepted lifesaver. Now he was determined to protect the reputation of the procedure, which he was afraid could be irreparably damaged if it was seen as worsening the spread of smallpox. For Thomas, even one death caused by inoculation was too many; in Lettsom's view, the purist stance was leaving the poor unable to protect themselves. The pair exchanged arguments in an unedifying pamphlet war, in which the younger man satirised 'The Great Inoculator, who claimed an exclusive right to the theory and practice of inoculation'. 'Remarks' and 'replies' flew between the two physicians, who bizarrely allowed each other to correct their manuscripts before publication.[46] After initial interest, the public grew bored of the row. In 1779, the *Monthly Review* summed up Lettsom's latest intervention as, 'More personal altercation, of a very disagreeable kind. We sincerely wish this may be the last publication in this very unimportant and degrading squabble.'

After two years, the two men made peace, warned by Fothergill that their spat was damaging the dignity of their profession.[47] Their reputations were dented, but survived, as did their friendship, with its strong Quaker underpinning. There were other battles to fight, where they were on the same side. By 1788, both were subscribers to the influential new Society for the Purpose of Effecting the Abolition of the Slave Trade, nine of whose twelve founders were Quakers.[48] Parliament never answered Thomas's call to back hospital-based inoculation of the poor, and Lettsom's vision of widespread outpatient treatment was hampered by Londoners' continuing suspicion of the practice.

'There never was in my opinion since the origin of physick, a medical controversy agitated of more consequence to mankind,' Black wrote of the challenge of urban inoculation. 'It is not only a political, but also a great national question.' Extending protection against smallpox to the whole population would not be achieved by inoculation, although the practice was critical in preparing the ground for the next, revolutionary stage in the fight against the brutal virus. Thomas would live, just, to see the emergence of a new, transformative technology built entirely on the foundations he and others had laid: vaccination.

Catherine II at Tsarskoe Selo, by Vladimir Borovikovsky. The
Italian greyhound at her feet is Zemira, a descendant of the
two dogs given to the Empress by Thomas Dimsdale.

10

The Last Meeting

'I shall never forget that he has preserved myself, my son and
my grandchildren from the dreadful disease of smallpox'
Catherine the Great[1]

In mid-June 1781, fierce summer storms battered the English Channel.
For several days, the packet ship bound for Ostend sheltered from the
weather in Dover harbour, passengers impatient for a break in the
clouds. Among them was Baron Thomas Dimsdale, setting out aged
sixty-nine on his second – and last – journey to Russia.

The circumstances were very different from the physician's first
visit thirteen years before, though the mission was the same: inoculation. Thomas had treated Catherine and her son Paul, and their
trust in his abilities was absolute. They had kept in touch, exchanging gifts, letters and family news. When the time came to inoculate
the next generation in line to the Russian Imperial throne – Paul's
sons Alexander, three, and his two-year-old brother Constantine –
they called for the English doctor.

Undeterred by another 3,400-mile round trip, Thomas had
instantly accepted the invitation, rushing to finish his fourth and
final publication in order to answer the Empress's summons. The
weighty 249-page *Tracts on Inoculation* had been completed 'with
some haste', he confessed to readers importantly, 'on account of a
sudden obligation to attend the court of Russia a second time'.[2] In
reality, he was flattered and happy to go. His new volume, dedicated
to Catherine, repaid the compliment with the same loyalty he had
always shown, praising:

the distinguished fortitude with which your Imperial Majesty exposed your person to the early experiment of a practice, before little-known in Russia . . . Under the influence of examples so illustrious as those of your Majesty, and his Imperial Highness, the Grand Duke, the introduction of inoculation has been facilitated within your Majesty's Dominions, and will, I trust, considerably promote the strength and happiness of the Empire.

The book finally fulfilled Thomas's promise to publish in English all five of the tracts he had written in St Petersburg on the Empress's orders, together with his account of the anxieties, secrecy and triumphs of the visit.

Thomas felt the same campaigning zeal to extend the practice of inoculation as when he had last seen Catherine, but the intervening years had brought change to his steady life. After the ill-tempered public debates over how best to protect the urban poor from smallpox, he had retired from regular medical practice as his sight became blurred by cataracts (an operation in 1783 would restore his vision). For now, he peered at the world through glasses. In 1780, a year that also saw the death of his close friend Dr John Fothergill, he stood as MP for Hertford. Thomas's local popularity and professional reputation swept him to election victory, buoyed by the town's strong Quaker vote. Had he still been a member of the sect, he could not have sworn the oath of allegiance to the King – a requirement that effectively barred Quakers from Parliament. He carried the pacifist principles of his upbringing with him to Westminster, voting to end the long and bloody war with America and grant independence to the colonies once settled by his ancestors.[3] Otherwise, his preference for face-to-face conversation over public speaking meant he was, literally, rarely heard in the chamber. A report of his one recorded speech, on tax, noted that he 'spoke for some time, but in so low a tone, that we could not distinctly hear him'.[4] 'Oratory is not one of his talents,' conceded the *English Chronicle*, but predicted he would 'vote upon every subject from the unbiassed influence of his principles and conviction'.[5]

Thomas's personal life, too, had altered dramatically. His beloved wife Ann, mother of his seven children, had died on 9 March 1779 after a long and painful period of ill health, reminding her husband in her final hours of her only request: to be buried in the Quaker burial ground at nearby Bishop's Stortford, 'as near to where you are to lye as possible'. Her touching wish was granted, and Thomas, bereft, wrote shortly afterwards:

> I lived in matrimony with this most excellent woman more than 32 years & half and during that whole time we never had any difference or one real unkind word passed between us and not long before her death as well as several times in our lives we have mutually declared that each can truly say that we had not only lived with harmony but neither ever was made unhappy by the other.[6]

The deep loneliness of a second widowhood did not suit a man who had always sought the love and close companionship of married life. Just eight months later, on 3 November, Thomas married again. His third wife, Elizabeth Dimsdale, was the unmarried Quaker daughter of his cousin and fellow doctor Joseph Dimsdale, twenty years younger than himself at forty-seven but already a friend who wrote him cheerful letters from trips abroad and – like Catherine – shared his fondness for pet dogs. Perhaps conscious of his apparent haste to marry, he wrote after the wedding to her brother John: 'The desire I had to make sure of a companion for life of the person I esteemed the most of anyone in the World & the certainty of its being agreeable to my whole Family were my inducements & I hope as reasonable as a man at my Time of Life can give.'[7]

Elizabeth, now Baroness Dimsdale, proved the partner Thomas wished for. She was affectionate, a capable household manager who later wrote her own recipe book, and with an adventurous spirit that saw her join him in his travelling post-chaise for the long journey to Russia.[8] The couple, who brought along their dog, Fox,[9] and a supply of hot chocolate, were also accompanied by their German servant, Henry, and, in a separate carriage, by the Reverend John Glen King, the former English chaplain at St Petersburg whom Thomas had met on his first visit.[10] Departing at last from stormy Dover, the party weathered a rough crossing and severe sea sickness and headed east via Brussels, Cologne and Dresden before reaching Königsberg and picking up Thomas's previous route along the wild Baltic coast to Riga. Elizabeth, with a more inquisitive nature and sharper eye for cost and social hierarchy than her husband, recorded the trip in her journal.[11] The Baron's fame guaranteed them a gracious reception from a succession of dignitaries and noble households across northern Europe, but the long distances between were punctuated by stays at inns and post houses, often dirty and sometimes dangerous. At one stop, Thomas's best hat and the Rev. King's wig were stolen, prompting a scramble to find replacements; afterwards, the Dimsdales often slept in their carriage. Elizabeth gamely endured the dangers of the roads, once losing a clog as she sank up to her knees in quicksand. She felt alarmed only when the chaise was ferried perilously across wide rivers at night or was washed axle-deep by waves along the exposed sands of the Curish Haff. The route crossed borders newly drawn even since Thomas's previous visit, as an ascendant Russia and Prussia each encroached into Polish territory.[12]

At last, after seven weeks on the road, the party arrived at one o'clock in the afternoon on Wednesday 8 August in St Petersburg.[13] Elizabeth, like so many previous English visitors, was entranced. The city, developed and expanded under the Empress's rule, was

> a much finer place than I expected. On my entering it appeared very grand, as all the steeples and spires are covered with tin and brass, and some of them gilt, the sun shining full upon them made a very gay appearance. The palace is a prodigious fine building and a great many elegant houses are dispersed about the city . . . The view upon the bank of the River Neva exhibited the grandest liveliest scenes I ever beheld.

The Dimsdales were again given the luxurious house on the Millionnaya, equipped with a large English bed with crimson silk hangings and staffed by an English housekeeper, 'an exceeding good plain cook'. Baroness Dimsdale was gratified to discover her rank entitled her to a coach drawn by up to six horses. 'We have everything very elegant and handsome,' she wrote home.[14]

Two days after their arrival, Thomas set out with Dr Rogerson, Catherine's physician, to visit the Empress and the Grand Duke at Tsarskoe Selo, where they were escaping the rigid formalities of the court and the heat of the city. The bond between doctor and patients, forged in the tense drama of the first inoculations, remained as strong as ever. For the Empress, his arrival revived memories of her fever and dizziness and the long walks she had taken in the palace gardens to help her recovery. Paul, his childhood scarred by his father's death, recalled the care and affection he had received from Thomas as a teenager. Both received the physician 'very graciously . . . like an old friend', he reported to his wife. 'They said many kind obliging things, that his visit afforded them great pleasure.'

While the Empress's two grandsons were prepared for their inoculation, Elizabeth seized every opportunity to explore St Petersburg. Touring the Hermitage, the art gallery and private apartments added by Catherine to the Winter Palace, she admired the diamond-encrusted crown jewels and 'a very fine picture of the Empress as large as life dressed like a man in the uniform of the Guards'. The Eriksen equestrian portrait, commissioned as part of Catherine's image-making after seizing the throne, had been designed to represent her 'masculine' leadership qualities. Symbol had now been replaced with reality after Russia's victory over the Turks – bringing control of Crimea and access to the Black Sea – and westward expansion into Poland. The Empress's ambitious Legislative Commission had crumbled when her attention turned to war, but she had since modernised provincial governance and administration across her unwieldy dominions. She would shortly embark on educational reform and a new charter to clarify the status and anchoring role of the nobility. Age had not slowed her: her drive to build and to improve was stronger than ever.

Elizabeth's curious eye took in examples of Catherine's soft power: she admired the stunning art collection amassed by Great Britain's first Prime Minister, Sir Robert Walpole, snapped up from his debt-ridden grandson by the Empress at a bargain price. The 6,800-book library of Voltaire, Catherine's correspondent and admirer who had died three years previously, was also now installed in full in St Petersburg, complete with his annotated texts on inoculation. Workmen on the Neva embankment were putting the final touches to Falconet's imposing new equestrian statue of Peter the Great, designed to connect Catherine explicitly in the public mind with her reforming predecessor, the founder of the city.

Elizabeth was enchanted by her tours of the Russian capital's palaces and liberal showpieces such as the Smolny Institute of Noble Maidens, Europe's first public educational establishment for girls. But she also saw the brutal underside of Catherine's enlightened despotism. 'The peasants, that is to say, the greater part of the subjects, are in an abject state of slavery, and are reckoned the property of the nobles, and considerable people to whom they belong, as much as their horses or dogs,' Elizabeth recorded. She quizzed the Empress's gardener about his team of labourers, learning that 'some of the masters of these poor slaves who are cruel men, allow them so little that they appear almost starved, and not able to do a day's work.' Masters dictated all aspects of their enslaved workers' lives, taking their produce, dictating their marriage partners and exacting taxes for male children.

The Dimsdales spent time in St Petersburg with the British prison reformer John Howard, in Russia to investigate prisons and penal policy, who described witnessing a beating with a knout, a hardened leather thong attached to a scourge-like whip.[15] A flogging, sometimes involving hundreds of blows, was usually fatal. Elizabeth added to her journal an eyewitness report she was given by an acquaintance of the blood-soaked public execution in 1775 of Yemelyan Pugachev, the Cossack leader who claimed to be the deposed Emperor Peter III and led a violent popular insurrection. The rebel leader's head was severed and impaled on a spike (Catherine insisted on quick beheading rather than the living torture sought by the baying crowd); then his hands and feet were cut off and displayed to the mob. The horror and speed of the uprising and the 'blindness, stupidity, ignorance and superstition' of her subjects had shaken the Empress deeply, prompting her drive to reorganise and strengthen provincial government.

On a visit to the Kunstkamera, the museum established by Peter the Great on the Neva embankment opposite the Winter Palace,

Elizabeth was shown the original handwritten manuscript of the Empress's *Nakaz* or *Great Instruction*: the compilation of enlightened political thought she had published in 1767 to guide the creation of a new legal code in Russia. Carefully preserved in a bronze casket and displayed at meetings of the Academy of Sciences, it had become more talisman than reform handbook, though its influence would reverberate into the next century. Its vision of Russia as an educated, tolerant European state was underpinned by a premise Catherine would always adhere to as she led her growing empire: 'A society of citizens, as well as every thing else, requires a certain fixed order. There ought to be some to govern, and others to obey.'

On 27 August, the Dimsdales travelled by coach to Tsarskoe Selo, where Elizabeth was finally presented to the Empress at a rare private audience. Catherine's warmth and charm, as always, worked their magic. 'I bowed down to kiss her hand, then she stooped and kissed my cheek,' Elizabeth wrote. 'She is a very fine looking woman, not so tall as I am, and lustier, very fine expressive blue eyes, and a sweet sensible look, that altogether she is a very fine handsome person.' Since Thomas's last visit, Catherine had maintained her appetite both for lovers and for hard work. The Dimsdales dined with Prince Grigory Potemkin, the Empress's beloved 'twin soul', conqueror of the Turks and perhaps her secret husband, and admired the magnificent outfit of her latest favourite Alexander Lanskoy, 'a very handsome young man' of twenty-three.

Neither sex nor friendship affected Catherine's disciplined daily regimen. 'The Empress is an early riser and very often in the garden a little after six, she walks in leather shoes and several dogs were with her,' the admiring Baroness recorded. Returning to her apartments in the centre of the extravagant palace, she lit her own fire, washed off the previous night's rouge and drank strong hot coffee while she fed her dogs and began work. Thomas was summoned to join her walk before seven o'clock one morning, with the sun barely up. The palace gardens, landscaped in the English style, still delighted Catherine in their late summer beauty, though the famously terrifying roller coaster, the joy of her thrill-seeking younger years, had now been all but decommissioned. A specially constructed stone pyramid awaited the interment of Sir Thomas and Lady Anderson, the two elderly and much-loved Italian grey-hounds given to the Empress by Thomas.

The two little princes – 'beautiful children and extremely sensi-ble and clever', according to Elizabeth – were doted on by their grandmother. The Empress gave them clockwork toys in solid gold and silver, their own apartments, servants and carriage, and a regiment apiece of boy soldiers: 'she cannot refuse them anything they ask for.' Catherine had seen her own son and heir taken from her at birth to be brought up by the Empress Elizabeth. Now it was she who directed her grandsons' education and upbringing rather than their parents, Paul and his second wife Maria Fedorovna, whom he had married shortly after his first wife's death in child-birth. The boys had been named in preparation for rule: Alexander was destined to become Paul's successor on the throne of Russia while his younger brother Constantine was intended to govern a recreated Byzantine empire from Constantinople. The so-called 'Greek Project' was a dream that eluded even Catherine and Potemkin.

At fifty-two, the Empress managed her grandmotherly role with a characteristic mixture of loving indulgence and brisk rigour. The young boys should be addressed simply by their first names, with-out titles, she instructed their two English governesses, warning that 'Pride would come fast enough without encouraging it.' She had begun to write a series of stories, historical dissertations and other works specifically to be used for the princes' education, and her continuing 'Anglomania' prompted her to ask Thomas for information on 'exactly the mode of treatment observed in the nursery of the royal family of England'. On his return to Hertford, he duly sent her a detailed description of the royal nursery's routine, provided by its head superintendent Miss Cheveley.[16] The regimen turned out to be a no-nonsense round of early rising, a wash in 'quite cold' water, flannel undergarments, long hearty walks twice daily in the fresh air (up to five miles a day even for three- and four-year-olds) and a plain diet with no butter or sugar. 'This is their constant living, the regularity of which, with air and exercise, makes them the healthiest family in the world,' concluded Miss Cheveley.

Grand Dukes Alexander and Constantine, grandsons of
Catherine II. Portrait by Richard Brompton, 1781.

The health of Alexander and Constantine was not so well
managed. As he checked the boys' medical notes in preparation for
their inoculations, Thomas discovered to his alarm that Constantine
had endured thirty-six purges in one year. At their grandmother's
table, their doctors reported, they were allowed to fill up on fruit,
and they often asked for bread between lunch and dinner, all of

which made them picky and reluctant to finish a full meal. Thomas was honest with the Empress. He outlined his concerns in a letter, highlighting her tendency to indulge the boys and recommending a more regular diet. Catherine immediately promised to have the regimen 'strictly observed', but avoided accepting personal responsibility for the children's poor eating habits. Instead, she blamed bad nursing and the stuffy bedrooms insisted on by the Russian doctors she distrusted so much.

The princes were inoculated by Thomas on Friday 7 September. There was none of the secrecy and extreme tension surrounding the Empress's treatment, but the pressure on the physician remained great. 'Alexander had the disorder very full for inoculation, tho' not one alarming symptom ever appeared, the Baron was naturally anxious until it was all over,' Elizabeth wrote in her journal. The stress was worsened by panicking attendants dashing breathlessly from the Grand Duke's rooms to find Thomas, only to ask if Alexander could be allowed to eat an orange. The little boy felt very unwell before his smallpox pustules appeared. One day, sitting miserably on his nurse's knee, he called for his purse and asked that the gold roubles inside could be distributed to the Empress, the Dimsdales and his favourite servants.[17] It seemed 'so much like a legacy', Elizabeth recorded, 'that I was much affected'.

Constantine, more boisterous than his older brother, breezed through the procedure and soon both children had recovered. They were never in danger, Thomas wrote home to his doctor cousin, adding: 'I continue to receive very distinguished marks of favour from the Empress and Grand Duke and Duchess and have the honour to dine with one or the other almost every day.'[18] Paul and Maria, filled with relief and gratitude, showered the Dimsdales with gifts, including yet another diamond-set snuffbox in blue enamel and gold, together with a diamond locket enclosing locks of the princes' light brown hair. After Elizabeth admired the boys' clothing, she was presented with an intricately embroidered suit and bonnet belonging to each, one accented with shimmering gold thread and one in silver, and a baby frock of Alexander's.

With the operation safely over, the Grand Duke and Duchess prepared to set out on a year-long tour of Europe, leaving their little sons behind. Maria was distraught, weeping desperately and begging Thomas to write to her every day with news of the children. Elizabeth too was caught up in the outpouring of emotion affecting much of the court, but the Empress walked calmly in the garden, pointing out that the trip was entirely the couple's own choice and they had no need to leave until her daughter-in-law was happy to go. Thomas, dry-eyed but with his own memories of being parted from his family while previously in Russia, understood their distress. He sent the Grand Duke and Duchess regular updates and received many emotional letters of thanks from both parents. Maria, writing in her distinctive untamed hand, wrote: 'I congratulate you with all my heart and my husband and I repeat to you a thousand times our thanks, and the assurance of our eternal gratitude.'[19]

On 6 October, as the days quickly shortened and the evenings grew cold, the royal party returned from Tsarskoe Selo to St Petersburg. The Empress's coach was drawn by ten horses and the Dimsdales' by six, and there were eight hundred more in the accompanying cavalcade as they left the palace to the sound of cannons and trumpets. Inoculation in Russia was still firmly yoked to spectacle; royal children undergoing the procedure provided a fresh opportunity to influence by example. Huge crowds turned out to see the little princes, who sat alongside their grandmother, and cheer the successful inoculations. 'In the evening the city was illuminated and there were great rejoicings,' wrote Elizabeth. There were more celebrations at a court ball the following evening, and on 14 October, when the official court calendar resumed after the inoculations, the nobles of the capital assembled at the Winter Palace to offer their congratulations. Elizabeth was delighted to be ushered past them, having been granted the honour of another private audience with the Empress to say her goodbyes before leaving for England the following morning. Catherine received the physician and his wife for the last time while dressing for court, standing before a large mirror while she pinned her robe of white and silver tissue. 'I was informed I could not have more respect shown than in taking leave of me in this private manner,' gushed Baroness Dimsdale. 'The Empress upon my bowing to kiss her hand, kissed my cheek on first going into the room, said many civil polite things, and several times wished me a good journey, hoped I should get home well etc.' Catherine was courteous to a fault to his wife, but she spoke at length to Thomas, whose friendship and honest advice she had valued for so long. 'The Baron and she had a great deal of conversation,' wrote Elizabeth. The meeting was their last. Though they would continue their correspondence across the wide continent between Hertford and St Petersburg, the Empress and her English doctor would never see each other again.

That evening, as the Dimsdales prepared for departure, they received a handwritten note from the Empress, scribbled in response to Thomas's warnings about her grandchildren's diet. As always, he had spoken the truth to her: a quality she valued greatly, yet rarely found. His paper, she wrote in French, was 'a fresh proof of the same zeal and attachment for my person and my family which he has never failed to testify since I have had the satisfaction to know him. He may also be assured of my sincere gratitude. I shall never forget that he has preserved myself, my son and my grandchildren from the dreadful disease of the smallpox.'[20]

The Dimsdales arrived at Dover on the evening of 30 November 1781, their cold, uncomfortable journey interrupted only briefly when a stout, threatening man tried to halt their carriage near Riga. Declining to use the guns carried in the chaise, Thomas calmly fended him off by waving a large stick and 'advancing resolutely', despite being barely able to see: he had forgotten his spectacles in St Petersburg. A servant was sent back for them and the journey continued.

Safely home in Hertford, and reunited with his glasses, the physician could return to promoting the book he had raced to complete before leaving for Russia. *Tracts on Inoculation* contained the accumulated knowledge of some forty-five years as an inoculator, and reflected the giant strides made in the understanding of smallpox and its prevention during his lifetime. Inoculation, Thomas stated categorically, was now 'infallible' if carried out correctly, and the technique was 'universally known in England'.[21] He had slimmed down even further the simplified method he had outlined in his first treatise and employed on his first visit to Russia. The puncture of the skin was now so slight it could be performed on sleeping children without waking them, and he no longer prescribed any medical or dietary preparation at all for healthy patients, though he still used mercury purges and a plain diet after the operation and recommended adapting the regime for 'tender and delicate persons'. Inoculation had become increasingly standardised, as doctors treated the specific disease rather than tailoring their therapy to individual patients with their imagined fluctuating humours.

Thomas believed his expertise still mattered for optimal inoculation results, but physicians' early monopoly over the practice had long gone. Even he recognised that the poor were often being successfully treated by 'persons totally unacquainted with medicine'. With no regulation of the medical profession, itinerant inoculators of varying abilities could ply their trade, and many mothers carried out the procedure on their children without mishap.[22] Sometimes, amateurs succeeded where trained professionals did not. In Scotland, religious objections among the poor meant inoculation never became as well established as in England.[23] Nevertheless, a self-taught doctor nicknamed Johnnie Notions managed to immunise some three thousand people in the Shetland Islands over the last two decades of the eighteenth century using his home-devised version of the Suttonian method.

Sometimes, even in supposedly expert hands, inoculation failed. George III and Queen Charlotte lost their one-year-old son Alfred in 1782 and his four-year-old brother Octavius the following year after they were inoculated by the court doctors.[24] The heartbroken royal parents, both committed supporters of inoculation, attributed the deaths to 'Providence' and never lost faith in the procedure.[25] The King wrote from Kew to his son Prince William: 'It has pleased the all-wise Director of all things to put a period to the life of dear little Alfred, who certainly was as fine a child as ever was seen.' Grief at the child's death would haunt the monarch as he descended into mental illness. But the public reputation of inoculation, always guarded so carefully by Thomas, was by now too powerful to be shaken by the family tragedy.

Tracts on Inoculation also addressed the causes of smallpox. Thomas systematically demolished traditional arguments that the disease was generated by a miasma – 'an epidemic state of the air' – or existed as dormant 'seeds' within every individual. Strict quarantine and isolation of the sick in pest houses had been shown to prevent smallpox, proving to observant doctors that the virus could not 'self-generate'. He wrote: 'I therefore maintain that smallpox is a poison or (if it will please better) a disease of the contagious kind, communicated either from an atmosphere infected with the effluvia of persons sick of that distemper, or by contact with substances that retain the fomes of infection.'[26] Although he could not explain the mechanism of contagion, he was effectively describing germ theory, eighty years before it was demonstrated by Koch and Pasteur.

Throughout his book, Thomas returned to the touchstones of the enlightened eighteenth-century natural philosopher: 'observation and plain reasoning', as opposed to inherited theory. Experience and close enquiry had not only established that smallpox spread by contagion, it also revealed that inoculation acted faster on the body than the natural infection, meaning patients accidentally exposed to the virus could still avoid succumbing if treated quickly. The most terrifying disease of the age could be stopped in its tracks by human intervention, even after it had invaded the body. The intense focus on smallpox was leading doctors to ask further important questions: could the virus be weakened by diluting it or using only variolous matter from the mildest cases? How, they wondered, did it relate to other, apparently similar diseases such as chickenpox, or even animal diseases such as swinepox or cowpox? Edward Jenner's world-changing discovery was moving closer.

Thomas explored the mechanisms of inoculation, but by now his priority was action. The technology existed and it worked; the challenge was to extend it throughout society. The wealthy had in general adopted the practice, and the middle class could now afford it, he wrote. 'The poor, whose situation renders them unable to bear expense, and who, if neglected, would be the greatest sufferers, have been much the objects of my attention; and I have endeavoured to afford them every assistance in my power.'[27] He had campaigned publicly on the risks of infection if inoculated people failed to isolate. Now he pressed again for a national programme of controlled general inoculations in which everyone in a community would be treated at once, with anyone declining the operation staying safely out of the way. There was still no state backing or funding for the practice, but campaigning doctors were beginning to instigate free outpatient inoculation programmes for the poor even in larger towns and cities, run by the emerging dispensaries and supported by charitable donations. 'The medical gentlemen of the cities of Chester, Bath and the populous town of Leeds, with several others, are of the number,' Thomas noted, urging other cities – including London – to learn from the successful, carefully controlled methods. Doctors were treating patients with 'due care', providing free medicine and food, instructing them to comply with isolation rules to prevent infection and rewarding those who could prove they had obeyed.

The scheme to inoculate the poor of Chester, in the north-west of England, was the most sophisticated and far-sighted of any in Britain. It was led by John Haygarth, Yorkshire-born physician to the Chester Infirmary and closely connected with the reformist network of dissenting scientists, including the Quaker doctors Fothergill and Lettsom. In a report on a smallpox epidemic in the town in 1774, he examined the mortality data and found almost one in six died, with children under two especially badly affected. His findings spurred him to establish the Small-Pox Society at Chester, funded by private subscription, which began inoculating poor children in their homes when a new epidemic wave hit in 1780. Enquiring further, Haygarth pursued every case to establish its origins, effectively inventing the system now known as contact tracing and proving that smallpox spread by close contagion. He published clear 'Rules of Prevention' focusing on isolation, fresh air and hand washing, and proposed that parents be paid to keep their inoculated offspring in isolation during the infectious period, while a system of surveillance by inspectors meant fines could be issued for rule-breakers.[28] Some queried whether the approach interfered with 'English liberty', but the physician argued the inspectors should be seen not as 'a spy to detect fraudulent gain, but a friendly monitor to warn the ignorant how to avoid poisoning their neighbours and friends.'[29]

The Chester model influenced similar programmes in Leeds and Liverpool, but in other cities, including London, Newcastle, Manchester and Glasgow, popular fear, apathy and fatalism prompted by the apparently constant presence of smallpox hampered the efforts of doctors and other campaigners to bring inoculation to the urban poor.[30] The problems of controlling infection still prevented the practice from being routinely provided to outpatients. Efforts were far more successful in market towns and villages, home to four-fifths of the population at the end of the century, where community-wide treatment conducted with the help of poor relief was markedly effective in driving down deaths from the disease and reducing its prevalence.[31] The south of England, where general inoculations had been adopted early, benefited most.[32] In Maidstone in Kent, as many as six hundred people died of smallpox in the thirty years before the town's first mass inoculation in 1766; in 1782, its vicar John Howlett reported that the total since was only about sixty: 'ample and satisfactory evidence of the vast benefit the town has received from this salutary invention!'[33] Once a community had experienced a successful general inoculation, it typically continued the practice whenever a smallpox epidemic threatened. As well as saving lives, there was an economic benefit: towns could preserve and boost their trade by publicising their efforts to drive out smallpox, and the costs of inoculations were far less than expensive treatment and burials of victims of the natural disease.

Where it was widely practised with careful controls to prevent cross-infection, inoculation could drive out smallpox from a community. That extraordinary truth led progressive doctors to the next logical step: the disease could be eradicated from the country entirely. In *A Sketch of a Plan to Exterminate the Casual Smallpox from Great Britain*, published in 1793, Haygarth – by now a Fellow of the Royal Society – proposed a nationwide, state-led programme of inoculation and enforcement through 'civil regulation': rewards and penalties underpinned by inspection. According to statistical calculations he commissioned, the scheme would increase the population of Britain from eight million to nine million in fifty years. The government, preoccupied with war with Revolutionary

France, did not take up the costly and politically contentious suggestion; it would be almost two hundred years before the World Health Organization finally achieved the global eradication of smallpox.

The decades of development of inoculation in Britain had contributed to new understanding reaching well beyond the procedure itself. Advances in the technology had extended medical knowledge: of contagion, of the processes of infection within the body and of comparative pathology. Campaigns by Thomas, Haygarth and others to extend its benefits to the poor had united scientific discovery with social action, driving forward the concept of public health as a political issue. And there was more: inoculation had also broken new ground in the use of data in medicine. From the first simple table drawn up by Thomas Nettleton in 1722, comparing the death rates of natural and inoculated smallpox, through the detailed analyses of the Bills of Mortality by James Jurin at the Royal Society and numerous subsequent calculations by Thomas and others, the case for inoculation had always been made using numerical arguments. Gradually, religious and superstitious objections were being chipped away by the reasoned conclusions of 'medical arithmetic'.[34] The term was coined by the physician William Black, Thomas's critic over how best to protect the London poor, who wrote in 1789: 'I believe the first dawn of medical arithmetick [sic] will be found in Dr Jurin, and was the last resource in support of inoculation, then in its infancy, but vilified in print by physicians and divines. It was by demonstrating in numbers the comparative success under inoculation, and the natural disease, that this inveterate conspiracy against the practice could be defeated.'[35] Data, he was confident, could triumph over prejudice.

As the century's end approached, some observers credited inoculation with another transformation: the rapid increase in the population of England and Wales, now nudging nine million (even without Haygarth's eradication plan) from six million only fifty years before.[36] In January 1796, a correspondent wrote to *The Gentleman's Magazine* to express a common interpretation of the trend: 'The increase of people within the last twenty-five years is visible to every observer . . . Inoculation is the mystic spell that has produced this wonder.' The true picture was far more complicated:

multiple economic and social factors affected patterns of death and disease in Britain, and growing efforts to improve medical and welfare provision were intricately interconnected. Nevertheless, inoculation had a definite impact on the incidence of smallpox and unquestionably reduced the mortality rate. It preserved hundreds of thousands of lives of all ages, and ensured more children survived to have children of their own.[37]

Every individual life saved and disability or disfigurement prevented represented a triumph for the power of inoculation. But the technology, the chief medical contribution of the Enlightenment, would prove most significant in its role as a crucial foundation for the world-changing development that came next.

When Edward Jenner, born in 1749 in Berkeley, Gloucestershire, was a young apprentice surgeon in the county, he heard a country girl observe that she could not be infected with smallpox because she had already had cowpox, a relatively mild disease caught from blisters on the teats of infected cattle.[38] The prophylactic power of cowpox had been noticed in England for over a century, and in other parts of the world for far longer, but the connection was not widely recognised or proven. In the early 1770s, a Gloucestershire inoculator called John Fewster presented the theory – suggested to him by some of his patients – to a local medical society to which Jenner belonged, but did not take his research further. A handful of experimenters informally tested the same idea, most famously the Dorset farmer Benjamin Jesty, who in 1774 used a stocking needle to scratch cowpox pus into the arms of his wife and children in the face of a smallpox epidemic.

The phenomenon became increasingly apparent to Jenner's probing and persistent mind at the same time, for a reason he highlighted later in his landmark 1798 paper *An Inquiry into the Causes and Effects of the Variolæ Vaccinæ*.[39] When, as a local doctor, he was invited to inoculate country patients, he found that the procedure often did not produce the usual mild case of the disease, even though the patients insisted they had never previously had smallpox. Something had been making them immune, but only inoculation – growing ever more popular thanks to the simpler Suttonian method – had exposed the fact by actively challenging

Dr Edward Jenner.

their immunity. 'These patients I found had undergone a disease they called the Cow Pox,' Jenner wrote. 'A vague opinion prevailed that it was a preventive of the Small Pox.'[40] The farmers had only recently made the connection, he found. 'Probably the general introduction of inoculation first occasioned the discovery.' He began to enquire more deeply into the nature and origin of cowpox, and its potential prophylactic properties.

Jenner collected and documented multiple case histories of individuals who proved immune to smallpox having previously caught cowpox, sometimes many years before. In 1796, by now aged forty-seven, he used the technology of inoculation to test his theory directly. On 14 May, he inoculated James Phipps, the eight-year-old son of his gardener, with cowpox lymph from a blister on the hand of Sarah Nelmes, a milkmaid who had recently been infected, reportedly by a cow named Blossom.[41] Nine days later, the boy experienced mild symptoms – including just one pock at the point of inoculation – and quickly recovered. On 1 July, he was inoculated in the normal way with smallpox, which produced no significant reaction: the child was immune. After twenty-seven years of research, Jenner had a result that would make history. He wrote to a friend: 'I have at last accomplished what I have been so long waiting for, the passing of the vaccine Virus from one human being to another by the ordinary mode of Inoculation . . . The Boy has since been inoculated for the small pox which as I ventured to predict produced no effect. I shall now pursue my Experiments with redoubled ardour.'[42]

He was true to his word. When cowpox struck nearby dairies again in spring 1798, Jenner conducted more trials, using pus directly from an infected cow to inoculate a five-year-old boy and then inoculating four more children, one from another, as each suffered mild symptoms. Again, the children proved immune when subsequently inoculated conventionally with smallpox. Now Jenner had shown that the protective power of the cowpox vaccine was retained even after arm-to-arm transmission between individuals, meaning that – if the chain could be kept going – it did not need to be sourced directly from cattle. Not only that, it was much safer than traditional inoculation, for those treated produced only one pock rather than disfiguring clusters, and – crucially – there was no risk of spreading smallpox to others in the community. That also made it cheaper, as patients had no need to isolate for two weeks to prevent infection.

The game-changing nature of Jenner's contribution, self-published in June in his *Inquiry* complete with his own hand-drawn illustrations of pocks, was recognised immediately. 'The substituting of cow-pox poison for the smallpox promises to be one of the greatest improvements that has ever been made in medicine,' wrote his friend Henry Cline, a surgeon who performed the first vaccination in London in July 1798.[43]

After a few months trialling the procedure on a larger scale, the capital's medical establishment threw its weight behind vaccination. The practice spread with remarkable speed in Britain, but also in inoculation-cautious Europe, North America, India, Spanish America and around the world. By 1801, Jenner claimed that over 100,000 people had been vaccinated in Britain, where the campaigning inoculators Haygarth and Lettsom became influential early supporters. Smallpox mortality in London would fall from an average 91.7 deaths in every 1,000 in the last quarter of the eighteenth century to 51.7 in the first quarter of the next, and to 14.3 by 1851–75.

In France, where Napoleon was a powerful advocate of the new technology, some 1.7 million people were vaccinated in the four years from 1808. Vaccination was introduced in North America in 1800, and again the medical and political establishments swiftly gave it their blessing. Thomas Jefferson, third President of the United States and another committed proponent, wrote to Jenner in 1806: 'You have erased from the calendar of human afflictions one of its greatest. Yours is the comfortable reflection that mankind can never forget that you have lived.'[44]

In 1801, samples of vaccine reached Russia, where the Imperial family was impatient to introduce the new procedure, already trialled in the Baltic provinces. Anton Petrov, a boy from the Moscow foundling house, was the first person in Russia to be vaccinated. Just as little Alexander Ospenniy had been given an inoculation-themed noble title by Catherine, the child was renamed Anton Vaktsinov in honour of the event. Lymph from the blister on his arm became a source of vaccine for chains of other patients. Vaccination spread out from the new and old capitals, reaching over 64,000 people in European Russia in 1804 alone before extending the following year across almost every province in the empire.[45]

The switch from inoculation was not always smooth. In Britain, fear of the cowpox vaccine, with its animal origin, prompted some wary patients – especially poor Londoners – to opt for the old, familiar technique, even when the new one was offered. Satirical cartoons depicted patients sprouting horns and hooves after being vaccinated. Concerns over the efficacy of the procedure and inconsistent vaccine quality prompted new questions over what, precisely, Jenner's vaccine was. Gradually, it emerged that its protection was not permanent, meaning patients would need booster doses. Within a few years of his discovery, an anti-vaccination movement had emerged that would ebb and flow but never disappear.

Despite some opposition, adoption of vaccination continued, and Jenner proved correct in his prediction, made in 1801, that 'It now becomes too manifest to admit of controversy, that the annihilation of the Small Pox, the most dreadful scourge of the human species, must be the final result of this practice.'[46] In 1980, after a campaign of vaccination and surveillance, smallpox was officially declared eradicated, in one of the greatest ever public health achievements.

Jenner's innovation would, rightly, bring him global fame as one of the most important figures in the history of medicine. Vaccination was a safe, affordable and effective preventative treatment against a devastating virus that had killed millions. But his discovery had not emerged from nowhere: it rested on the insight, determination, courage and sheer labour of countless men and women before him who had developed the foundational technology of inoculation. The observations of Thomas Dimsdale, Daniel Sutton and all the other experimental inoculators; the campaigning courage of Lady Mary Wortley Montagu, Catherine II of Russia, Voltaire and their fellow advocates; the painstaking analysis of Jurin, Nettleton, Haygarth and the other data collectors; the centuries of protective care provided by so many uncelebrated 'amateur' inoculators in continents beyond Europe – all had created the stepping stones across which Jenner could stride.

The early vaccinators inherited the technique of inoculation, but also a constituency of patients and practitioners already familiar with the concept of preventative medicine. The core principle of deliberately infecting a healthy individual to protect them from a far greater risk was well established, even if it was a risk not everyone chose to take. Thanks to the efforts of Thomas and his fellow campaigners, the scientific and humane arguments for ensuring all strata of an unequal society had access to vaccination had been won.

Jenner, himself an inoculator, stood on many shoulders to envisage a world safe from smallpox. Without inoculation, there would have been no vaccination.

Thomas Dimsdale, his long life spanning most of the eighteenth century and the decades of inoculation in Britain, lived to see the introduction – and triumph – of vaccination. His attitude to the innovation is not recorded, though he would have had many questions about the development and, in his meticulous way, queried Jenner's methodological shortcomings. Aged eighty-six by the time the *Inquiry* was published, he was a figure from an earlier scientific era. Criticism by Lettsom, Black and other younger men over his resistance to outpatient inoculation in crowded cities had bruised his reputation, yet the success of vaccination rested precisely on its capacity to bypass the problem of cross-infection with smallpox.

After serving a second term in Parliament, Thomas had stepped down as an MP in 1790, and had spent time in the fashionable spa town of Bath, where he had a house on the Royal Crescent. He maintained his medical interests as a governor of the town's general hospital. During the winter, he lived in London, at his home on Red Lion Square.

Following his second visit to St Petersburg in 1781, he had maintained his Russian connections. Thomas acted as go-between in the purchase by Catherine of botanical drawings collected by John Fothergill and sold by his sister Ann, with valuation advice from Joseph Banks and Daniel Solander. He remained concerned for the Empress's health, prescribing a 'pleasant and agreeable' magnesia medicine to cure her stomach ache and sending over a pony and two little greyhounds for her grandsons. In 1785, despite recovering from a serious illness, he offered to make a third trip to Russia to inoculate two of the Grand Duke's daughters – a proposal that was, perhaps fortunately, never taken up.

In October 1793, Thomas received his last message from the Empress, thanking him for a gift of six engravings portraying views of London, a city she had never seen. A letter written on her instruction underlined the unbreakable connection that had now bound them for twenty-five years. It read: 'apart from the pleasure that she has in receiving such a pretty novelty, she has much pleasure in this mark of your remembrance. Her Majesty always preserves the same feeling for you and the esteem in which she holds you.'[47]

By now, increasingly unwell, distanced from her son Paul and horrified at the disorder and terror of Revolutionary France, Catherine was no longer the ruler Thomas had known. Her faith in the philosophes shaken, and perhaps unwilling to acknowledge her own unfulfilled ambitions, she had banned Alexander Radishchev's 1790 polemic *Journey from St Petersburg to Moscow*, with its radical critique of serfdom, corruption and war. Still accompanied by much younger favourites, she had lost her beloved Potemkin, brought down not by battle but sickness as he oversaw peace talks with the twice-vanquished Ottoman Empire. Crimea and yet more Polish territory was hers, but Russian expansion was now provoking the European rivals she had sought to impress with her enlightened rule. English caricaturists linked her insatiable imperial ambitions with her sexual appetite, depicting her as a colossal figure striding determinedly between Russia and Constantinople while below her the Lilliputian – all male – sovereigns of Europe shared crude innuendoes as they peered up her skirts.[48]

An Imperial Stride! – satirical print published by William Holland, 1791.

In her English doctor's memory, though, Catherine was unchanged. She remained forever the same charismatic, generous, supremely intelligent woman who had quizzed him about medicine and his Quaker origins, urged him to take courage and carry out her secret inoculation, and paced out her recovery to the stories of Voltaire in the gardens of Tsarskoe Selo. The Empress had given him riches, a title and fame he had never imagined, but most importantly she had trusted him with her body and her life. He had repaid her, protecting her and her son and helping her lift her inoculation from private act to symbolic statement and public example. Their friendship, forged in defiance of death, had lasted a lifetime.

On the morning of Wednesday 5 November 1796, Catherine – now aged sixty-seven – rose at six as usual, drank some black coffee and settled to her papers. When a chamberlain entered after nine, he found her body on the floor of the adjacent closet. She fell into a coma and Dr Rogerson, unable to extract the thick, dark blood from her veins, diagnosed a stroke. The Empress was given communion and anointed with holy oil, and Paul and his wife Maria Fedorovna kept vigil overnight beside her bed. The following day, at a quarter to ten in the evening, she died.

Thomas heard the news in Hertford. He wrote to Paul, congratu-lating him on his accession to the Imperial throne, and wishing continuing good health to the new Emperor and his family. In his last letter to the Imperial Court, written in the French he had never quite mastered, he declared: 'Handicapped at present by the weight of years, I do not and never shall lose the memory of all the evidence of this inexpressible goodwill, and never broken during the whole time I had had the happiness of living with your Imperial Majesty: evidence which has filled me and will fill me until my last breath with the most lively feelings and the most respectful gratitude.'[49]

The Cow-pock, or the Wonderful Effects of the New Inoculation – satirical
cartoon by James Gillray ridiculing anti-vaccination sentiment, 1802.

Epilogue

The Legacy

'The world and all its peoples have won freedom from small-pox, which was a most devastating disease sweeping in epidemic form through many countries since earliest time, leaving death, blindness and disfigurement in its wake.'

Resolution adopted by the thirty-third
World Health Assembly, Geneva, 8 May 1980

On 30 December 1800, as the old century pivoted into the new, Thomas Dimsdale died at his home in Hertford. Aged eighty-eight, he had outlived his most famous patient – the Empress of Russia, two wives, and the life-saving innovation he had done so much to promote. Barely two years after Jenner's *Inquiry*, vaccination was already displacing inoculation, the technology on which it was founded.

Science marched on, but Thomas's reputation remained. In his 1796 *History of the Inoculation of the Small-pox in Great Britain*, William Woodville had written that Baron Dimsdale's 'works are well entitled to public thanks; and will be a lasting monument of his judgement, discrimination and candour'.[1] His landmark *Present Method* treatise, read around the world, had not only set him on his journey to Russia but had 'met with the universal approbation of the faculty; and the instructions it contains have, almost without exception, deservedly continued ever since to regulate the practice of inoculation'.

Thomas's long life had seen dramatic change in the technology that defined his career. Imported from Turkey by Mary

Wortley Montagu and backed by Caroline of Ansbach, it owed its adoption in Britain to the vision of influential women. Pioneering doctors and scientists saw its potential, evaluated its success and faced down sceptics and fierce opponents, sharing their discoveries via a remarkable international social network. The simplicity and safety of the inoculation method established for centuries in parts of Asia and Africa was lost in the West as doctors tried to reconcile it with the norms of humoral medicine, only to be found again by the entrepreneurial Daniel Sutton, bringing him a fortune and opening the way to widespread availability.[2] Thanks to Thomas, the 'new' technique was explained and publicised, and his voice joined others to campaign for universal free access to inoculation. When Edward Jenner successfully tested the belief that cowpox provided immunity to smallpox, he brilliantly modified existing technology and convinced an audience already accustomed to the idea of preventative medicine.

Thomas brought the same qualities to his work as a doctor as he demonstrated in the rest of his life. His independence of mind had seen him withdraw from the Quaker faith in order to marry as he chose. He had resisted pressure to back down, just as he had held to his uncompromising views on the importance of isolation after inoculation to prevent infection. Though uncomfortable on a public platform, he was – as Catherine and so many others recognised – principled and utterly firm in his convictions, whether in medicine, pacifism or opposition to the slave trade. He drew his conclusions, as a true man of the Enlightenment, from his own observations and experiments rather than from theory, and – unlike Sutton – he made them known for the public good. In the introduction to his final publication, he invited readers to investigate and challenge his findings. 'Though I may have been mistaken in the theoretical and speculative part, I can truly assure the reader, that I have been scrupulously careful to relate nothing as fact, which I was not myself an eye-witness of, or had good authority for.'[3]

He was scrupulous, too, in his dealings with patients. His connection with the Empress of Russia was unique, forged in extremity and accompanied by exceptional anxiety and reward. But he brought the same humanity to the poor of Hertford, wading through snow to ease the suffering of ten-year-old George Hodges, and to Omai, the frightened young man from Tahiti who to most of Thomas's countrymen was no more than a scientific specimen. As a father, son and husband three times over, he had loved and been loved.

Nathaniel wrote with news of his father's death to the Emperor Paul I, the ruler he had inoculated long before as a young medical student. 'I must also bear witness in memory of my late father that he lived and died with feelings of the most respectful and profound attachment for Her Imperial Majesty, and I beg it to be believed that these sentiments will be hereditary in our family, and that I will preserve them to the end of my days.'[4] Thomas's Russian title passed to his eldest son, John, and on down the family line. Nathaniel died unmarried in 1811 and his own baronetcy ended with him.

Vaccination made rapid progress in Russia, where it spread in the established – though sometimes faded – tracks of inoculation, but it would not be Paul who led the change. The man overshadowed for almost all his life by a mother determined not to cede him power was assassinated just a few months later in March 1801, less than five years after taking the throne. He was succeeded by his reformist son Alexander I, Catherine's preferred heir and, as a little boy, Thomas's inoculation patient who had given the doctor and his wife gold coins.

Paul's widow, the Dowager Empress Maria Fedorovna, energetically promoted the new weapon in the fight against smallpox, just as her formidable mother-in-law had endorsed its predecessor. Children at the St Petersburg Foundling House were quickly vaccinated from those in Moscow, and both institutions provided Maria with monthly updates on numbers. The first original work on vaccination in Russian, published in 1801, was dedicated to her.[5] The following year, in an echo of the gifts showered on Thomas and Nathaniel Dimsdale, she sent Edward Jenner a diamond ring in recognition of his discovery and a personal note detailing her efforts to follow his example. Jenner thanked her, declaring that her support would help 'extinguish prejudice, and hasten the universal adoption of vaccine inoculation'.[6]

Advised by the College of Medicine in St Petersburg, Czar Alexander issued a state edict endorsing vaccination in 1801. The following year, a detailed plan was set in motion to take cowpox arm to arm via vaccinated patients across every province of the Russian empire, establishing permanent vaccination programmes and setting up hospitals en route. Inevitably, the initiative met resistance from wary parents, but by 1805 it had carried vaccine as far north as Archangel, south to Kazan and east to Irkutsk – where the indigenous population continued to support it – and the frontier with China. Inoculation was banned in Russia in the same year, thirty-five years before the same step was taken in England. In 1811, Alexander issued a second decree, this time making vaccination mandatory and ordering all Russians to undergo the procedure within three years. Religious resistance and sheer weight of numbers made such a feat impossible, but even in the face of Napoleon's invasion, total vaccinations exceeded an astonishing 1.6 million in Russia by 1812. State-imposed enforcement now eased as the Czar's government made way for medical leadership of the programme, but vaccination retained his personal support. When he met Jenner in London in 1813, Alexander told him – albeit optimistically – that the vaccine had 'nearly subdued the small-pox' in his Empire.

Catherine's sponsorship of inoculation had helped beat the path for vaccination in Russia, but the new technology spread with remarkable speed even in countries where its predecessor had been resisted. As early as 1803, it was solidly established in western Europe, taking off in Sweden, Italy, Germany and Austria, and soon afterwards in France, where it was strongly endorsed by Napoleon and promoted by the state.[7] From Spain, where Carlos IV had ordered the introduction of vaccination in royal orphanages as early as 1798, the vaccine made its way by ship to the colonies of South America, preserved through consecutive arm-to-arm vaccination of twenty-two orphan children on board. By the end of the campaign, some 300,000 people in countries from

Mexico and Venezuela to the Philippines and China had been vaccinated.

The same human chain principle was used to distribute vaccine in India after it arrived via Iraq in 1802, and to bring the protective lymph to colonial outposts in Africa, Australia and Indonesia. In America, where the Reverend Cotton Mather and Dr Zabdiel Boylston's far-sighted experiments had contributed to the earliest research on inoculation, vaccination also spread quickly, helped by President Jefferson's active support for the procedure. Adoption of inoculation had never been universal in America, where it often faced public resistance, though George Washington had ordered the mandatory inoculation of all troops in 1777 after recognising the advantage immunity to smallpox gave the British forces in the War of Independence.

In Britain, the global centre of inoculation science and birthplace of Jenner's great breakthrough, vaccination met some of its fiercest early opposition. While the wealthy and middle classes quickly switched to the new method, the poor in London, in particular, resisted it and clamoured for the old. At the London Smallpox Hospital, many parents insisted they only wanted inoculation for their children and would rather risk smallpox than accept vaccination. Mercenary inoculators, loath to lose business, were accused of spreading the disease by allowing patients to infect others. An 1808 satirical print by Isaac Cruikshank showed Jenner challenging the old-style practitioners with their blood-soaked knives, begging, 'Oh brothers, brothers, suffer the love of gain to be overcome by compassion for your fellow creatures.'[8] Lettsom, who had once campaigned for outpatient inoculation in London, now argued that inoculators who caused death by spreading infection were effectively murderers.[9] Jenner was – eventually – rewarded by Parliament for his discovery but he was unable to speed up its adoption in Britain. He wrote in frustration in 1815: 'Take a survey of Europe and you will find that while we [have been] fighting our battles with antivaccinists, they have been fighting with the smallpox and have vanquish'd the monster.'[10]

Only in 1840, after a smallpox epidemic that caused forty thousand deaths, did the British government finally legislate to ban inoculation and provide for free universal vaccination. With thousands still dying of the disease, further laws from 1853 onwards made childhood vaccination compulsory, only to prompt a widespread backlash on grounds including safety, bodily auton-omy and personal freedom from an interfering state. Opponents of inoculation had been free to avoid it; though some had proposed compulsion as a means of beating back the disease, Thomas – like Catherine – had always believed incentives, persuasion and free access to the procedure were more effective. Now mandatory vaccination, enforced by fines, provoked organised opposition and new social movements such as the National Anti-Vaccination League. Ultimately, the government backed down and permitted conscientious objection, though compulsion was not legally ended in Britain until 1948 with the establishment of the National Health Service.[11]

By the early 1950s, smallpox was declared eliminated in North America and Europe, but it remained endemic in South America and Asia, with around fifty million cases a year. Governments brought together by the newly founded World Health Organization began to discuss the possibility of eradication, but the proposal only gained real impetus in 1958, when the Soviet scientist Viktor Zhdanov made the case for a four-year global vaccination campaign to wipe out the virus. Zhdanov convinced the WHO member states, but the programme – which brought nations together across the Cold War divide – did not begin in earnest until 1966. It soon became clear that mass vaccination would not be feasible in the densely populated countries where smallpox remained endemic, and the strategy shifted to a combination of surveillance, containment and targeted vaccina-tion that bore strong similarities to the plan put forward by the Chester physician John Haygarth over 150 years before.

The WHO team, led by Donald Henderson, gradually tight-ened the noose on smallpox. In late 1975, three-year-old Rahima Banu from Bangladesh was the last person in the world to have naturally acquired variola major, while in October 1977 Ali Maow Maalin, a hospital cook from Somalia, was the last to have natu-rally acquired smallpox caused by the far less virulent variola minor. Both survived. In 1978, Janet Parker, a medical photographer at Birmingham University, became the last person ever to die of smallpox after coming into contact with the virus used for research in the microbiology department below her office. Her death was the final tragedy in a litany of loss that is beyond imagining. An estimated 300 million people died of the disease during the twentieth century, and half a billion in the last hundred years of its existence.[12]

Almost two centuries after Jenner dared to hope that vaccination could annihilate smallpox, and over 250 years after British doctors first recognised the potential of inoculation, the thirty-third World Health Assembly of the WHO declared the world free of the disease on 8 May 1980. Its eradication is widely seen as the greatest public health achievement in history. No other human disease has been eliminated, although vaccination has brought the eradication of polio within sight.

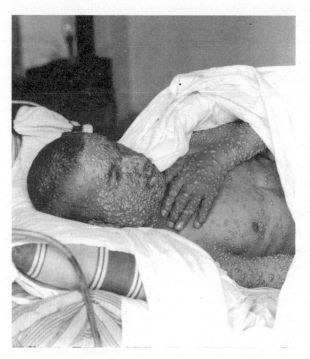

Boy with smallpox, early twentieth century.

The WHO decided in 1999 that all remaining stocks of the smallpox virus should be destroyed, but fears of bioterrorism, a leak from forgotten samples or even the thawing of bodies of victims of the disease in the melting permafrost of Siberia have prevented the recommendation ever coming into effect. Samples remain for research purposes in tightly controlled laboratories at the Centers for Disease Control and Prevention in the US city of Atlanta, and the VECTOR Institute in Koltsovo, Russia.

Today, over forty years after its eradication, the reality of smallpox, with its monstrous death toll, is almost forgotten. Few people alive still bear the scars that once ensured the disease was always, terrifyingly, visible, and no one is routinely vaccinated against it.[13] Inoculation, too, has slipped out of sight, its history obscured by a successor technology with an appealing pastoral narrative of cows and pretty milkmaids.

Vaccination, however, remains an unparalleled global health and development success story, saving between two and three million lives every year. There are now vaccines to prevent more than twenty life-threatening diseases, including polio, diphtheria, tetanus, pertussis, influenza and measles. During the writing of this book, vaccines were developed, trialled and approved at record speed to tackle Covid-19, a coronavirus disease that has caused the greatest global health crisis in a century.

Yet despite this unprecedented progress, there is no neat resolution to the vaccination story. Shortly before the coronavirus pandemic, global coverage had stalled, and in some countries take-up had gone into reverse.[14] For the inoculators of the eighteenth century, fear of an ever-present deadly disease acted as a powerful incentive, persuading patients to put aside their doubts and protect themselves and their families. Today, when the terrible effects of smallpox or polio are – thanks to vaccination – no longer an inescapable presence, complacency can kick in. Without the focusing effect of imminent risk, anti-vaccination sentiment, now amplified through social media, is more easily spread.

The new threat presented by Covid-19 has powerfully refocused attention on the life-saving power of vaccines. The world's affluent nations have rushed to protect their populations but, just as in the eighteenth century, the benefits of the technology are far from equally distributed. And even in a global pandemic that has claimed more than 5.5 million lives,[15] fear and distrust of authority have again led to vaccine hesitancy and refusal. The qualities – and failings – of those in power have been ruthlessly exposed. As world leaders roll up their sleeves to be vaccinated on camera, the power of example is as important as ever.

Inoculation, like its successor, vaccination, occupied the shadowy borderland between the rigour of science and the infinite complexities of human nature. On one side of that frontier lay the data-driven, coolly rational comparison of figures, the 'merchant's logick' summoned three hundred years ago by Thomas Nettleton, the pioneering Yorkshire inoculator who had seen too many patients fall prey to the Speckled Monster. Inoculation, even in its flawed early form, was always less dangerous than natural smallpox: choosing it improved an individual's chances in the 'forced lottery' of death conjured by the French philosophe Charles-Marie de La Condamine.

On the other side of the border lay the fear, disbelief and resistance to the laws of probability that make humans such poor assessors of risk. A parent's decision over whether to inoculate a child is 'not a question in morality, it is a matter of calculation', La Condamine insisted. That was always wishful thinking: emotion clouded decisions and alarm skewed the scales. Where the prospect of death or harm seemed imminent, given shape by superstition or misinformation, a more distant threat – though greater, and almost unavoidable – seemed preferable to many.

Catherine II of Russia understood this duality and herself encompassed it. Her order-loving mind welcomed the stark clarity of a comparison table: by 1768, with the new, simplified method established, deaths from inoculation were close to zero in healthy patients while smallpox killed one in five or six. Daniel Sutton challenged critics to prove his treatment ever directly caused a fatality, and by 1781 Thomas Dimsdale, a far more cautious man, declared the new method 'infallible' if carried out safely. Today, that record is almost entirely forgotten. Any 'reasonable man', seeing two dangerous paths in front of him, would take the least risky if all other things were equal, Catherine wrote to Frederick the Great after her inoculation. She not only understood and trusted the data: once convinced, she stuck by her decision, even when Thomas wavered. Scientists must doubt; politicians look for certainty. Catherine's assessment of the scientific odds ran alongside political calculation: her legitimacy as ruler was derived from her son, and protecting her heir helped secure her own power.

The Empress's accounts of her inoculation spoke of reason, but she acknowledged the role of emotion too. She had wrestled with a 'horrible fear' of smallpox all her life, she told Frederick, and had 'a thousand difficulties' mastering her terror. When the disease threatened her son and the possibility of inoculating him was raised for a second time, she could bring herself to take the step only if she underwent the procedure first. Their relationship would grow ever more distant, but she was a mother and Paul was her child. When she urged Thomas to dismiss his worries over the unsatisfactory trial inoculations, she may have spoken as much to her own deepest fears as to her doctor.

Catherine's personal response to inoculation combined with her acute political instincts to help her promote the practice in Russia. Understanding the importance of trust in medical decisions, she recognised the power of her example to overcome doubt. She used all the tools at her disposal – religious mystery, art, allegorical symbolism and firework-filled celebration – to draw attention to her message and influence her people. Her image-making skill presented her at once as Good Shepherd to her flock, wise and warlike Minerva and reassuring Matushka, Little Mother to her adoptive nation.

Among the nobility, Catherine could set a fashion, and she could direct her health reforms to begin the harder task of introducing inoculation throughout her empire. But the significance of her action went far beyond the promotion of a medical procedure. As she wrote with faux flippancy to Voltaire, she had sought to create an example 'that might be useful to mankind' and inoculation had come to mind. The procedure, newly developed through observation rather than ancient theory, was the perfect symbol of enlightened thinking, precisely fitting the image she sought for her country and herself. By adopting it, she could not only please the philosophes whose approval she sought but symbolically earn a place in their ranks.

Catherine was a masterly maker of her own image, but her self-creation battled, as it still does today, with the versions of others. As Grand Duchess and Empress, she was constantly observed, her combination of intellectual command and personal charm – and even her looks – often defined in terms of 'masculine' and 'feminine' qualities. She consciously played with those stereotypes, riding astride and dressing in men's clothing to symbolise the power associated exclusively with male leadership. But in death, she could no longer respond when biographers and commentators accused her of moral and physical feminine weakness, rushing out salacious accounts of her allegedly rapacious sexual appetite. Henry Hunter, English translator of a 1797 biography by the French writer Jean Henri Castéra, declared that 'she contrived to blend the most daring ambition, that ever distinguished the male character, with the grossest sensuality that ever dishonoured the vilest of her sex.'[16] Among the depictions was the notorious misogynistic myth that has smeared her memory ever since: the invented claim that, during an orgy of bestiality, the Empress had been crushed to death by a stallion suspended by a harness above her.

Throughout her life, Catherine's body was often out of her control. As a child, her curved spine was smeared with saliva and strapped with black ribbon; as a new wife ignored by her husband, she was encouraged to have sex with another man; court doctors in Russia bled her almost to death, dangerously mishandled her miscarriage and pulled out part of her jawbone. In her sexual relationships, she found physical pleasure, but could not control the judgement and lies of others. By her inoculation, she made her own decision to treat her body as she chose. 'My life is my own,' she told Thomas, overriding his doubts and summoning him to conduct the procedure. The lancet pierced her arms, and the blisters wrote their pattern on her skin, telling a story she made her doctor record in detail. Then she published every word. In place of the falsehoods about her body in death, the truth about the action that protected her life and set an example in Russia and beyond deserves to be remembered.

The final resting places of the Empress of Russia and her English doctor could not be more different. Catherine lies in the golden-spired Peter and Paul Cathedral in St Petersburg, the traditional burial place of the Romanov rulers and set within the fortress whose cannons fired to mark her inoculation. Her white marble tomb is next to that of her husband Peter III, reburied beside her by their son Paul, as if the two had reigned together. In the act of death, her life was rewritten. Catherine, who always resisted the title 'Great' in her lifetime, had once jotted down her own epitaph, jokingly basing it on one composed for Sir Thomas Anderson, the greyhound Thomas had given her. It included the lines: 'Here lies Catherine the Second ... Arrived on the throne of Russia, she desired its good and sought to procure for her subjects happiness, liberty and propriety. She forgave easily and hated no one; indulgent, easy to live with, naturally cheerful, with a republican soul and a good heart.'[17]

Thomas Dimsdale, born a Quaker, disowned by the sect but shaped by its values, is buried – as he wished – in the modest Quaker Burial Ground on a side street in the Hertfordshire town of Bishop's Stortford. According to Friends' tradition, the grave itself is unmarked: in death, as in life, Quakers believe in equality of status. Thomas has no epitaph, though an early line from his final treatise might sum up his belief in the processes of scientific progress: 'Some of the opinions advanced may appear singular and disputable. I shall only say, that as enquiries tend to the discovery of truth, I willingly submit them to investigation.'

Thomas's name is engraved on a stone set into a wall in the neatly tended garden, one of many Dimsdales commemorated there, including his wives Mary and Ann, who died before him, and Elizabeth, who outlived him. The stone is weathered and the letters are almost illegible, but when the sun shines at the right angle the worn-down names appear, cast by shadow into the light.

Acknowledgements

My warmest thanks for help in writing this book are owed to some-one I sadly never met: the late Robert Dimsdale, direct descendant of Thomas and an expert on his ancestor's extraordinary life and the wider history of his remarkable family. His meticulous research is the foundation of this account. I am immensely grateful to the Dimsdale family, particularly Annabel, Edward, Wilfrid and Françoise, for their generosity in sharing their collection of Thomas's correspondence, medical notes and other papers with me, and trusting me to tell his story. Their help, given amid all the chal-lenges of the Covid-19 pandemic, was invaluable.

Equally generous was Professor Anthony Cross of Fitzwilliam College, University of Cambridge, who passed on to me his burst-ing file of documents relating to the story of the Empress and the English doctor. His findings gave me a flying start as I began my own research, and his enthusiasm for the lives of the many British citizens who passed through Russia in the eighteenth century captured my imagination.

Many other people freely lent me their time and expertise. Jonathan Ball, Professor of Molecular Virology at the University of Nottingham, was an especially helpful guide on the history of viruses and vaccines, while Professor Ben Pink Dandelion, Director of the Centre for Postgraduate Quaker Studies at the University of Birmingham, shed invaluable light on Thomas Dimsdale's Quaker heritage. Owen Gower, manager of Dr Jenner's House, trawled the museum's archives for me when it was not possible to visit, while authors Michael Bennett, Gavin Weightman and Jennifer Penschow generously shared findings from their own research into the history of inoculation. Helen Esfandiary shared her expertise on mothers and inoculation in elite Georgian society, while Jon Dunn gave me wise authorial advice and ensured the Shetlands made it into this book.

In St Petersburg, Natalia Sorokina provided a home away from home and a sense of personal connection to the city, while Valentina Danilova's historical and cultural expertise brought the Hermitage and the royal estates around St Petersburg to life. Thank you to the curators of the Voltaire Library for hunting down texts on inocula-tion, complete with Voltaire's handwritten notes, and to Harriet Swain for putting up with my relentless palace-hopping.

Back in the UK, I am very grateful to Gill Cordingley for her tour of Hertford's top Dimsdale locations and the loan of her books. Thanks too to Marilyn Taylor and Jean Purkis Riddell, and to Kathie Moy for the introductions. Bonnie West of the Hertfordshire Archives located important Quaker records for me when the archive was closed during the pandemic. Archivists at Yale University, the Russian State Archive of Ancient Acts (RGADA), the Library at Friends House in London, the Royal Society of Physicians, the University of Aberdeen and University College London (home to the archive of St Thomas's Hospital) were all exceptionally helpful in difficult conditions. Hayley Wilson dug out archival treasures and joined me on research visits, while Martyn Everett directed me to the wonders contained in the Gibson Library in my home town of Saffron Walden.

Colleagues at Gonville & Caius College and many others at Cambridge offered me encouragement and expert knowledge. Thank you in particular to Hugo Larose and Valerio Zanetti, and to Dr David Secher. I am also greatly indebted to Tatiana King, who provided the Russian translations for the book and worked through *Ospa i ospoprivivanīe* with me. Never have so many hours been spent on Zoom talking about pustules.

Many friends patiently put up with my inoculation fixation. Thank you especially to Sheila Gower Isaac, Victoria Skinner, Alison Mable, Clare Mulley, Sarah Stockwell, Katherine Whitbourn and Joyce Harper. My former *Guardian* colleague Patrick Barkham and Rebecca Ostrovsky of Pushkin House helped set me on my way and Rachel Wright encouraged me throughout. Simon and Katya Cherniavsky lent me their home and, with the expert help of Irina Shkoda, translated eighteenth-century handwritten Cyrillic, while Tav Morgan kindly paid my RGADA bill (cash only) in Moscow.

Past influences were important too. Beryl Freer, my school history teacher, set alight my interest in Catherine the Great. Sadly she died shortly before publication of this book; I would have loved to show it to her. Siân Busby, too, is no longer with us, but her kindness and her wholly original books had a great impact on me.

When I first proposed this book to Cathryn Summerhayes, my agent at Curtis Brown, the Covid-19 pandemic was just weeks away. Neither of us knew the story would soon have new resonance. I am immensely grateful for her faith in me. Sam Carter, my editor at Oneworld, has been exceptionally patient and generous, supporting me in writing and editing during lockdown and beyond. Holly Knox and Rida Vaquas were perceptive and meticulous. The book is much improved thanks to all of you; its shortcomings are all mine.

Lastly, thank you to my family. Pauline, David and Tom Ward and Robert Smith read, advised and encouraged. Most of all, Liam, Ailis, Maeve and Ned put up not only with a modern pandemic but with a partner and mother obsessed with a previous one. And Rosie, Milo and Mishka sat patiently by my side, wondering if I would ever get up and walk them.

Further Reading

The Empress and the English Doctor is not only about a pandemic; it was written during one. In Britain and beyond, the doors of archives and libraries clanged shut as lockdown was imposed, turning out the lights on everything from state papers to Quaker lists of 'sufferings'. Fortunately, a treasure trove of material is available online, for free, in digitised archives. The original letters from British diplomats in Russia quoted extensively in the book are held in the National Archives at Kew and the British Library, but most can also be found online in *Sbornik Imperatorskago Russkago Istoricheskago Obshchestva* (*SIRIO*), the mighty 148-volume collection of archival documents and correspondence published by the Imperial Russian Historical Society. *SIRIO* also includes the Russian-language version of Thomas's original account of his trip and much more. The *Kamer-fur'erskii tseremonialnyi zhurnaly*, the Imperial Court records listing ceremonies and banquets, are also accessible online.

Likewise, numerous eighteenth-century medical treatises, pamphlets and articles relating to the debate over smallpox inoculation, the development of the method and the debates over how best to extend it to the poor in Britain are digitised. Reading them provides a direct line to the excitement of the controversial new technology and the passion with which it was discussed – as well as a powerful sense of familiarity with many of the debates over risk and lesser harm. Thomas Dimsdale's publications, including his landmark treatise *The Present Method of Inoculating for the Small-Pox* and *Tracts on Inoculation*, detailing his visit to Russia, can all be found online in the Wellcome Collection, along with Jenner's

Inquiry, de La Condamine's address to the French Academy of Sciences and many other texts from the period. The online archive of the Royal Society is another excellent source of original documents including the very first reports of inoculation to reach Britain, as are the Royal College of Physicians and the James Lind Library, which charts the development of fair tests of treatments in healthcare.

Discussion of inoculation reached far beyond the medical world in the eighteenth century. Oxford University's Electronic Enlightenment online database (accessible by subscription) is an invaluable repository of correspondence from over ten thousand early modern figures, and includes many references to the topic. Eighteenth Century Collections Online hosts thousands of texts printed in Britain and America, including poems and plays featuring inoculation, while the Georgian Papers Online contains documents from the Royal Archives relating to the deaths of two sons of George III after they underwent the procedure. Newspapers of the period – digitised in several subscription-based databases – reflect the boom in inoculation through advertisements and news reports, while journals such as *The Gentleman's Magazine* (accessible for free in the HathiTrust Digital Library) track the development of the technology.

In addition to this wealth of digitised primary sources, numerous books and articles illuminated the story of the Empress and her English doctor. Below is a small selection of the texts I found most useful, grouped by theme.

History of smallpox and inoculation

Bennett, M. *War Against Smallpox: Edward Jenner and the Global Spread of Vaccination*. (Cambridge: Cambridge University Press, 2020)

Bishop, W. 'Thomas Dimsdale, M.D., F.R.S. (1712–1800): And the Inoculation of Catherine the Great of Russia.' *Annals of Medical History*, 4, No. 4, 1932, pp. 321–38

Boylston, A. W. *Defying Providence: Smallpox and the Forgotten 18th Century Medical Revolution*. (North Charleston, SC: CreateSpace, 2012)

Brunton, D. *Pox Britannica: Smallpox Inoculation in Britain, 1721–1830*. (Philadelphia: University of Pennsylvania Press, 1990)

Dimsdale, R. *Mixed Blessing: The Impact of Suttonian Smallpox Inoculation in the Later Eighteenth Century*. (Neuchâtel: 2016)

Eriksen, A. 'Cure or Protection? The Meaning of Smallpox Inoculation, ca 1750–1775.' *Medical History*, 57, No. 4, 2013, pp. 516–36

Grant, A. *Globalisation of Variolation: The Overlooked Origins of Immunity for Smallpox in the 18th Century*. (London: World Scientific Europe, 2018)

Grundy, I. *Lady Mary Wortley Montagu*. (Oxford: Oxford University Press, 1999)

Hopkins, D. R. *The Greatest Killer: Smallpox in History*. (Chicago: University of Chicago Press, 2002)

Miller, G. *The Adoption of Inoculation for Smallpox in England and France*. (Philadelphia: University of Pennsylvania Press, 1957)

Razzell, P. *The Conquest of Smallpox*. (Firle: Caliban Books, 1977)

Shuttleton, D. *Smallpox and the Literary Imagination 1660–1820*. (Cambridge: Cambridge University Press, 2007)

Smith, J. R. *The Speckled Monster: Smallpox in England 1670–1970, with Particular Reference to Essex*. (Chelmsford: Essex Record Office, 1987)

Weightman, G. *The Great Inoculator: The Untold Story of Daniel Sutton and his Medical Revolution*. (New Haven: Yale University Press, 2020)

Catherine the Great and eighteenth-century Russia

Catherine the Great: Selected Letters, trans. A. Kahn and K. Rubin-Detlev. (Oxford: Oxford University Press, 2018)

The Memoirs of Catherine the Great, trans. M. Cruse and H. Hoogenboom. (New York: Modern Library, 2006)

Alexander, J. T. *Catherine the Great: Life and Legend*. (New York: Oxford University Press USA, 1989)

Cross, A. G. (ed.). *An English Lady at the Court of Catherine the Great: The Journal of Baroness Elizabeth Dimsdale, 1781*. (Cambridge: Crest Publications, 1989)

Cross, A. G. *By the Banks of the Neva: Chapters from the Lives and Careers of the British in Eighteenth-Century Russia*. (Cambridge: Cambridge University Press, 1997) de Madariaga, I. *Russia in the Age of Catherine the Great*. (London: Phoenix, 2003)

Dixon, S. *Catherine the Great*. (London: Profile Books, 2009)

Greenleaf, M. 'Performing Autobiography: The Multiple Memoirs of Catherine the Great (1756–96).' *The Russian Review*, 63, No. 3, 2004, pp. 407–26

Maroger, D. (ed.) *The Memoirs of Catherine the Great*, trans. M. Budberg. (London: Hamish Hamilton, 1955)

Massie, R. *Catherine the Great: Portrait of a Woman*. (London: Head of Zeus, 2019)

McBurney, E. 'Art and Power in the Reign of Catherine the Great: The State Portraits.' 2014. Dissertation. Columbia University, New York

Proskurina, V. 'Catherine the Healer', *Creating the Empress: Politics and Poetry in the Age of Catherine II*. (Boston, MA: Academic Studies Press, 2011), pp. 86–108

Rounding, V. *Catherine the Great: Love, Sex and Power*. (New York: St Martin's Press, 2006)

Sebag Montefiore, S. *Catherine the Great and Potemkin: The Imperial Love Affair*. (London: Weidenfeld & Nicolson, 2000)

Smallpox in Russia

Alexander, J. 'Catherine the Great and Public Health.' *Journal of the History of Medicine and Allied Sciences*, 36, No. 2, 1981, pp. 185–204

Bartlett, R. 'Russia in the Eighteenth-Century European Adoption of Inoculation for Smallpox.' *Russia and the World of the Eighteenth Century*. (Columbus, OH: Slavica Publishers, 1988), pp. 193–213

Clendenning, P. 'Dr Thomas Dimsdale and Smallpox Inoculation in Russia.' *Journal of the History of Medicine and Allied Sciences*, 28, No. 2, 1973, pp. 109–25

Gubert, V. O. *Ospa i ospoprivivanīe*. (St Petersburg: Sojkin, 1896)

Schuth, S. O. 'The Formation of the Russian Medical Profession: A Comparison of Power and Plagues in the Eighteenth and Nineteenth Centuries.' 2014. Dissertation. William & Mary, Virginia

Eighteenth-century health, medicine and thought

Bynum, W. F., Porter, R. (eds) *William Hunter and the Eighteenth Century Medical World*. (Cambridge: Cambridge University Press, 1985)

Cunningham, A., French, R. (eds) *The Medical Enlightenment of the Eighteenth Century.* (Cambridge: Cambridge University Press, 1990)

Dobson, M. J. *Contours of Death and Disease in Early Modern England.* (Cambridge: Cambridge University Press, 2009)

Gottlieb, A. *The Dream of Enlightenment: The Rise of Modern Philosophy.* (New York: Liveright, 2016)

Porter, R. *Enlightenment.* (London: Penguin, 2000)

Porter, R., Conrad, L. I., Neve, M., Wear, A., Nutton, V. *The Western Medical Tradition: 800 BC to AD 1800.* (Cambridge: Cambridge University Press, 1995)

Roberts, M. K., *Sentimental Savants: Philosophical Families in Enlightenment France.* (Chicago: University of Chicago Press, 2016)

Robertson, R. *The Enlightenment: The Pursuit of Happiness 1680–1790.* (London: Penguin, 2020)

Rusnock, A. *Vital Accounts: Quantifying Health and Population in Eighteenth-Century England and France.* (Cambridge: Cambridge University Press, 2002)

Tröhler, U. *To Improve the Evidence of Medicine: The 18th Century British Origins of a Critical Approach.* (Edinburgh: Royal College of Physicians of Edinburgh, 2000)

Wear, A. *Medicine in Society: Historical Essays.* (Cambridge: Cambridge University Press, 1992)

Other

Biss, E. *On Immunity: An Inoculation.* (Minneapolis, MN: Graywolf Press, 2014)

Connaughton, R. *Omai: The Prince Who Never Was.* (London: Timewell Press, 2005)

Notes

Introduction: The Speckled Monster

1 Macaulay, T., *The History of England from the Accession of James the Second*, ed. C. H. Firth (London: Macmillan & Co. Limited, 1913–15), vol. 5, pp. 2468–70.

2 *The Memoirs of Catherine the Great*, trans. M. Cruse and H. Hoogenboom (New York: Modern Library, 2006), p. 23.

3 On 9 December 1979, a global commission certified that smallpox had been eradicated. The certification was officially accepted by the 33rd World Health Assembly in 1980.

4 Source: World Health Organization.

5 Behbehani, A. M., 'The Smallpox Story: Life and Death of an Old Disease', *Microbiological Reviews* (December 1983): 455–509. See also Miller, G., *The Adoption of Inoculation for Smallpox in England and France* (Philadelphia: University of Philadelphia Press, 1957), p. 26.

6 The Rector of Little Berkhamsted Richard Levett's afterthought noted in a Parish Register. Hertfordshire Archives and Local Studies (HALS), DP/20/1/2.

7 Letter, Catherine the Great to Frederick II of Prussia, 5 December 1768, in *Catherine the Great: Selected Letters*, trans. A. Kahn and K. Rubin-Detlev (Oxford: Oxford University Press, 2018), p. 70.

8 Source: World Health Organization, 'Poliomyelitis – Key Facts', 22 July 2019, www.who.int/news-room/fact-sheets/detail/poliomyelitis.

9 Vaccine Confidence Project, *State of Vaccine Confidence 2016: Global Insights through a 67-Country Survey*, September 2016. DOI: 10.1016/j.ebiom.2016.08.042.

10 Larson, H., 'The State of Vaccine Confidence', *The Lancet*, 392, 10161 (2018): 2244–6, DOI: 10.1016/S0140-6736(18)32608-4.

11 Dimsdale, T., *Thoughts on General and Partial Inoculations* (London: William Richards, 1776), p. 63.

1 The Doctor

1 A copy of Thomas's birth certificate, made by his mother, and other documents are part of the privately held Dimsdale family collection, drawn on throughout this book.

2 From information held in Hertfordshire Archives and Local Studies (HALS), gathered by Robert Dimsdale in his unpublished and unfinished family memoir, *Inheritance*, December 2018. Thomas's great-grandfather, also Robert, was described in a 1630 court indictment as a barber – a role that could extend from haircutting and shaving to minor operations such as lancing boils and setting bones.

3 From information held in Essex Record Office, cited in Dimsdale, R., *Inheritance*.

4 Dimsdale, T., *A Tribute of Friendship to the Memory of the Late Dr. John Fothergill*. This short tribute – one of several celebrating the remarkable life and work of Dr John Fothergill – was printed privately by Thomas in 1783. The document is mentioned by R. Hingston Fox in *Dr. John Fothergill and His Friends* (London: Macmillan, 1919), pp. 416–17, and forms the basis of much of that book's chapter on Thomas Dimsdale. The original text is in the Dimsdale family collection.

5 Dimsdale, R., *Inheritance*.

6 Essex Record Office, DP 152/12/1, 2 and 3.

7 Brunton, D., *Pox Britannica: Smallpox Inoculation in Britain, 1721–1830* (Philadelphia: University of Pennsylvania Press, 1990), p. 137.

8 Smith, J. R., *The Speckled Monster: Smallpox in England, 1670–1970* (Chelmsford: Essex Record Office, 1987), p. 17.

9 Bennett, M., *War Against Smallpox: Edward Jenner and the Global Spread of Vaccination* (Cambridge: Cambridge University Press, 2020), p. 24.

10 Unable to work the treadle on the wheel, Wedgwood could not throw pots and applied his talents instead to the technology of colour and glaze, to design and to branding. He built his business into a world-famous enterprise that would attract the patronage of Catherine the Great.

11 Glynn, I. and J., *The Life and Death of Smallpox* (London: Profile Books, 2004), pp. 21–2. Abū Bakr Muḥammad ibn Zakariyyā al-Rāzī, generally known in the West as Rhazes, was born in Rayy, Persia, in *c.* 854 CE. He spent most of his life in Baghdad, where he directed a hospital.

12 Hopkins, D. R., *The Greatest Killer: Smallpox in History* (Chicago: University of Chicago Press, 2002), p. 43.

13 This account of the famous duel is drawn from *The Roll of the Royal College of Physicians of London* by William Munk (commonly referred to as Munk's Roll), vol. II, 1701–1800 (London, 1878), https://archive.org/stream/rollofroyalcolleo2royaiala/rollofroyalcolleo2royaiala_djvu.txt. It represents a slightly punchier version of Woodward's own contemporary account, published in a letter of 13 June 1719, which in turn challenged another telling with a less favourable spin.

14 Croton, a poisonous plant from the *Euphorbiaceae* family, has violent purgative properties. Scammony is the common name of *Convolvulus scammonia*, a

bindweed native to the eastern Mediterranean which was used medicinally as a purgative and to kill roundworm and tapeworm.

15 Jenkins, J. S., 'Mozart and Medicine in the Eighteenth Century', *Journal of the Royal Society of Medicine* 88 (1995): 408–13, 410. See also Glynn, I. and J., *The Life and Death of Smallpox*, p. 1.

16 Dimsdale, T., *Tracts on Inoculation, Written and Published at St Petersburg in the Year 1768, by Command of Her Imperial Majesty, the Empress of All the Russias: With Additional Observations on Epidemic Smallpox, on the Nature of that Disease, and on the Different Success of the Various Modes of Inoculation* (London: W. Owen, 1781), p. 151.

17 Figures taken from Guy, W. A., 'Two Hundred and Fifty Years of Smallpox in London', *Journal of the Royal Statistical Society* XLV (1882): 431–3, quoted in Brunton, D., *Pox Britannica*, pp. 10, 253–4, and in Miller, G., *The Adoption of Inoculation for Smallpox*, pp. 33, 291.

18 Hoole, J., *Critical Essays on some of the Poems of Several English Poets: by John Scott, Esq. with an Account of the Life and Writings of the Author; by Mr Hoole* (London: J. Phillips, 1785), pp. i–lxxxix.

19 La Condamine, C-M. de., *A discourse on inoculation, read before the Royal Academy of Sciences at Paris, the 24th of April 1754*, trans. M. Maty (London: P. Vaillant, 1755), p. 50.

20 Figures drawn from Fenner, F. *et al.*, *Smallpox and Its Eradication* (Geneva: World Health Organization, 1988), p. 231.

21 Smith, J. R., *The Speckled Monster*, p. 24.

22 Ibid.

23 *Ipswich Journal*, 9 June 1764.

24 *London Gazette*, issue 7379, 22 February 1734, p. 1.

25 *Ipswich Journal*, 3 February 1733.

26 Quoted in *Smallpox in Poetry*, from the podcast series *History of the Eighteenth Century in Ten Poems*, Faculty of English Language and Literature, University of Oxford.

27 Montagu, M. W. [Autobiographical romance: fragment], in *Lady Mary Wortley Montagu: Essays and Poems and Simplicity, A Comedy*, ed. R. Halsband and I. Grundy (Oxford: Clarendon Press, 1993), p. 77.

28 Letter, Mary Wortley Montagu to Sarah Chiswell from Adrianople, 1 April 1718. Montagu, M. W., *The Turkish Embassy Letters* (London: Virago, 1994), pp. 80–2. Sarah would later die of smallpox.

29 Maitland, C., *Mr Maitland's Account of Inoculating the Small Pox* (London: J. Downing, 1722), https://wellcomecollection.org/works/v9stfkzk, quoted in Boylston, A. W., *Defying Providence* (North Charleston, SC: CreateSpace, 2012). This was not the first official inoculation of a British subject: Alicia Grant points out that the two sons of Mr Hefferman, secretary to the British ambassador, were inoculated in Turkey in 1715 or earlier. They were sent to Britain and members of the Royal Society were invited to view them and see whether inoculation protected against a second attack of smallpox. The Society's members never took up the invitation. Grant, A., *Globalisation of Variolation: The Overlooked Origins of Immunity for Smallpox in the 18th Century* (London: World Scientific Europe, 2019), p. 31.

30 Maitland, C., *Account*.

31 Record of the inoculation of Mary Montagu by Charles Maitland, Royal Society Archive, reproduced in online exhibit *Women and the Royal Society*, https://artsandculture.google.com/exhibit/women-and-the-royal-society-the-royal-society/ogJSHD47mg0ZLQ?hl=en.

32 Maitland, C., *Account*.

33 Timonius, E., 'An Account of History, of the Procuring the Small Pox by Incision, or Inoculation: As It Has for Some Time Been Practised at Constantinople', *Philosophical Transactions* 29 (1714): 72–82. The Latinisation of Timoni's name followed common scholarly practice, especially in scientific contexts. Latinisation produced names that were internationally consistent.

34 Pylarini, G., 'Nova et tuta variolas excitandi per transplantationem methodus; Nuper inventa et in usum tracta: qua rite peracta immunia in posterum praeservantur ab hujusmodi contagio corpora', *Philosophical Transactions* 29 (1716): 393–9.

35 Grundy, I., *Lady Mary Wortley Montagu: Comet of the Enlightenment* (Oxford: Oxford University Press, 1999), pp. 218–19.

36 *The London Gazette*, 10 March 1722, p. 6.

37 Born Claudius Amyand in France, Amyand, a Huguenot, fled to London to escape religious persecution in 1685 and was appointed Serjeant Surgeon to George I in 1715, continuing in the post under George II. On 5 April 1716 he was elected a Fellow of the Royal Society under the name Claude Amyand.

38 The exhibition *Enlightened Princesses: Caroline, Augusta, Charlotte and the Shaping of the Modern World* (2017) at Kensington Palace, London, showcased books featuring choreographic notation of dances performed by the children.

39 Letter, King George I to his daughter Sophia Dorothea, Queen of Prussia, 26 May 1724, Wellcome Collection MS.9212/1. Sophia Dorothea's eldest son, the young Prince Frederick, later Frederick II 'the Great' of Prussia, had suffered an attack of smallpox. The King recommended inoculation for the rest of her children, explaining it had been successfully practised on his grandson (Frederick Louis, later Prince of Wales, 1707–51) at Hanover.

40 Wagstaffe, W., *A Letter to Dr. Freind; Shewing the Danger and Uncertainty of Inoculating the Small Pox* (London: Samuel Butler, 1722).

41 Sparham, L., *Reasons against the Practice of Inoculating the Small-pox: As also a Brief Account of the Operation of This Poison, Infused after This Manner into a Wound* (London: J. Peele, 1722).

42 Massey, E., *A Sermon against the Dangerous and Sinful Practice of Inoculation* (London: W. Meadows, 1721).

43 Arbuthnot, J., *Mr Maitland's Account of Inoculating the Smallpox Vindicated from Dr Wagstaffe's Misrepresentations of that Practice; With Some Remarks on Mr Massey's Sermon* (London: J. Peele, 1722).

44 Dimsdale, T., *Tribute*.

45 Dimsdale family collection.

46 Thomas Dimsdale from the Enfield Monthly Meeting (Middlesex), Hertfordshire Archives and Local Studies (HALS), NQ2/5F/53.

2   The Deadly Lottery

1   La Condamine, C-M. de, *Discourse on Inoculation*, p. 51.

2   Hertfordshire Archives and Local Studies (HALS), NQ2/1A/15 and NQ2/1A/16.

3   Dimsdale, T., *Tribute*.

4   Ibid.

5   Ibid.

6   Letter, Thomas Dimsdale to his children, 20 March 1779, Dimsdale family collection.

7   Dimsdale family collection.

8   Nettleton, T., 'A Letter from Dr. Nettleton, Physician at Halifax in Yorkshire, to Dr. Whitaker, Concerning the Inoculation of the Small Pox', *Philosophical Transactions* 32 (1723): 35–48.

9   Nettleton, T., 'A Letter from the Same Learned and Ingenious Gentleman, Concerning His Farther Progress in Inoculating the Small Pox, To Dr. Jurin R. S. Secr', *Philosophical Transactions* 32 (1723): 49–52.

10 Miller, G., *The Adoption of Inoculation for Smallpox*, pp. 111–17. Boylston, A. W., *Defying Providence*, p. 103. Rusnock, A., *Vital Accounts: Quantifying Health and Population in Eighteenth-Century England and France* (Cambridge: Cambridge University Press, 2002), p. 44, makes the same argument but places Arbuthnot and Jurin as the pioneers. However, Jurin's comparative calculations came after Nettleton's. Either way, the early debates over inoculation were critical in establishing the use of numerical evidence in medicine.

11 Jurin, J., 'A Letter to the Learned Dr. Caleb Cotesworth, F. R. S., of the College of Physicians, London, and Physician to St. Thomas's Hospital; Containing a Comparison between the Danger of the Natural Small Pox, and of That Given by Inoculation', *Philosophical Transactions* 32 (1723): 213–27.

12 Onesimus was a Guaramante from what is now southern Libya. He had been 'given' to Mather by his parishioners in 1707.

13 Jurin, J., 'A Letter to the Learned Dr Caleb Cotesworth', p. 215.

14 Ibid.

15 Scheuchzer, J. G., *An Account of the Success of Inoculating the Small-pox in Great Britain, for the Years 1727 and 1728. With a Comparison between the Mortality of the Natural Small-pox, and the Miscarriages in that Practice; As Also Some General Remarks on Its Progress and Success, since its First Introduction* (London: J. Peele, 1729). Scheuchzer, a Swiss naturalist and physician, took on the onerous task of documenting every inoculation because he wished to see the project continue and, after Jurin stepped down, 'nobody else seem'd disposed to engage in it'. Introducing his report, he wearily concluded that, 'I am very sensible, that it will be extremely difficult for me to content the two opposite parties, which have hitherto appeared, not without a good deal of Zeal and Warmth, one for, the other against inoculation.'

16 Rusnock, A., *Vital Accounts*, p. 67.

17 Hill, A., *The Plain Dealer: Being Select Essays on Several Curious Subjects: Relating to Friendship, . . . Poetry, and Other Branches of Polite Literature. Publish'd Originally*

in the Year 1724. And Now First Collected into Two Volumes (London: S. Richardson and A. Wilde, 1724).

18 Voltaire, *Letters Concerning the English Nation* (London: C. Davis and A. Lyon, 1733), published in French in 1734 as *Lettres philosophiques*. The book was banned in France but became a bestseller in England. 'On Inoculation' is the eleventh of twenty-four numbered letters, positioned between letters on trade and on the philosopher Francis Bacon.

19 *Daily Advertiser*, 15 November 1743. The newspaper also reported the birth of George's younger brother, Prince William Henry, and the appointment of his wet nurse.

20 Frewen, T., *The Practice and Theory of Inoculation: With an Account of Its Success; In a Letter to a Friend* (London: S. Austen, 1749).

21 Report of the governors of the Middlesex County Hospital for Smallpox and Inoculation, 1759–60, quoted in Green, F. H. K., 'An Eighteenth Century Small-Pox Hospital', *British Medical Journal* 1, 4093 (1939): 1245–7.

22 *The Gentleman's Magazine* 22 (1752), p. 511.

23 Kirkpatrick, J., *The Analysis of Inoculation: Comprizing the History, Theory, and Practice of it: With an Occasional Consideration of the Most Remarkable Appearances in the Small Pox* (London: J. Millan, 1754).

24 *Annals of the Royal College of Physicians* XII (1755): 41–2.

25 Voltaire, *Letters Concerning the English Nation*, Letter XI.

26 Du Marsais, C. C., 'Philosopher', in *The Encyclopedia of Diderot & d'Alembert Collaborative Translation Project*, trans. D. Goodman (Ann Arbor: Michigan Publishing, University of Michigan Library, 2002). Trans. of 'Philosophe', in *Encyclopédie ou Dictionnaire raisonné des sciences, des arts et des métiers*, vol. 12 (Paris, 1765).

27 La Condamine, C-M. de, *Discourse on Inoculation*, p. 50.

28 Taschereau, J.-A., Chaudé, A., Meister, J.-H., von Grimm, F., Melchior, F. and Diderot, D., *Correspondance littéraire, philosophique et critique de Grimm et de Diderot, depuis 1753 jusqu'en 1790* (Paris: Furne, 1829), p. 460.

29 *Correspondance de Frédéric II avec Louise-Dorothée de Saxe-Gotha (1740–1767)*, ed. M.-H. Cotoni (Oxford: Oxford University Press, 1999), p. 10. Louise-Dorothea von Meiningen, Duchess of Saxe-Gotha, an intellectual with a passionate interest in literature and philosophy, corresponded regularly with Voltaire. Their exchanges, particularly on philosophical Optimism, are thought to have influenced his satirical novella *Candide*, which Catherine the Great later read while recovering from her inoculation (Dawson, D., 'In Search of the Real Pangloss: The Correspondence of Voltaire with the Duchess of Saxe-Gotha', *Yale French Studies* No. 71, *Men/ Women of Letters* (New Haven: Yale University Press, 1986), pp. 93–112.

30 Bernoulli, D., 'An Attempt at a New Analysis of the Mortality Caused by Smallpox and of the Advantages of Inoculation to Prevent it', *Histoire de l'Academie Royale des Sciences* 1–45 (1760/1766).

31 d'Alembert, J. le Rond, 'Onzième mémoire: sur l'application du calcul des probabilités à l'inoculation de la petite Vérole', in *Opuscules mathématiques* (Paris: David, 1761), vol. II, pp. 26–46.

32 Gatti, A., *New Observations on Inoculation*, trans. M. Maty (Dublin: John Exshaw, 1768).

33 Ibid., p. 65.

34 Ibid.

35 Letter, Galiani to Mme de Belzunce, of Naples, 27 September 1777, quoted in Rusnock, A., *Vital Accounts*, p. 90.

36 *The Gentleman's Magazine* 23 (May 1753), pp. 216, 217, quoted in Smith, J. R., *The Speckled Monster*. Smith also notes that Pugh was another pioneering doctor in the provinces, designing a set of curved forceps and an early proponent of dieting as a means of losing weight.

37 Dimsdale family collection.

3   The Empress

1 Letter, Thomas Dimsdale to Henry Nicols, 8 September 1768, Dimsdale family collection.

2 *The Memoirs of Catherine the Great*, trans. M. Cruse and H. Hoogenboom, p. 11.

3 Quoted in Dixon, S., *Catherine the Great* (London: Profile Books, 2009), p. 41.

4 Letter, Catherine the Great to Johanna Bielke, 13 July 1770, *Catherine the Great, Selected Letters*, trans. A. Kahn and K. Rubin-Detlev, p. 90.

5 Rounding, V., *Catherine the Great: Love, Sex and Power* (New York: St Martin's Press, 2007), p. 24.

6 *The Memoirs of Catherine the Great*, trans. M. Cruse and H. Hoogenboom, p. 16.

7 Massie, R. K., *Catherine the Great: Portrait of a Woman* (London: Head of Zeus, 2011), p. 384.

8 Brückner, A., *Die Ärzte in Russland biz zum Jahre 1800*, quoted in Alexander, J. T., 'Catherine the Great and Public Health', *Journal of the History of Medicine and Allied Sciences* 36 (1981): 185–204.

9 Letter, Lord Cathcart toViscount Weymouth, 12 August 1768, *SIRIO*, xii:348. Much of the diplomatic correspondence of British ambassadors and envoys at the Russian Court is contained in the *Sbornik Imperatorskago Russkago istoricheskago obshchestva (SIRIO)* – the Collection of the Imperial Russian Historical Society, one of imperial Russia's most important scholarly bodies. The collection consists primarily of archival documents and correspondence, the bulk of which concerns the diplomatic history of the period stretching from Peter the Great to the Napoleonic Wars. The series includes a large number of documents from foreign as well as domestic archives, many of which have not been published elsewhere.

10 Gubert, V. O., *Ospa i ospoprivivanïe* (St Petersburg: Sojkin, 1896).

11 Ibid.

12 Grant, A., *Globalisation of Variolation*, p. 140.

13 Alexander, J. T., 'Catherine the Great and Public Health', p. 200.

14 Müller, G., *Ezhemesyachnie Sochineniya* (1755), St Petersburg part 1, p. 37. Quoted in Grant, A., *Globalisation of Variolation*, p. 139.

15 Ibid., p. 143.

16 Modern Tartu in Estonia.

17 Grant, A., *Globalisation of Variolation*, p. 150.

18 Bartlett, R. P., 'Russia in the Eighteenth Century European Adoption of Inoculation for Smallpox', in *Russia and the World of the Eighteenth Century*, ed. R. P. Bartlett *et al.* (Columbus, OH: Slavica, 1986), p. 196.

19 *The Despatches and Correspondence of John, Second Earl of Buckinghamshire, Ambassador to the Court of Catherine II of Russia 1762–1765*, ed. for the Royal Historical Society with introduction and notes by A. D'Arcy Collyer (London: Royal Historical Society, 1902), vol. 2, p. 177.

20 Massie, R. K., *Catherine the Great*, p. 386.

21 Ibid.

22 *SIRIO*, xii:331.

4   The Invitation

1 Dimsdale, T., *Tracts on Inoculation*, p. 4.

2 Ibid., p. 5.

3 Ibid., p. 5.

4 Ibid., p. 6.

5 John Fothergill was one of the wealthiest physicians in England, but would slip banknotes into the hands of poor patients when taking their pulse. 'I climbed over the backs of the poor into the pockets of the rich,' he said (cited in Deutsch, A., 'Historical Inter-Relationships between Medicine and Social Welfare', *Bulletin of the History of Medicine* 11, 5 (1942): 485–502, www.jstor.org/stable/44440720, quotation p. 491). He made important contributions to the study of diphtheria, scarlet fever, migraine and other conditions, as well as strongly advocating inoculation. He was also part of a network of Quaker botanists; the specialism was popular within the sect as it was useful and could be studied without going to university. Like many of his fellow Quakers, including Thomas Dimsdale, Fothergill was a supporter of anti-slavery and prison reform movements.

6 Dimsdale, T., *Tribute*.

7 Dimsdale, T., *Tracts on Inoculation*, p. 6.

8 Ibid., p. 7.

9 Dimsdale, T., *The Present Method of Inoculating for the Small-Pox* (London: W. Owen, 1767), p. 7.

10 Ibid., p. 55.

11 Ibid., p. 56.

12 Ibid., p. 26.

13 Ibid., p. 5.

14 Ibid., pp. 5, 6.

15 *Ipswich Journal*, 16 April 1757. This was the first advertisement for inoculation in the *Ipswich Journal*. It was repeated in several issues, followed by a series of similar notices offering more details of Sutton's offering.

16 *Ipswich Journal*, 25 September 1762. Two months later, Robert Sutton placed a new advertisement in the *Journal* stating that he had now successfully inoculated 453 patients in under a year, including children.

17 *Ipswich Journal*, 5 November 1763.

18 *Chelmsford Chronicle*, October 1764, quoted in Weightman, G., *The Great Inoculator* (New Haven: Yale University Press, 2020), p. 41.

19 Smith, J. R., *The Speckled Monster*, p. 74.

20 Weightman, G., *The Great Inoculator*, pp. 44–7.

21 Smith, J. R., *The Speckled Monster*, pp. 48–9.

22 Sutton appeared before a grand jury in the Essex town of Chelmsford, accused of causing a public nuisance by spreading infection. He argued that inoculation was widely practised by apothecaries in the town and was acquitted of all charges.

23 Houlton, R., *The Practice of Inoculation Justified: A Sermon Preached at Ingatestone, Essex, October 12, 1766, in Defence of Inoculation. To Which Is Added an Appendix on the Present State of Inoculation; with Observations, &c / by Robert Houlton* (Chelmsford: Lionel Hassall, 1767), p. 29.

24 Ibid., p. 40. Houlton gushingly continued: 'The pleasing conversation of the company, added to their various amusements, makes the time glide away imperceptibly.'

25 *Short Animadversions Addressed to the Reverend Author of a Late Pamphlet, Intituled [sic]: the Practice of Inoculation Justified* (London: S. Bladon, 1767), p. 33.

26 Houlton, R., *Indisputable Facts Relative to the Suttonian Art of Inoculation. With Observations on Its Discovery, Progress, Encouragement, Opposition, etc. etc.* (Dublin: W. G. Jones, 1798), p. viii.

27 *Letters of Horace Walpole, Earl of Orford, to Sir Horace Mann His Britannic Majesty's Resident at the Court of Florence, from 1760 to 1785* (London: R. Bentley, 1843), vol. 1, p. 368.

28 Jones, H., *Inoculation or Beauty's Triumph: A Poem, in Two Cantos* (Bath: C. Pope, 1768).

29 Baker, G., *An Inquiry into the Merits of a Method of Inoculating the Small-Pox, Which Is Now Practised in Several Counties of England* (London: J. Dodsley, 1766), p. 1.

30 Houlton, R., *Indisputable Facts*, p. 18.

31 Ibid., p. 28.

32 Ibid., p. 31.

33 Ibid., p. 32.

34 Watson, W., *An Account of a Series of Experiments, Instituted with a View of Ascertaining the Most Successful Method of Inoculating the Smallpox* (London: J. Nourse, 1768).

35 Dimsdale, T., *Tracts on Inoculation*.

36 Ibid.

37 Dimsdale, T., *Thoughts on General and Partial Inoculations*, p. 9.

38 *Oxford Journal*, 14 November 1767.

39 *Leeds Intelligencer*, 3 May 1768.

40 Letter, Joseph Cockfield to the Reverend Weeden Butler, 26 March 1766, quoted in Abraham, J. J., *Lettsom: His Life Times Friends and Descendants* (London: William Heinemann, 1933), p. 195.

41 *Leeds Intelligencer*, 5 July 1768.

42 Piozzi, H. L., *Dr Johnson by Mrs Thrale. The Anecdotes of Mrs Piozzi in Their Original Form* (London: Chatto & Windus, 1984), p. 17.

43 Duncan, W., *et al.*, 'The Opinion of His Majesty's Physicians and Surgeon Given Jan. 23, 1768, in Regard to Messrs Sutton's Practice in Inoculation . . .', *The Gentleman's Magazine* 38 (February 1768), p. 75.

44 *The Town and Country Magazine, Or, Universal Repository of Knowledge, Instruction, and Entertainment*, June 1769, p. 309.

45 Princess Ekaterina Dashkova, close friend of Catherine and her accomplice during the coup, also acquired a copy of the treatise. She was later appointed Director of the Imperial Academy of Arts and Sciences (known now as the Russian Academy of Sciences) – the first woman in the world to head a scientific academy. She met Thomas Dimsdale in St Petersburg and corresponded with him.

46 Fox, R. H., *Dr. John Fothergill and His Friends; Chapters in Eighteenth Century Life* (London: Macmillan and Co., 1919), p. 85.

47 Smith, J. R., *The Speckled Monster*, p. 88. Source for conversion: MeasuringWorth.com.

48 Dimsdale, T., *The Present Method*, p. 81.

49 Announcement placed by Richard Lambert in the *Newcastle Weekly Courant* (Newcastle-upon-Tyne), 16 April 1768, p. 2.

50 *Salisbury and Winchester Journal*, 18 July 1768, p. 3.

51 Letter, Joseph Cockfield to the Reverend Weeden Butler, 8 August 1768, 'Letters of Mr. Joseph Cockfield', in Nichols, J., *Illustrations of the Literary History of the Eighteenth Century*, vol. 5 (London: J. B. Nichols and Son, 1828), p. 785. Joseph Cockfield wrote several letters praising Thomas Dimsdale's abilities as an inoculator, and detailed his own headache and sore right arm after Thomas successfully inoculated him in April 1766. In February of that year he wrote: 'When it is considered that of two thousand inoculated at the Small-pox Hospital in Cold Bath-fields, London, not more than two have expired, who can refrain from paying a tribute of praise to the Creator of the Universe? Who can remain unconvinced of the general utility of this new invented method adopted from the oriental nations?'

52 Letter, Thomas Dimsdale in St Petersburg to Henry Nicols, 8 September 1768 (OS), Dimsdale family collection.

53 Modern Gdańsk in northern Poland.

5   The Preparations

1 Count Nikita Panin's speech to Thomas Dimsdale, quoted by Thomas in *Tracts on Inoculation*, p. 10.

2 Richardson, W., *Anecdotes of the Russian Empire: In a Series of Letters, Written, a Few Years Ago, from St. Petersburg* (London: W. Strahan and T. Caddell, 1784), pp. 13–14.

3 William Coxe, historian, priest, tutor and travelling companion to the nobility, *Travels into Poland, Russia, Sweden, and Denmark: Interspersed with Historical Relations and Political Inquiries*, vol. 2, third edition (London: T. Cadell, 1787), p. 268.

4 Description of Panin's wig and courtier's clothing by Princess Ekaterina Dashkova, quoted in Rounding, V., *Catherine the Great: Love, Sex and Power*, p. 132.

5 Dimsdale, T., *Tracts on Inoculation*, p. 12.

6 Letter, Thomas Dimsdale to Henry Nicols, 8 September 1768, Dimsdale family collection.

7 Thomas's account published in his treatise *Tracts on Inoculation* in 1781 is a double translation. The original, contemporaneous document, written in his poor French in December 1768, was then translated into Russian at Catherine's instruction. It can be found in the Russian State Archives, *SIRIO*, ii:295–322. Thomas, having lost his original version, had the Russian text translated back into English for publication thirteen years after the event. *Tracts on Inoculation* also included a reprint of his 1776 treatise *Thoughts on General and Partial Inoculations*.

8 Letter, Thomas Dimsdale to Henry Nicols, 8 September 1768, Dimsdale family collection.

9 Dimsdale, T., *Tracts on Inoculation*, p. 16.

10 Ibid., p. 17.

11 Ibid.

12 Ibid., p. 18.

13 Ibid.

14 Cross, A., *By the Banks of the Neva* (Cambridge: Cambridge University Press, 1997), pp. 55–8.

15 Charles Cathcart was shot in the face at the Battle of Fontenoy, a major engagement in the War of the Austrian Succession, in 1745. Joshua Reynolds' portrait (painted 1753–5) shows the patch on his cheek.

16 Dates of events in Russia during Thomas Dimsdale's first visit are given in the Old Style Julian calendar. Thomas Thynne, 1st Marquess of Bath and 3rd Viscount Weymouth, was Secretary of State for the Northern Department. Before 1782, the responsibilities of the two British Secretaries of State for the Northern and the Southern departments were divided geographically. The Secretary of State for the Southern Department, the more senior, was responsible for Southern England, Wales, Ireland, the American colonies (until 1768 when the responsibility was given to the Secretary of State for the Colonies), and relations with the Roman Catholic and Muslim states of Europe. The Secretary of State for the Northern Department, the more junior, was responsible for Northern England, Scotland, and relations with the Protestant states of northern Europe. In 1782, the two Secretaries of State were reformed as the Secretary of State for the Home Department and the Secretary of State for Foreign Affairs.

17 *SIRIO*, xii:363. All ambassadorial despatches quoted can be found in the same volume.

18 Letter, Thomas Dimsdale to Henry Nicols, 8 September 1768, Dimsdale family collection.

19 Ibid.

20 Dr John Rogerson, a Scottish doctor at Catherine's court who by 1776 was her personal physician. He was responsible for checking the Empress's various lovers for signs of venereal disease. Letter, John Rogerson to Thomas Dimsdale, 26 August 1770 (OS), Dimsdale family collection. Thomas Dimsdale had been suffering from kidney or bladder stones and Rogerson emphasised Thomas's generally healthy diet and lifestyle. 'No person certainly merits it [the stone] less; nor do I recollect anything in your way of living that can contribute to it, setting aside your predilection in favour of malt liquors.'

21 Letter, John Thomson to Dr James Mounsey, physician to Empress Elizabeth of Russia. Quoted in Thomas, G. C. G., 'Some Correspondence of Dr James Mounsey, Physician to the Empress Elizabeth of Russia', *Scottish Slavonic Review* 4 (1985): 11–25.

22 The Anglo-Russian commercial treaty of 1766, negotiated on the Russian side by Count Panin and by Ambassador George Macartney on behalf of the British. Britain's Industrial Revolution was heavily dependent on Russian raw materials, including iron, timber, hemp and flax (Cross, A., *By the Banks of the Neva*, p. 48).

23 Ibid., p. 19.

24 Letter, Lord Cathcart to the Earl of Rochford, 12 October 1770 (OS), *SIRIO*, xix:123–4. Quoted in ibid, p. 37.

25 Letter, Thomas Dimsdale to Henry Nicols, 6 October 1768 (OS), Dimsdale family collection.

26 Health questionnaire filled in by Catherine for Thomas Dimsdale, Dimsdale family collection.

27 Ibid.

28 Report by 'G. Foussadier', St Petersburg, 23 September 1768, Dimsdale family collection.

29 Dimsdale, T., *Tracts on Inoculation*, p. 23.

30 Ibid., p. 24.

31 Ibid., p. 25.

32 Ibid.

33 Letter, Thomas Dimsdale to Henry Nicols, 27 October 1768, Dimsdale family collection.

34 Dimsdale, T., *Thoughts on General and Partial Inoculations*, p. 16. This volume included two of five tracts Thomas prepared in St Petersburg on the Empress's instruction. All five had been translated into Russian and published in St Petersburg in 1770, but none had previously been published in English.

35 The estimate of two million deaths per year appeared in Thomas's *Thoughts on General and Partial Inoculations*, published in 1776. When the book was republished together with the account of the imperial inoculations as *Tracts on Inoculation* in 1781, Thomas added a note acknowledging that some believed his estimate much too large. 'Perhaps it may be so, the conjecture was hastily written, at a time when my mind was deeply impressed with the ravages of the small-pox in Russia.' Population figure taken from Macartney, G., *Some Account of the Public Life, and a Selection from the Unpublished Writings, of the Earl of Macartney*, ed. J. Barrow (Cambridge: Cambridge University Press, 2011).

36 Dimsdale, T., *Thoughts on General and Partial Inoculations*, p. 17.

37 Ibid.

38 Dimsdale, T., *Tracts on Inoculation*, pp. 31–2.

39 Ibid., p. 34.

40 Letter, Thomas Dimsdale to Henry Nicols, 27 October 1768, Dimsdale family collection.

41 Notes headed 'Regime', Dimsdale family collection.

42 Letter, Catherine the Great to Count Ivan Chernyshëv, 14 December 1768, *Pis'ma imperatritsy Ekateriny II k grafu Ivanu Grigor'evichu Chernyshevu (1764–1773)*, RA, 9 (1871), p. 1325.

43 The story of the coach and horses waiting to rush the Dimsdales to safety appears in many accounts of Catherine's inoculation but in no direct source. An important essay by Philip H. Clendenning, 'Dr Thomas Dimsdale and Smallpox Inoculation in Russia' (published in the *Journal of the History of Medicine and Allied Sciences* 28, (1973): 109–25), gives the source of the claim as a letter from Viscount Weymouth to Lord Cathcart on 18 October 1768. However, the referenced State Papers in the National Archives (SP 91/91) do not contain the letter. A letter of that date (7/18 October 1768) from Cathcart to Weymouth in a different volume (SP 91/79) does not include any reference to the plan. The coach is not mentioned in Thomas's account. The English author and politician Nathaniel Wraxall recorded in his memoirs the story of the yacht, which he had heard from one of Thomas Dimsdale's sons over forty years before (Wraxall, Sir N. W., *Posthumous Memoirs of My Own Life, III* (London: T. Cadell and W. Davies, 1836), p. 199). The yacht makes more sense as a means of escape to England than a carriage travelling overland, and the Dimsdales would certainly have needed a coach to reach it from Tsarskoe Selo.

44 Letter, Lord Cathcart to Viscount Weymouth, 7/18 October 1768, National Archives SP 91/79: 262.

45 Dimsdale, T., *Tracts on Inoculation*, p. 40.

6 The Inoculations

1 Dimsdale, T., medical notes for Saturday 18 October 1768 (OS), Dimsdale family collection.

2 Dimsdale, T., medical notes on the Empress's inoculation, Dimsdale family collection.

3 Dimsdale, T., *Tracts on Inoculation*, p. 73.

4 Thomas recorded the temperature outside as five or six degrees according to Réaumur's thermometer, a scale used widely in eighteenth-century Europe. This alcohol-based device used a temperature scale for which the freezing and boiling points of water were defined as 0 and 80 degrees respectively. The temperature of the Empress's apartment was between 12 and 14 degrees – a bracing 16 or 17 degrees Celsius.

5 Letter, Catherine the Great to Voltaire, 6 July 1772, in *Catherine the Great: Selected Letters*, trans. A. Kahn and K. Rubin-Detlev, pp. 123–4.

6   Letter from Catherine the Great to Johanna Bielke, 28 April 1772, in *Catherine the Great: Selected Letters*, trans. A. Kahn and K. Rubin-Detlev, pp. 122–3.

7   Letter, Catherine the Great to Voltaire, 6 July 1772, in *Catherine the Great: Selected Letters*, trans. A. Kahn and K. Rubin-Detlev, p. 123.

8   Letter, Catherine the Great to Johanna Bielke, 4 March 1769, *SIRIO*, x:332.

9   Dimsdale, T., medical notes for 15 October 1768, Dimsdale family collection.

10 Dixon, S., *Catherine the Great*, pp. 265–6.

11 Obituary of Thomas Dimsdale, *The European Magazine, and London Review* 42 (August 1802): 85.

12 Dimsdale, T., *Tracts on Inoculation*, p. 41.

13 Dimsdale, T., medical notes, Dimsdale family collection.

14 Dimsdale, T., *Tracts on Inoculation*, p. 41.

15 Dimsdale, T., medical notes, Dimsdale family collection.

16 Catherine's menstruation is not referred to in Thomas's public account of her recovery in *Tracts on Inoculation*, but it is mentioned in his contemporaneous medical notes with reference to the implications for purging. A note dated 26 October states: 'Her Majesty was perfectly well insomuch that I should have advised the taking of something purging the next morning only her menses were not quite gone'. Five days later, on 31 October, Thomas noted: 'Her Majesty continued very well but omitted taking a second dose of purging salts as she had a return of her menses'. The basic procedure of inoculation was the same for men and women, but preparation and aftercare were adapted for the two sexes, and for children.

17 Dimsdale, T., medical notes, Dimsdale family collection.

18 Dimsdale, T., *Thoughts on General and Partial Inoculations*, p. 59.

19 Ibid.

20 Letter, Thomas Dimsdale to Henry Nicols, 27 October 1768, Dimsdale family collection.

21 Letter, Catherine the Great in Tsarskoe Selo to Count Petr Saltykov, 27 October 1768, in *Letters of the Empress Catherine the Great to Field Marshal Count P. S. Saltykov 1762–1771* (Moscow: В Унив. тип. (М. Катков), 1886), p. 72, Letter 129. Available in digitised format on the website of the Boris Yeltsin Presidential Library: www.prlib.ru/en/node/436953.

22 Letter, Catherine the Great to Étienne Falconet, 30 October 1768, *SIRIO*, xvii:61.

23 Letter, Catherine the Great to Johanna Bielke, 1 November 1768, *SIRIO*, x:302.

24 Dimsdale, T., *Tracts on Inoculation*, p. 80.

25 Details of the court celebrations around the inoculation are drawn from the *Kamer-fur'erskii tseremonialnyi zhurnal* for 1768, the official Imperial Court record.

26 Letter, Lord Cathcart to Viscount Weymouth, 1 November 1768, *SIRIO*, xii:394.

27 Letter, Count Solms to Frederick II, 26 October 1768, *SIRIO*, xvii:163.

28 Letter, Lord Cathcart to the Earl of Rochford, 10 November 1768, National Archives SP 91/79: 357.

29 Ibid.

30 Letter, Earl of Rochford to Lord Cathcart, 20 December 1768 (9 December according to the Russian calendar), National Archives SP 91/79: 72–3.

31 Letter, Lord Cathcart to Viscount Weymouth, 7 November 1768, *SIRIO*, xii:403–4.

32 Graham, I. M., 'Two Hertfordshire Doctors', *East Hertfordshire Archaeological Society Transactions* 13 (1950): 44–54.

33 More standard transliterations would be: Naryshkins, Shcherbatovs, Golitsyns, Vorontzovs, Buturlins, Stroganovs.

34 From Thomas's Memorandum on his visit to Russia, written in his poor French and translated into Russian by M. Zlobin, *SIRIO*, ii:295–322. The observation does not appear in the English version that he eventually published as part of *Tracts* in 1781.

35 Letter, Lord Cathcart to Viscount Weymouth, 7/18 November 1768, *SIRIO*, xii:402.

36 Letter, Catherine the Great to Frederick II, 14 November 1768, in *Catherine the Great: Selected Letters*, trans. A. Kahn and K. Rubin-Detlev, pp. 68–70.

37 Letter, Catherine the Great to George Browne, 16 November 1768, quoted in Bishop, W. J., 'Thomas Dimsdale MD FRS (1712–1800) and the Inoculation of Catherine the Great of Russia', *Annals of Medical History* 4, 4 (July 1932):332.

38 Letter, Catherine the Great to Ivan Chernyshëv, 17 November 1768, quoted in Proskurina, V., 'Catherine the Healer', in *Creating the Empress: Politics and Poetry in the Age of Catherine II* (Boston, MA: Academic Studies Press, 2011), pp. 93–4.

7 The New Fashion

1 Letter, Catherine the Great to Ivan Chernyshëv, 17 November 1768, quoted in Proskurina, V., 'Catherine the Healer', pp. 93–4.

2 In Eastern Christianity, an iconostasis is a wall of icons and religious paintings, used to separate the nave (the main body of the church where most of the worshippers stand) from the sanctuary (the area around the altar, east of the nave).

3 This feast, marking the presentation of Mary by her parents into the Jewish Temple in Jerusalem as a little girl, is celebrated on 21 November according to the old Julian calendar. An Afterfeast is a period of celebration attached to Great Feasts, in this case lasting until 25 November.

4 Richardson, W., *Anecdotes of the Russian Empire*, Letter V, p. 33.

5 Richardson, unfamiliar with Orthodox rites and places of worship, interpreted the service through British eyes. By altar, he noted, he meant 'the place corresponding to the altar in English churches'. He also had little appreciation for icons, which he dismissed as 'glaring and ill-executed pictures of Russian saints'.

6 Details of the court ceremonies are drawn from the *Kamer-fur'erskii tseremonialnyi zhurnal* 1768. Details of the celebrations, speeches and poetry marking the Empress's inoculation are drawn from Gubert, V. O., *Ospa i ospoprivivanīe*, Chapter 12.

7 Soloviev, S. M., *Istoriia Rossii s drevneishikh vremen* (originally published in 29 vols., St Petersburg, 1851–79), vol. 28, Chapter 1, p. 365, cited in Proskurina, V., 'Catherine the Healer', p. 90.

8 Dimsdale, T., *Tracts on Inoculation*, p. 58.

9 *SIRIO*, x:305. Gospel of John 10:1–21.

10 Catherine had celebrated the Great Feast on 21 November with a sleigh ride after divine liturgy. *Kamer-fur'erskii tseremonialnyi zhurnal*, p. 229.

11 *Kamer-fur'erskii tseremonialnyi zhurnal*, 22–4 November 1768; Gubert, V. O., *Ospa i ospoprivivanīe*, pp. 275–6.

12 Jaques, S., *The Empress of Art* (Cambridge: Pegasus, 2016), p. 97.

13 Dixon, S., *Catherine the Great*, p. 190.

14 The Order of St Catherine was an award of Imperial Russia, instituted on 24 November 1714 by Peter the Great on his marriage to Catherine I of Russia. Aside from the Insignia of St Olga, in existence only from 1916 to 1917, it was the only award for women.

15 Dimsdale, T., *Tracts on Inoculation*, p. 10.

16 Letter, Lord Cathcart to the Earl of Rochford, 25 November 1768 (OS), *SIRIO*, xii:405–7.

17 Catalogue accompanying *Two Eighteenth Century Visits to Russia*, an exhibition held by Robert Dimsdale in July 1989 to showcase items linked to his ancestor Thomas Dimsdale's two trips to St Petersburg; hereafter referred to as Dimsdale exhibition catalogue.

18 Ibid.

19 Source for conversion: MeasuringWorth.com, comparing relative income value between 1768 and 2020.

20 Letter, Thomas Dimsdale to Henry Nicols, 25 November 1768 (OS), Dimsdale family collection.

21 The set, still almost complete, is on display with its case in the State Hermitage Museum, St Petersburg.

22 Thomas and Nathaniel were both given personal shooting permits while in Russia. Handwritten in Russian, they remain in the Dimsdale family collection.

23 He listed the weapons as: 'two fouling pieces, a bullet gun and a brace of pistols, exceeding fine, and she also told me she had shot with them herself and proved them to be good ones'. She had the pistols inscribed 'To Baron Dimsdale'. Letter, Thomas Dimsdale to John Dimsdale, December 1768, Dimsdale family collection.

24 Dimsdale exhibition catalogue.

25 *SIRIO*, xii:427, 17 March 1769.

26 Proskurina, V., *Creating the Empress: Politics and Poetry in the Age of Catherine II* (Brighton, MA: Academic Studies Press, 2011), pp. 90–1; Dixon, S., *Catherine the Great*, p. 191.

27 Gubert, V. O., *Ospa i ospoprivivanīe*, Chapter 12, pp. 269–72.

28 Ibid., p. 270.

29 Ibid., pp. 271–2.

30 Richardson, W., *Anecdotes of the Russian Empire*, Letter 6, p. 38.

31 *Sankt-Peterburgskie Vedomosti*, quoted in Gubert, V. O., *Ospa i ospoprivivanīe*, p. 278. The paper, established by Peter the Great in 1702, was the first to be printed in Russia. It is still published today.

32 Tooke, W., *View of the Russian Empire during the Reign of Catharine II and to the Close of the Present Century* (London: T. N. Longman, 1799).

33 *The Memoirs of Catherine the Great*, trans. M. Cruse and H. Hoogenboom, pp. 199–200.

34 Letter, Catherine the Great to Frederick II, 5 December 1768, in *Catherine the Great, Selected Letters*, trans. A. Kahn and K. Rubin-Detlev, pp. 70–1.

35 'The Mountain in Labour', one of Aesop's Fables, describes a mountain groaning terribly before cracking and releasing a tiny mouse. The story warns against building excessive expectations and delivering little.

36 Letter, Catherine the Great to Voltaire, December 1768, in *Catherine the Great, Selected Letters*, trans. A. Kahn and K. Rubin-Detlev, pp. 72–4.

37 Letter, Thomas Dimsdale to Henry Nicols, 16 November 1768, Dimsdale family collection.

38 Letter, Voltaire to Catherine the Great, 26 February 1769, Electronic Enlightenment Scholarly Edition of Correspondence, ed. R. McNamee *et al.* Vers. 3.0 (University of Oxford, 2018).

39 Ibid.

40 Tronchin, T., 'Inoculation', in *The Encyclopedia of Diderot & d'Alembert Collaborative Translation Project*. Trans. of 'Inoculation', *Encyclopédie ou Dictionnaire raisonné des sciences, des arts et des métiers*, vol. 8 (Paris, 1765).

41 *The Scots Magazine*, 1 December 1768 (NS).

42 *Bath Chronicle and Weekly Gazette*, 29 December 1768.

43 Letter, Horace Walpole to Sir Thomas Mann, 2 December 1768, Lewis Walpole Library, Yale.

44 Letter, Voltaire to Prince Dimitri Alexeievich Galitzin, 25 January 1769 (NS), Electronic Enlightenment Scholarly Edition of Correspondence.

45 Dimsdale, T., *Tracts on Inoculation*, p. 216.

8 The Impact

1 Letter, Voltaire to Catherine the Great, 26 February 1769, Electronic Enlightenment Scholarly Edition of Correspondence.

2 Dimsdale, T., *Tracts on Inoculation*, p. 62.

3 Ibid., p. 60.

4 Letter, Thomas Dimsdale to John Dimsdale(?) in Hitchin, December(?) 1768, Dimsdale family collection.

5 Dimsdale, T., *Tracts on Inoculation*, p. 62.

6 Ibid.

7 The girl's name and many other details not included in the 1781 *Tracts* are mentioned in Thomas's original reports, written in his bad French and translated into Russian by K. K. Zlobin for publication in 1770. *SIRIO*, ii:295–322.

8 *Novago voiazhirova leksikona na frantsusskom, nemetskom, latinskom i rossiiskom iazykakh*, trans. S. S. Volchkov (St Petersburg: Tip. Imp. Akademii nauk, 1764). Volchkov (1707–73) was a translator for the Imperial Academy of Sciences from 1736. He produced the first major Russian translations of the works of the Spanish Jesuit philosopher Baltasar Gracian and of Montaigne.

9 Dimsdale, T., *Tracts on Inoculation*, pp. 64–5.

10 Letter, Catherine the Great to Voltaire, 15 April 1769, in *Catherine the Great, Selected Letters*, trans. A. Kahn and K. Rubin-Detlev, p. 74.

11 Richardson, W., 'The Russian Winter, February 1769', from *Anecdotes of the Russian Empire*, p. 53.

12 From Thomas's original manuscript of his report for Catherine, not included in the published *Tracts*. *SIRIO*, ii:317.

13 Thomas's original report, translated into Russian. *SIRIO*, ii:318.

14 Merridale, C., *Red Fortress* (London: Allen Lane, 2013), p. 191.

15 Letter, Catherine the Great to Voltaire, 6 October 1771 (OS), cited in Merridale, C., *Red Fortress*, p. 195.

16 Mertens, C., *An Account of the Plague which Raged at Moscow* (London: F. and C. Rivington, 1771), p. 25. The population of Moscow was fluid and no precise figures can be calculated.

17 Gubert, V. O., *Ospa i ospoprivivanie*, p. 277.

18 Dimsdale, T., *Tracts on Inoculation*, p. 67.

19 Letter, Ann Dimsdale to Lady Jane Cathcart, 4 April 1769, Dimsdale family collection.

20 *SIRIO*, ii:318–19.

21 Dimsdale, T., *Thoughts on General and Partial Inoculations*, pp. iii–iv.

22 Huhn, O. von, *Die Allgemeine Einführung der Schutzpocken im Europäischen und Asiatischen Russland* / Повсемѣстное введение предохранительной оспы: в Европейской и Азиятской России (Moscow, 1807).

23 Dimsdale, T., *Thoughts on General and Partial Inoculations*, p. 17.

24 Ibid., p. 16.

25 Dimsdale, T., *Tracts on Inoculation*, p. 93, 'A Short Account of the Regulations in the Medical College of St Petersburg in 1768'.

26 Dimsdale, T., *Thoughts on General and Partial Inoculations*, p. 11.

27 Ibid., p. 9.

28 Tooke, W., *View of the Russian Empire*, vol. 2, p. 206.

29 Cross, A., *By the Banks of the Neva*, p. 141.

30 Tooke, W., *View of the Russian Empire*, vol. 2, p. 207.

31 Ibid., p. 204.

32 Hilton, A., *Russian Folk Art* (Bloomington: Indiana University Press, 1995), p. 112.

33 Gubert, V. O., *Ospa i ospoprivivanie*, p. 228.

34 Bennett, M., *War Against Smallpox*, p. 233.

35 Tooke, W., *View of the Russian Empire*, vol. 2, p. 208.

36 Alexander, J. T., *Bubonic Plague in Early Modern Russia: Public Health and Urban Disaster* (Baltimore: Johns Hopkins University Press, 1980); Tooke, W., *View of the Russian Empire*, vol. 1, pp. 565–7.

37 Grot, J., *Petersburgische Kanzelvorträge* (Leipzig and Riga: Johann Friedrich Hartknoch, 1781).

38 Storch, H., *Tableau historique et statistique de l'empire de Russie à la fin du dix-huitième siècle* (Basel: J. Decker, 1800); Bartlett, R., 'Adoption of Inoculation for Smallpox', in *Russia and the World of the Eighteenth Century*.

39 Gubert, V. O., *Ospa i ospoprivivanie*, p. 235.

40 Letter, Lord Cathcart to Viscount Weymouth, 1/12 November 1768, National Archives SP 91/79: 302.

41 Letter, Catherine the Great to Thomas Dimsdale, 8 July 1771 (OS), Dimsdale family collection.

42 Letter, Catherine the Great to Piotr Aleksandrovich Rumiantsev, 20 April 1787. The letter, signed by the Empress and owned by a private collector, was sold by MacDougall's auction house in December 2021. Auctioned together with a portrait of the Empress, it was bought by an unnamed buyer for almost $1.3 million. Letter translation by MacDougall's. The doctor in Novgorod Severskii whom Catherine proposed should conduct the inoculations seems to have been Samuel Hunt, a British graduate of Gonville & Caius College, Cambridge, and the first Cambridge-educated doctor to work in Russia in the eighteenth century (*By the Banks of the Neva*, p. 156).

43 Storch, H. F., *Historisch-statistisches Gemälde des Russischen Reichs am Ende des achtzehnten Jahrhunderts*, vol. 1 (Riga: Hartnoch, 1797), p. 425.

44 Bartlett, R., 'Adoption of Inoculation for Smallpox', p. 197.

45 Parkinson, J. (ed.), *A Tour of Russia, Siberia and the Crimea 1792–1794* (London: W. Collier, 1971), p. 51, quoted in Grant, A., *Globalisation of Variolation*, p. 162.

46 Clarke, E. D., *Travels in Various Countries of Europe, Asia and Africa: Russia, Tahtary, and Turkey* (London: T. Cadell and W. Davies, 1816), p. 350.

47 Dimsdale, T., *Tracts on Inoculation*, p. 68.

48 Ibid.

49 Ibid., p. 69. Thomas was typical for his time: bleeding remained a common treatment for fever and inflammation throughout the century, favoured by such eminent figures as the Scottish surgeon John Hunter. It was contentious only when used to excess: Wolfgang Amadeus Mozart and George Washington were both subjected to severe bloodlettings shortly before they died. In the mid-nineteenth century, the practice came under greater scrutiny and was shown to be ineffective and often dangerous. Louis Pasteur (1822–95) and Robert Koch (1843–1910) proved conclusively that inflammation resulted from infection and thus was not susceptible to bloodletting.

50 Letter, Catherine the Great to Johanna Bielke, 4 March 1769, *SIRIO*, x:332.

51 Letter, Lord Cathcart to Sir Andrew Mitchell, British envoy to Prussia, in Berlin, 28 February 1769, quoted in Dimsdale exhibition catalogue. The letter was written at the point of Thomas's abortive first departure, which he cancelled to care for the Empress. See also Bisset, A., *Memoirs and Papers of Sir Andrew Mitchell, K. B.: Envoy Extraordinary and Minister Plenipotentiary from the Court of Great Britain to the Court of Prussia, from 1756 to 1771*, vol. 2 (London: Chapman and Hall, 1850).

52 The story of Catherine throwing the fur from her sleigh was passed down through the Dimsdale family. Dimsdale exhibition catalogue.

53 Letter, Stratford Canning to his father, also Stratford Canning, from Danzig, 12 April 1769, Dimsdale family collection. The author of the letter was father to a third, and more famous, Stratford Canning, 1st Viscount Stratford de Redcliffe, a British diplomat best known as ambassador to the Ottoman Empire.

54 Mittau, some twenty-five miles south west of Riga, is modern Jelgava, in Latvia. The Prussian town of Memel is now Klaipėda, the third largest city in Lithuania. The Curish Haff is the Curonian Spit, which runs from Lithuania to Kaliningrad Oblast, the westernmost territory of Russia. It is designated a UNESCO World Heritage Site. Königsberg, in Prussia, became the Russian city of Kaliningrad in 1946. Danzig is now Gdańsk, in northern Poland.

55 Bisset, A., *Memoirs and Papers of Sir Andrew Mitchell*, p. 516.

56 Shoberl, F., trans. Campbell, T., *Frederick the Great, His Court and Times*, vol. 4 (London: Henry Colburn, 1842), p. 333.

57 From Thomas's original manuscript of his report for Catherine, not included in the 1781 *Tracts*. *SIRIO*, ii:321.Translation from Brayley Hodgetts, E. A., *The Life of Catherine the Great of Russia* (New York: Brentano's, 1914), p. 247.

58 *SIRIO*, ii:322. Translation from Brayley Hodgetts, E. A., *The Life of Catherine the Great*, p. 248.

59 *SIRIO*, ii:322. Translation from Brayley Hodgetts, E. A., *The Life of Catherine the Great*, p. 249.

60 Letter, Stratford Canning to his father, 14 July 1769, Dimsdale family collection.

9   The Celebrity

1 Dimsdale, T., *Thoughts on General and Partial Inoculations*, p. viii.

2 Galton was one of the 'Lunar Men': a member of the Lunar Circle, later the Lunar Society of Birmingham, an informal learned society of prominent figures in the Midland Enlightenment. Members, who included industrialists and natural philosophers, held their meetings around the time of the full moon, allowing them light to ride home by. Other key figures in the Society were Joseph Priestley, Erasmus Darwin (a doctor and committed advocate of inoculation; grandfather of Charles Darwin), James Watt and Josiah Wedgwood.

3 Library of the Society of Friends, London (Euston), Betty Fothergill, Diary (LSF, 1769–70).

4 Thomas's other two eminent supporters were Richard Brocklesby, a Quaker physician educated at Edinburgh and Leiden and a former surgeon general of the British Army, and the Dutch Huguenot physician Matthew Maty, Secretary of the Royal Society, who had translated into English the landmark address of the French inoculation advocate Charles-Marie de La Condamine.

5 Thomas's sons succeeded him, and the bank remained a Dimsdale family enterprise for generations until in 1891 it merged with Prescott, Cave, Buxton, Loder & Co. to form what became Prescott's Bank, a constituent bank of NatWest.

6 Letter, Duchess of Portland to 3rd Duke of Portland, William Henry Cavendish-Bentinck, 17 March 1777, University of Nottingham Library, Portland Papers, Pw F 10679. Thomas continued to treat the couple's children: on 29 August of the same year Dorothy wrote to her husband that 'one dose of Baron Dimsdale's Powder has brought a worm from William of I dare say six inches in length, this happen'd yesterday & I never saw any thing so much changed for the better as the child is already.' University of Nottingham Library, Portland Papers, Pw F 10694.

7 Letter, Grand Duke Paul to Thomas Dimsdale, 2 September 1769, Dimsdale family collection.

8 Letter, Grand Duke Paul to Thomas Dimsdale, 8 March(?) 1776, Dimsdale family collection.

9 Letter, Count Vladimir Orlov to Thomas Dimsdale, October 1769, Dimsdale family collection.

10 Letter, Count Vladimir Orlov to Thomas Dimsdale, 22 January 1772, Dimsdale family collection.

11 Letter, Count Vladimir Orlov to Thomas Dimsdale, 3 June 1770(?), Dimsdale family collection.

12 Letter, Thomas Dimsdale to Catherine the Great, 25 June 1771 (in French, author's translation), Dimsdale family collection.

13 Letter, Catherine the Great to Thomas Dimsdale, 8 July 1771, Dimsdale family collection.

14 Catherine immortalised her beloved greyhounds through a variety of decorative objects: they appeared as figurines and on vases, paperweights and inksets. At the Imperial Porcelain Factory, head of the sculpture workshop Jean-Dominique Rachette made a life-size sculpture of Zemira lying on a cushion. In the closing scenes of Alexander Pushkin's novella *The Captain's Daughter*, Catherine is depicted with 'a little white dog of English breed' in the park at Tsarskoe Selo.

15 Siberian pine, or *Pinus sibirica*, is part of the Pinaceae family. It grows in Siberia, and in parts of Kazakhstan and Mongolia. Its edible seeds, often called cedar nuts, are probably those Catherine sent to Voltaire (see p. 155).

16 Letter, Dr John Rogerson to Thomas Dimsdale, 26 August 1770, Dimsdale family collection.

17 *Encyclopédie, ou dictionnaire raisonné des sciences, des arts et des métiers, etc.*, ed. Denis Diderot and Jean le Rond d'Alembert (Chicago: University of Chicago ARTFL Encyclopédie Project, Spring 2021 Edition), ed. R. Morrissey and G. Roe http://encyclopedie.uchicago.edu, vol. 8, p. 768; quoted in Roberts, M. K., *Sentimental Savants: Philosophical Families in Enlightenment France* (Chicago: University of Chicago Press, 2016), p. 77.

18 Roman, Jean-Joseph-Thérèse (M. l'abbé Roman), *L'inoculation, poème en quatre chants* (Amsterdam: Lacombe, 1773). The poet added a note on vocabulary letting readers know his poem did not include the term 'petite vérole', French for smallpox. He also left out the word 'inoculation' which, though less shocking, he explained was too long to fit the rhythm of his verse. Finally, he defended his decision to describe a 'hideous disease' at all, arguing that the horror it inspired contributed to the effect of the poem.

19 Hopkins, D. R., *The Greatest Killer*, p. 70.

20 Previous deaths were: Joseph I, Holy Roman Emperor (1711); King Luis I of Spain (1724); Emperor Peter II of Russia (1730); and Ulrika Eleonora, Queen of Sweden and then queen consort (1741). Maximilian III Joseph, Elector of Bavaria, would die of smallpox in 1777.

21 Letter, Catherine the Great to Friedrich Grimm, 19 June 1774 (OS), *SIRIO*, xiii:407–10.

22 In the language of Tahiti, the prefix O means 'it is', so Omai's real name was Mai. He was referred to by Thomas and in all letters and publications in Britain as Omai (sometimes spelt Omaih) so for clarity that name has been used here. Similarly, he was generally referred to as 'The man from Otaheite', referring to Tahiti.

23 Rousseau is often wrongly associated with the phrase 'noble savage'; he never used the term. It first appeared in English in John Dryden's heroic play *The Conquest of Granada* (1672), where it was used in reference to newly created man.

24 Joseph Banks was yet another friend of Dr John Fothergill, an avid plant collector whose garden at Upton in Essex Banks was judged to be second only to Kew in the whole of Europe. As Banks prepared for departure on the *Endeavour*, Fothergill sent him provisions intended to prevent scurvy, including six gallons of lemon juice evaporated down to less than two. Banks also took Fothergill's black servant, Richmond, with him on the expedition. Richmond died of exposure in heavy snow during a trip ashore in Tierra del Fuego. An artist on the ship, the Quaker Sydney Parkinson, broke the sad news to Fothergill, writing, 'I feel his loss very much'. Parkinson too would die after falling ill on the voyage. Ms autograph letter, Sydney Parkinson to John Fothergill, Batavia, 16 October 1770, Library of the Society of Friends, London. An image of the original letter can be seen on the Library's blog: https://quakerstrongrooms.org/2019/11/08/dr-john-fothergill/.

25 The first Cook expedition, lasting from 1768 to 1771, set out to observe the transit of Venus across the sun, a phenomenon that would allow measurement of the distance from Earth to the sun. The Royal Society had petitioned King George III, himself interested in astronomy, to commission the expedition. Catherine II also despatched scientists to observe the transit from Siberia and other locations. The second goal of the Cook voyage was to seek evidence of the hypothetical landmass *Terra Australis Incognita* or 'unknown southern land'.

26 Quoted in Connaughton, R., *Omai: The Prince who Never Was* (London: Timewell Press, 2005), p. 61.

27 Cartwright made a second visit to Labrador and in December 1773 brought back another Inuit boy, Noozelliack, aged about twelve. On landing, he took him straight to Daniel Sutton in Knightsbridge to be inoculated. Sutton carried out the procedure, but the boy died shortly after the pustules emerged. Cartwright was frustrated at a lost opportunity to increase his understanding of the Inuit people and their homeland. He wrote: 'This was a very great mortification and disappointment to me; for, as I intended, at a future period, to have visited all the northern tribes of Eskimo, I had brought home this boy, in order to put him to school to be instructed in the English language; intending him for my interpreter. Through him I should have been enabled to have gained full information of their religion, customs and manners. At the same time, I should have improved myself in their language, my dealings with his countrymen would've been greatly facilitated, and I should've acquired much knowledge of the northern part of the coast.' Cartwright, G., *A Journal of Transactions and Events During a Residence of Nearly Sixteen Years on the Coast of Labrador*, vol. 1 (Newark: Allin and Ridge, 1792), pp. 286–7.

28 Letter from Catherine Cartwright, sister of Captain George Cartwright, to Margaret Stowe, 20 June 1773. Quoted in Stopp, M. and Mitchell, G., ' "Our Amazing Visitors": Catherine Cartwright's Account of Labrador Inuit in England', *Arctic* 63, 4 (December 2010): 399–413. Catherine Cartwright had grown to know the Inuit party well and was distressed at news of their deaths. 'How I have grieved for these objects of my affection: and how my very heart doth bleed with sorrow for their sakes.'

29 *The Craftsman; or SAY's Weekly Journal*, 6 August 1774.

30 Thomas Dimsdale notes and fair copy, labelled 'Respecting Omaih', Dimsdale family collection.

31 By the 1770s, wealthy individuals expected their servants to be inoculated if they had not already had smallpox so that they could not pass on the disease. It is highly likely that Dr John Fothergill's servant Richmond, who had died on the first Cook voyage, would have been inoculated if he was not already immune since his employer was a doctor and advocate of the practice. Britain had a black population of over 20,000 people by the 1780s; some, especially those in service, are likely to have undergone the procedure. Enslaved people in British colonies were inoculated at their masters' command for economic reasons, without their own consent.

32 *Autobiography, Letters and Literary Remains of Mrs Piozzi (Thrale)*, ed. A. Hayward (London: Longman, Green, Longman & Roberts, 1861). Hester Thrale's comment relates to a chess game in which Omai beat the writer and translator Giuseppe Baretti – perhaps the chess match witnessed by Thomas. Samuel Johnson often teased Baretti over his defeat by a 'savage', prompting a lifelong feud between the two men.

33 Boswell, S., *The Life of Samuel Johnson* (London: Henry Baldwin, 1791), p. 577. Boswell, a supporter of Cook's voyages, argued that the people of Tahiti 'could not be reckoned savages', but gave up the debate when it was clear Johnson would not change his view.

34 Boswell, S., *The Life of Samuel Johnson*, p. 316.

35 Hetherington, M. and McCalman, I., *Cook & Omai: The Cult of the South Seas* (Canberra: National Library of Australia, 2001), p. 31.

36 Published in *The Gentleman's Magazine* 53 (October 1783), p. 869.

37 Letter, *The Gentleman's Magazine* 49 (April 1779), pp. 192–3. Dr Pugh introduced himself as 'an old correspondent . . . I was among the first inoculators in England, a strong advocate for it, and shall continue so as long as I live, being convinced, by experience, of the truth of what I shall advance'.

38 Hanway, J., *The Defects of Police: the Cause of Immorality and the Continual Robberies Committed: Particularly in and about the Metropolis* (London: J. Dodsley, 1775), Letter XI, pp. 89–92. Hanway was a prolific social commentator and had travelled widely, including in Russia. He was also known for being a fierce opponent of tea drinking and for being the first man in London to carry an umbrella.

39 Dimsdale, T., *Thoughts on General and Partial Inoculations*, p. 65.

40 Ibid., pp. 62–4.

41 Hopkins, D. R., *The Greatest Killer*, p. 74.

42 Watkinson, J., *An Examination of a Charge Brought against Inoculation, by DeHaen, Rast, Dimsdale, and Other Writers* (London: J. Johnson, 1778).

43 Dimsdale, T., *Observations on the Introduction to the Plan of the Dispensary for General Inoculation with Remarks on a Pamphlet Entitled 'An Examination of a Charge Brought against Inoculation by DeHaen, Rast, Dimsdale, and Other Writers' by John Watkinson MD* (London: W. Richardson, 1778), p. 2.

44 Dimsdale, T., *Thoughts on General and Partial Inoculations*, p. 22.

45 Black, W., *Observations Medical and Political: On the Small-Pox and Inoculation and on the Decrease of Mankind at Every Age* (London: J. Johnson, 1781), p. 75.

46 Bishop, W. J., 'Thomas Dimsdale MD FRS (1712–1800) and the Inoculation of Catherine the Great of Russia', *Annals of Medical History* 4, 4 (July 1932): 334.

47 Letter, Ann Fothergill, sister of Dr John Fothergill, to Thomas Dimsdale, 1783, Friends MS Portfolio 23/18. Thomas had claimed in a memorial article following Fothergill's death that his friend corrected all his pamphlets before publication; Ann pointed out that her brother had not approved of the row with Lettsom and would not have become involved with that exchange.

48 Minute books of the Committee for the Abolition of the Slave Trade, British Library Add. MSS 21254–21256.

10 The Last Meeting

1 Letter from Catherine the Great, given to Thomas Dimsdale the evening before his departure from St Petersburg, 14 October 1781, Dimsdale family collection.

2 Dimsdale, T., *Tracts on Inoculation*.

3 The refusal to swear the oath of allegiance kept Quakers out of Parliament until an alternative was finally found in the nineteenth century. The election of the Quaker Joseph Pease (1799–1872) to represent South Durham in 1832 catalysed change. The resulting 1832 Reform Bill enabled Quakers to express their loyalty through affirmation rather than an oath, and Pease duly became the first Quaker MP to take his seat. To this day, many Quakers affirm in several contexts where oath taking is the norm.

4 *The Parliamentary Register; Or, History of the Proceedings and Debates of the House of Commons [and of the House of Lords] Containing an Account of the Interesting Speeches And Motions . . . During the 3rd Session of the 15th Parliament of Great Britain* (London: printed for J. Almon, 1775–1804), vol. 10, p. 161.

5 Quoted in *The History of Parliament*. The *English Chronicle* was an evening paper founded in London in 1779 and published three times a week. *The History of Parliament* is a research project creating a comprehensive account of parliamentary politics in England, then Britain, from their origins in the thirteenth century. It includes studies of elections and electoral politics in each constituency, and accounts of the lives of everyone elected to Parliament in the period, together with surveys drawing out themes of the research. Forty-one volumes covering ten periods and 326 years of parliamentary history have already been published. The project is also online at www.historyofparliamentonline.org.

6 Dimsdale family collection.

7 Dimsdale family collection.

8 The handwritten Receipt Book of Baroness Elizabeth Dimsdale, written from around 1800 to 1808, included 700 recipes, including what is believed to be the first recipe for doughnuts. There was also a recipe for 'Russia cucumbers', learned from an acquaintance at the Russian Embassy, and a selection of practical household advice, including ways to clean brass and protect a henhouse from vermin. *The Receipt Book of Baroness Elizabeth Dimsdale, c.1800*, ed. H. Falvey, (Rickmansworth: Hertfordshire Record Society, 2013), p. 145.

9 The Reverend King was returning to the Russian capital to sell a collection of ancient coins; he did not travel back with the Dimsdales. A parcel of receipts for the journey, mainly for tolls, postillions, carriage repairs and coffee, includes a bill for

'Washing dog and both carriages'. Incredibly, Fox had puppies en route. Dimsdale family collection.

10 Elizabeth refers to taking 'some of Sir Hans Sloane's hot chocolate with me, which I found a great comfort from'. Sloane, the President of the Royal Society and early supporter of inoculation, was introduced to cocoa while working as a doctor in Jamaica. He found it unpalatable unless mixed with milk, and brought the recipe back to Britain, where it was manufactured and initially sold as a medicine. As well as hot chocolate, the Dimsdales always carried a bottle of water and a piece of butter in their travelling tea chest while on the road.

11 Cross, A. G. (ed.), *An English Lady at the Court of Catherine the Great: The Journal of Baroness Elizabeth Dimsdale, 1781* (Cambridge: Crest Publications, 1989). The journal is referred to throughout the chapter.

12 The First Partition of Poland, in 1772, was first of three partitions that eventually erased the Polish–Lithuanian Commonwealth from the map by 1795. Over 200,000 km^2 was ceded to Russia, Prussia and Austria in the first partition.

13 Elizabeth uses a mix of Old and New Style dating in her journal. New Style predominates and this is used here for all dates on the second visit to Russia.

14 Letter, Elizabeth Dimsdale to her brother and sister, St Petersburg, 9 August 1781, Dimsdale family collection.

15 Howard, in whose name the campaigning organisation now known as the Howard League for Penal Reform was founded, investigated prisons in England and Wales and across Europe. During his stay in St Petersburg, he rejected Thomas's offer to introduce him to the Empress, telling him, 'My object is not to see great people.' He met the Dimsdales often but shared a meal with them only occasionally, complaining that their 'dinners were too good' and eating only bread pudding and potatoes. Howard would die in Kherson in the Ukraine of 'gaol fever', a form of typhus, in January 1790. A monument was erected there to mark his life and achievements. Cross, A. G. (ed.), *An English Lady at the Court of Catherine the Great*, p. 49.

16 Miss Cheveley's account, Dimsdale family collection.

17 A gold rouble dating from 1779 was passed down in the Dimsdale family, but is thought to have been given to the Baroness by Constantine, who copied his older brother and handed out his own coins.

18 Letter from Thomas Dimsdale at Tsarskoe Selo to John Dimsdale(?), 28 September 1781, Dimsdale family collection.

19 Letter, Maria Fedorovna to Thomas Dimsdale, September 1781, Dimsdale family collection.

20 Cross, A. G. (ed.), *An English Lady at the Court of Catherine the Great*, p. 84.

21 Dimsdale, T., *Tracts*, pp. 218 and 245.

22 Razzell, P., 'The Decline of Adult Smallpox in Eighteenth Century London: A Commentary', *The Economic History Review* 64, 4 (2011): 1329.

23 Brunton, D., *Pox Britannica*, Chapter 7.

24 The court doctors may have been using old-fashioned – and more dangerous – inoculation methods. In 1768, at the Queen's instruction, her brother, her son and Charlotte Albert, the daughter of one of her attendants, were all inoculated. The latter later wrote that the procedure involved drawing a thread soaked in pus under

her skin – a technique that had been widely abandoned by doctors some years before. It did not work: seven years later, Miss Albert suffered a severe case of smallpox.

25 Esfandiary, H., '"We Could Not Answer to Ourselves Not Doing It": Maternal Obligations and Knowledge of Smallpox Inoculation in Eighteenth-Century Elite Society', *Historical Research* 92 (2019): 754–70.

26 Dimsdale, T., *Tracts on Inoculation*, p. 157. Fomes, or fomites, are inanimate objects that, when contaminated with or exposed to infectious agents (such as pathogenic bacteria, viruses or fungi), can transfer disease to a new host. Clothing or bedding, for example, could transfer smallpox infection. The term, meaning *tinder* in Latin, appears to have been first used in this sense by the Italian scholar and physician Girolamo Fracastoro in his essay on contagion, *De Contagione et Contagiosis Morbis*, published in 1546.

27 Dimsdale, T., *Tracts on Inoculation*, p. 110.

28 Haygarth, J., *A Sketch of a Plan to Exterminate the Casual Small-pox from Great Britain; and to Introduce General Inoculation* (London: J. Johnson, 1793), vol. 1, pp. 62–5.

29 Ibid., vol. 1, p. 177.

30 Brunton, D., *Pox Britannica*, pp. 165–6.

31 Dobson, M. J., *Contours of Death and Disease*, pp. 481–2.

32 Razzell, R., *The Conquest of Smallpox* (Firle: Caliban Books, 1977); Smith, J. R., *The Speckled Monster*; Brunton, D., *Pox Britannica*; and Mercer, A., *Infections, Chronic Disease, and the Epidemiological Transition: A New Perspective* (Rochester, NY: University of Rochester Press, 2014) all offer detailed accounts of the impact of inoculation on communities in England during the later eighteenth century.

33 Howlett, J., *Observations on the Increased Population . . . of Maidstone* (1782), p. 8, quoted in Razzell, P., *The Conquest of Smallpox* (Firle: Caliban Books, 1977), p. 152.

34 Rusnock, A., *Vital Accounts*, p. 106.

35 Black, W., *An Arithmetical and Medical Analysis of the Diseases and Mortality of the Human Species* (London: J. Johnson, 1789), p. iii.

36 Smith, J. R., *The Speckled Monster*, p. 66.

37 Dobson, M. J., *Contours of Death and Disease*, p. 483; Smith, J. R., *The Speckled Monster*, p. 66; Hopkins, D. R., *The Greatest Killer*, pp. 76–7.

38 Hopkins, D. R., *The Greatest Killer*, p. 77.

39 Jenner published the *Inquiry* privately after an earlier, weaker version was rejected in 1797 by Sir Joseph Banks, by now President of the Royal Society. Jenner's misleading translation of cowpox as *variolæ vaccinæ*, literally smallpox of the cow, implied a common ancestor for the viruses, which he could not prove.

40 Jenner, E., 'On the Origin of the Vaccine Inoculation', *Medical and Physical Journal* 5, 28 (1801): 506.

41 It was not the first time Jenner had inoculated with pox virus from an animal: he inoculated his own son with swinepox in 1789. He would later inoculate a younger son with cowpox. His experiments defy modern ethical standards but in both cases he knew the disease to be mild in humans. In challenging his patients through inoculation with live smallpox, he was of course using an entirely standard preventative procedure.

42 Jenner introduced the terms 'vaccine virus' and 'vaccine inoculation'. The word 'vaccination' was coined in 1800 by Jenner's friend, the surgeon Richard Dunning, in his paper 'Some Observations on Vaccination or the Inoculated Cow-Pox'. Bennett, M., *War Against Smallpox*, p. 86.

43 Hopkins, D. R., *The Greatest Killer*, p. 81.

44 Letter, Thomas Jefferson to Edward Jenner, Monticello, 14 May 1806, from the Thomas Jefferson Papers at the Library of Congress, https://www.loc.gov/item/mtjbib016128/, Series 1: General Correspondence. 1651–1827.

45 Bennett, M., *War Against Smallpox*, p. 232.

46 Jenner, E., 'On the Origin of the Vaccine Inoculation', p. 508.

47 Letter, 5 October 1793, Dimsdale family collection. Signature unclear: possibly Alexander Count Bezborodko, Grand Chancellor of the Russian Empire.

48 *An Imperial Stride*, etching, 12 April 1791. Published by William Holland. British Museum Collection.

49 Letter, Thomas Dimsdale to Emperor Paul I, 5 January 1797 (NS), Dimsdale family collection.

Epilogue: The Legacy

1 Woodville, W., *The History of the Inoculation of the Small-pox, in Great Britain*, vol. 1 (London: James Phillips, 1796), p. vi.

2 Daniel Sutton finally published details of his method in his book, *The Inoculator*, in 1796 – the year Jenner proved cowpox conferred immunity to smallpox, and some thirty years after he had promised to make his discoveries known. On the title page, he described himself as 'Daniel Sutton, Surgeon, who introduced the New Method of Inoculation into this Kingdom in the year 1763'. Complaining about rumours 'that for many years I quitted my profession and was long since dead', Sutton wrote testily: 'What opinion the Faculty at large may entertain of my theory, or speculative reasoning, I know not; nor am I very solicitous about it.'

3 Dimsdale, T., *Tracts on Inoculation*, pp. ix–x.

4 Letter, Nathaniel Dimsdale to Emperor Paul I, 21 February 1801 (NS), Dimsdale family collection.

5 Bennett, M., *War Against Smallpox*, p. 228.

6 Baron, J., *The Life of Edward Jenner*, vol. 1 (London: H. Colburn, 1827), p. 463.

7 Napoleon's admiration for Jenner was so great that, during the Napoleonic Wars, he released several English prisoners in response to petitions from the doctor, on one occasion declaring, 'Ah, Jenner, I cannot refuse Jenner anything!' Quoted in Hopkins, D. R., *The Greatest Killer*, p. 82.

8 Cruikshank, I., *Vaccination against Small Pox, or Mercenary & Merciless Spreaders of Death & Devastation Driven Out of Society* (1808), British Museum collection.

9 Razzell, P., 'The Decline of Adult Smallpox'.

10 Fisher, R. B., *Edward Jenner: A Biography* (London: André Deutsch, 1991), p. 245.

11 The 1946 National Health Service Act repealed previous Vaccine Acts. It also strengthened the policy for subsequent introductions of childhood vaccinations

and allowed the National Health Service to take responsibility for co-ordinating both current and future vaccination programmes.

12 Henderson, D. A., 'The Eradication of Smallpox – An Overview of the Past, Present, and Future', *Vaccine* 29 (2011): D7–D9; Henderson, D. A., *Smallpox: The Death of a Disease – The Inside Story of Eradicating a Worldwide Killer* (Buffalo, NY: Prometheus Books, 2009).

13 Exceptions are laboratory staff working with the virus. The United States government maintains stocks of smallpox vaccine for use in the case of bioterrorism or other crisis.

14 See WHO, 'Vaccines and immunization', www.who.int/health-topics/vaccines-and-immunization#tab=tab_1. The WHO website states: 'In some countries, progress has stalled or even reversed, and there is a real risk that complacency will undermine past achievements.'

15 Figure from Our World in Data, ourworldindata.org, 11 January 2022.

16 Quoted in Cross, A., 'Catherine the Great: Views from the Distaff Side', in *Russia in the Age of the Enlightenment: Essays for Isabel de Madariaga*, ed. R. Bartlett and J. M. Hartley (London: Palgrave Macmillan, 1990), pp. 203–21.

17 Quoted in Rounding, V., *Catherine the Great: Love, Sex and Power*, p. 505.

Index

References to images are in *italics*.

© Ailis Halligan

LUCY WARD is a writer and former journalist for the *Guardian* and *Independent*. As a Westminster Lobby correspondent, she campaigned for greater women's representation. From 2010–12, she lived with her family in Moscow, renewing her interest in Russian history. After growing up in Manchester, she studied Early and Middle English at Balliol College, Oxford. She now lives in Essex.